CATHOLIC RECORD SOCIETY PUBLICATIONS

PUBLICATIONS

(MONOGRAPH SERIES) VOLUME 4

EDMUND PLOWDEN.
From the portrait by an unknown artist, at Plowden Hall.
(*Reproduced by permission of William Plowden, Esq.*)

EDMUND PLOWDEN

An Elizabethan Recusant Lawyer

by

Geoffrey de C. Parmiter

CATHOLIC RECORD SOCIETY
1987

ISBN 0 902832 11 5

Printed in Great Britain by
Hobbs the Printers of Southampton

(3310/86)

CONTENTS

PREFACE

Although the name of Edmund Plowden is well known as a great Elizabethan lawyer, no biography of him exists. That is not so surprising as it seems. The professional life of a lawyer is largely composed of a substantial number of cases, each of which has little or no relation to any of the others, so that an account of such a life tends to be fragmentary, as the biography of any modern lawyer will show. In the case of Edmund Plowden, however, the situation is much worse. The surviving accounts of the cases in which he was engaged are, for the most part, in Law French, a strange language which most writers do not find congenial, and in many instances they are incomplete. Moreover, much that would have assisted a biographer of Plowden has disappeared, immeasurably increasing the fragmentation. Such sources as still exist are widely scattered and relate almost entirely to his professional life, and many of the relevant records of the Middle Temple, where he was a dominating figure for many years, are missing. Worse still, with very few exceptions, his personal papers and correspondence have not survived; that is all the more unfortunate as it deprives any would-be biographer of one of the best means of estimating his character. It is not difficult to form an opinion of Plowden as a lawyer but, in the absence of his personal papers, it is much harder to discover the kind of man he was.

In this book I have tried to assemble as much of the surviving evidence as possible, scattered and fragmentary though it is, and to construct from it a biography that has some sort of unity. Plowden was a remarkable man who lived in a remarkable age. Of his contemporaries in his profession there were few who were his equal and probably none that were greater, yet most of his professional life was passed under a regime which proscribed the religion to which he adhered. Plowden made no secret of his Catholicism and, although his religion prevented his achieving the high position in his profession to which his gifts and learning entitled him, he succeeded in living a long and busy life without incurring the serious penalties which befell many of his fellow Catholics.

In quoting from books or manuscripts I have adopted a compromise. When the quotations occur in the text I have, in most cases, expanded contractions, modernized the spelling and normalized the punctuation and capitalization, but when the quotations occur in the footnotes I have left them as I found them in the originals. Dates are Old Style, save that the calendar year has been taken to begin on 1 January. References to printed works have either been abbreviated according to the List of Abbreviations, or given in a shortened form of which the full form can be found in the Bibliography at the end of the book.

I am indebted to many people for assistance in writing this book. They are too numerous to mention individually, but I should like to offer my special thanks to Mr. W. F. G. Plowden of Plowden Hall, Dr. Alan Davidson, and the staff of Duke Humphrey's Library in the Bodleian where much of my work was done. Finally, I should like to express my gratitude to the British Academy for a grant towards the costs of my research.

Geoffrey de C. Parmiter

LIST OF ABBREVIATIONS

A.I.T.   *Antiquities of the Inns of Court and Chancery*, by W. Herbert, London, 1804.

Anderson   Anderson's Reports, Common Pleas, 1534–1605.

A.P.C.   *Acts of the Privy Council of England*, ed. J. R. Dasent, 32 vols., London, 1890–1907.

A. & R.   *A Catalogue of Catholic Books in English printed abroad or secretly in England*, by A. F. Allison and D. M Rogers, Bognor Regis, 1956 [*R.H.*, iii, 119–187].

Athen. Oxon.   *Athenae Oxonienses*, by Anthony Wood. Ed. by Philip Bliss, 4 vols., Oxford, 1813–20.

Bacon Rep.   The Report made to Henry VIII by Nicholas Bacon, Thomas Denton and Robert Carey, as printed in D. S. Bland, "Henry VIII's Royal Commission on the Inns of Court" in *Journal of the Society of Public Teachers of Law*, new ser., x (1969), at pp. 183–94, from Waterhous, *Fortescutus Illustratus*, 543–6.

B.B.   *Records of the Honourable Society of Lincoln's Inn: The Black Books*, ed. J. D. Walker, W. P Baildon and R. F. Roxburgh, 5 vols., London, 1897–1968.

B.C.   *Handbook of British Chronology*, by F. M. Powicke and E. B. Fryde, 2nd ed., London, 1961 (Royal Historical Society Guides and Handbooks, no. 2).

Blakeway, *Isle*   'The Isle, anciently Up Rossall' by J. B. Blakeway, in *Transactions of the Shropshire Archaeological Society*, 2nd. ser., ix (1897), 107 et seq.

Blunden's MS   MS written by Andrew Blunden, printed as appendix to Blakeway, *Isle*, pp. 122–49 (and, in part, in Blakeway, *The Sheriffs of Shropshire*, Shrewsbury, 1831).

B.M.B.   Bench Minute Books, Middle Temple, London.

B.M.P.   *Records of the Plowden Family*, by B. M. P. [Barbara Mary Plowden], privately printed, 1887.

Br. Lib.   The British Library, London.

Burghley Papers   *A Collection of State Papers, from Letters and Memorials left by William Cecil, Lord Burghley*, 2 vols., London: vol. 1, ed. by S. Haynes, 1740; vol. 2, ed. by W. Murdin, 1759.

Cal. B.P.   *Calendar of Letters and Papers relating to the Affairs of the Borders of England and Scotland preserved in*

	Her Majesty's Public Record Office (1560–1603), 2 vols., Edinburgh. 1894–6.
Camb. L.J.	*Cambridge Law Journal.*
Co. Inst.	*Institutes of the Laws of England*, by Edward Coke.
Co. Litt.	*Coke upon Littleton*, the common name for 1 Co. Inst.
Co. Rep.	The Reports of Sir Edward Coke, 1572–1616.
C.P.R.	*Calendar of the Patent Rolls, 1232–47.* etc.
Cro. Eliz.	Croke's King's Bench Reports, temp. Elizabeth I.
C.R.S.	Publications of the Catholic Record Society:

Vol. 1 *Miscellanea I*, 1905.

     2 *Miscellanea II*, 1906.

  13 *Miscellanea VIII*, 1913.

  22 *Miscellanea XII*, 1921.

  39 *Letters and Memorials of Father Robert Persons, S.J., 1578–1588*, ed. L. Hicks, 1942.

  53 *Miscellanea: Recusant Records*, ed. Claire Talbot, 1960.

  57 *Recusant Roll No. 2 (1593–1594). An abstract in English*, ed. Hugh Bowler, 1965.

  58 *Letters of William Allen and Richard Barrett, 1572–1598*, ed. P. Renold, 1967.

  69 *St. Omers and Bruges Colleges, 1593–1773. A Biographical Dictionary*, ed. Geoffrey Holt, 1979.

C.S.P.D.	*Calendar of State Papers, Domestic Series, 1547–1580* etc.
C.S.P.F.	*Calendar of State Papers, Foreign Series*, 1547–1553 etc.
C.S.P.S.	*Calendar of Letters, Dispatches and State Papers relating to the Negotiations between England and Spain, preserved in the Archives at Simancas and elsewhere, 1485–1509* etc.
C.S.P.V.	*Calendar of State Papers and Manuscripts relating to English Affairs, existing in the Archives and Collections of Venice, and in other Libraries in Northern Italy. 1202–1509* etc.
D.N.B.	Dictionary of National Biography.
D.O.J.	*Origines Juridiciales*, by William Dugdale, London, 1666.
Dyer	Dyer's Reports, 1513–1582.

E.H.R.	*English Historical Review.*
Foley, *Records*	*Records of the English Province of the Society of Jesus*, by Henry Foley, 7 vols., London, 1877–83.
G.I.P.B.	*The Pension Book of Gray's Inn (Records of the Honourable Society)*, ed. R. J. Fletcher, 2 vols., London, 1901–10.
Gillow	*A Literary and Biographical History, or Bibliographical Dictionary, of the English Catholics from the Breach with Rome to the present time*, by Joseph Gillow, 5 vols., London, 1885–1903.
H.E.L.	*A History of English Law,* by W. S. Holdsworth, 13 vols., London, 1922–52 (vol. 1, 7th ed., revised, 1956).
H.M.C.	Publications of the Historical Manuscripts Commission.
Inq. p. m.	Inquisition post mortem.
I.T.R.	*A Calendar of the Inner Temple Records*, ed. F. A. Inderwick, 5 vols., London, 1896–1937.
Jenk.	*Eight Centuries of Reports*, by David Jenkins, London, 1661.
L. & P.	*Calendar of Letters and Papers, Foreign and Domestic, Henry VIII, 1509–1547*, ed. J. S. Brewer, James Gairdner and R. H. Brodie, 21 vols. in 33 parts, London, 1862–1910; 2nd ed. of vol. 1, in 3 parts, 1929–32.
Leon.	Leonard's King's Bench Reports, 1540–1615.
L.Q.R.	*The Law Quarterly Review.*
Moore	Sir Francis Moore's King's Bench Reports, 1512–1621.
M.T.	Middle Temple, London.
M.T.R.	*Middle Temple Records. Minutes of Parliament of the Middle Temple*, ed. C. H. Martin, 4 vols., London, 1904–05.
N. & Q.	*Notes and Queries.*
Neale I	*Elizabeth I and her Parliaments, 1559–1581*, by J. E. Neale, London, 1953.
O.R.	*Return of the Name of every Member of the Lower House of Parliament, 1213–1874*, House of Commons Parliamentary Papers, 69, 69–I, 69–II, 69–III of 1878.
P.C.C.	Prerogative Court of Canterbury.
Plowd.	Plowden's Commentaries (or Reports).

Poph.	Popham's King's Bench Reports, 1592–1597, followed by cases reported by others, 1618–1627.
P.R.O.	The Public Record Office, London.
R.A.M.T.	*Register of Admissions to the Honourable Society of the Middle Temple. From the Fifteenth Century to the year 1944*, ed. H. A. C. Sturgess, 3 vols., London, 1949.
R.H.	*Recusant History*, published by the Catholic Record Society [the first three volumes were published under the title *Biographical Studies*].
S.T.C.	*A Short-Title Catalogue of Books printed in England, Scotland and Ireland. And of English Books printed Abroad. 1475–1640*, comp. by A. W. Pollard and G. R. Redgrave, London, 1926.
T.R.P.	*Tudor Royal Proclamations*, ed. Paul L. Hughes and James F. Larkin, 3 vols., Yale, 1964–69.
T.S.A.S.	*Transactions of the Shropshire Archaeological and Natural History Society*, ser. 1, vols. 1–11 (1878–88); ser. 2, vols. 1–12 (1889–1900); ser. 3, vols. 1–10 (1901–10); ser. 4, vols. 1–12 (1911–30); *Transactions of the Shropshire Archaeological Society*, vols. 46– (1931–).
V.C.H.	*The Victoria History of the Counties of England.*
W.H.T.	*The History of the Temple, London. From the Institution of the Order of the Knights of the Temple to the close of the Stuart Period*, by J. Bruce Williamson, London, 1924.

I

PLOWDEN

Edmund Plowden was a Shropshire man who came of an ancient if not distinguished family long settled in the south-western part of the county of Salop, not far from the Montgomeryshire border. The Plowden family estate, Plowden Hall, lies about a mile to the east of the village of Lydbury North on a level stretch of ground between the surrounding hills. The village was part of the old manor of Lydbury North which once covered more than 18,000 acres.[1] From very early times the manor had formed part of the estates of the see of Hereford and as those estates extended over many thousands of acres along the Welsh border the bishops of Hereford became marcher lords with a feudal obligation to defend the Marches against inroads from the West. For that purpose a castle was built within the boundaries of the manor and it gave its name to the small town of Bishop's Castle which lies to the west of the village of Lydbury North and some four miles from Plowden Hall, over the Oakeley Mynd.[2]

It seems likely that the Plowdens took their name[3] from the place and not the other way about, as did their neighbours the Oakeleys and the Walcots.[4] The first Plowden of whom we have any knowledge is Roger de Plowden who is said to have been present at the siege of Acre in 1191 and to have received from the king, as a reward for his services, the grant of two fleurs de lys as an augmentation of his arms. Mr. Eyton observed that if Roger were present at the siege of Acre he must have been there as one of the vassals of the bishop of Hereford, William de Vere, and he suggested that a more likely origin for the fleurs de lys in the arms of Plowden (which also appear in arms of Oakeley and Walcot) is the presence of fleurs de lys in the arms of the bishop of Hereford who was suzerain of all three families.[5] There is a local tradition (which Mr. Cranage was unable to confirm) that a Plowden, a Walcot and an Oakeley went together to the Holy Land on one of the Crusades, and each made a vow to found an altar in his parish church if he returned safe; Plowden and Walcot carried out their vows, but Oakeley did not. If there be any substance in that

1. The manor is called Lydbury North to distinguish it from another episcopal manor, Lydbury South, some distance to the south of Hereford, and now called Ledbury; see Eyton, *Antiquities*, xi, 195.
2. See Anderson, *Shropshire*, 471, 472. In the 12th cent. the castle was known as Lydbury Castle, but in the course of the 13th cent. it acquired its present name of Bishop's Castle; see Eyton, *Antiquities*, xi, 203.
3. 'Plowden' signifies a 'valley where sports were held, or where deer played' and is derived from the Old English word 'plega' meaning 'play, sport, game'; see Ekwall, *English Place-Names*, 368, 369.
4. Oakeley is some 4 miles north-west, and Walcot about 1½ miles south-west of Plowden Hall; they are separated by Oakeley Mynd. The Oakeley estate was sold in the second half of the 18th cent. to Lord Clive, governor of Bengal, who was the son of an impoverished Shropshire squire. For the Oakeley family, see Oakeley, in T.S.A.S., 4th ser., vi (1916–17), 147–60; for the Walcot family, see Burton, *History of the Family of Walcot*.
5. *B.M.P.*, 5, 6; Eyton, *Antiquities*, xi, 219.

1

tradition, it might account for the building of the two transepts of the parish church of Lydbury North where the Plowdens worshipped; the south transept is known as the Walcot chapel, and the north transept as the Plowden chapel which is still owned by that family and occasionally used for Roman Catholic services.[6]

The first mention of Plowden in contemporary documents seems to be in 1203 when William Plowden (or de Plowden) was sued at the October Assizes by one Henry fitz Roger 'for four acres of land and one acre of bosc in Plowden. . . . The plaintiff was nonsuited.'[7] In view of the later close connection between Edmund Plowden and the Sandford family, it is of interest to note that in 1337 one John de Plowden was granted a protection to go to Ireland on the king's service, and that among those who went with him was Giles de Sandford.[8]

For centuries affrays, fighting and violence of all kinds had been a familiar feature of life in the Welsh Marches, and early in the fifteenth century it involved the Plowdens. The assize rolls for 1414 record a presentment that in 1399 'John Plowden of Co. Salop Esquire at Ludlow feloniously slew John Caumville.' No particulars are given, but it appears that retribution followed. On Good Friday, 6 April 1414, when John Plowden was going to church at Lydbury, he was killed by John Abrahall and others. The companions of Abrahall were described as of 'Irchenfield sondeours',[9] whom Mr. Weyman plausibly suggested were apparitors of the bishop; if that suggestion is right it provides a clue to the nature of the incident. In 1411 John Plowden had been appointed by the bishop of Hereford, Robert Mascall, to be warden of Ashwood. John Abrahall was a man of high standing in the county, and as he sat in the parliament of 1419 for the city of Hereford and in that of 1431 for the county, it is clear that he was not convicted of the murder. As he was accompanied by apparitors it seems probable that he was sent by the bishop to investigate some complaint against the warden of Ashwood who was killed in a sudden affray or in resisting arrest.[10]

Later in the century other members of the family were involved in another affray which ended fatally. At about four o'clock in the afternoon of Saturday, 21 August 1462, Edward Plowden, who seems to have been accompanied by Roger Plowden, attacked William Walcot 'with bills and bows' in a lane called Marsh Lane in Walcot, a mile or two from Plowden Hall. In the course of the attack Edward Plowden threw a bill at Walcot and so seriously injured him that he died of his wound ten days later. An inquest was subsequently held at Ludlow and evidently the matter was treated as more than an ordinary stabbing affray since the jury included

6. Cranage, *Churches of Shropshire*, i, 411, 412, and information from Mr. W. F. G. Plowden; *cf. B.M.P.*, 6.

7. Eyton, *Antiquities*, xi, 219, 220.

8. *C.P.R., 1334–1338*, p. 525.

9. 'Sondeours' appears to mean messengers. 'Irchenfield' is Archenfield, a deanery of the diocese of Hereford.

10. Weyman, in *T.S.A.S.*, 4th ser., vi (1916–17), 193–200, at p. 197.

some of the chief men of the county such as John Leighton, one of the knights of the shire for Shropshire and Sheriff of the county, Roger Eyton who was sheriff in 1466, and Robert Cresset, sheriff in 1469. They found that Edward Plowden had murdered William Walcot, and they declared that another Edward Plowden and John Plowden, Robert Corbet of Bishop's Castle, and Richard Burley of Shrewsbury, and Roger Betley of Betley had received and comforted the murderer. The Controlment Rolls show that the case never came to trial as the Plowdens concerned disappeared. Edward Plowden and Roger Plowden were indicted for 'certain felonies and murders', and the other Edward Plowden, together with John Plowden, Roger Corbet, Richard Burley, Roger Betley and John Blyke were charged with being accessories. None of them appeared after being called in the usual manner at successive courts, and they were outlawed. The origin of the quarrel is obscure, but it may have been connected with the animosities and lawlessness engendered by the Wars of the Roses, as the Walcots had Lancastrian sympathies.[11] A local tradition, on the other hand, attributes the quarrel to gaming debts incurred at the cockpit of the Red House, about half a mile from Lydbury North; the Red House was once a coaching inn but is now a farm house on the Plowden estate where the cockpit is still in existence.[12]

The old border violence was still to be met with in those parts when Edmund Plowden himself was a youth. For instance, Sir Edward Croft wrote to Thomas Cromwell to inform him that the king's commissioners had issued a proclamation forbidding anyone to carry weapons in fairs or markets in the Marches of Wales but, despite that order, a great affray had occurred in the market of Bishop's Castle on Friday, 3 July 1534, when many people had been maimed.[13]

By the middle of the fifteenth century the Plowdens were in possession of a town house in Shrewsbury which may have been the house now known as the Council House.[14] The Council House, so called because it was one of the meeting places of the Council in the Marches of Wales, still stands, much altered, in a courtyard off Castle Street, and is now the residence of the Catholic bishop of Shrewsbury.

At the end of the century, in 1495, an Edmund Plowden was recorded in the burgess roll of Shrewsbury, which also noted his children, John, Rowland, Richard, Ann, Sybil and Alice. The John Plowden there mentioned was the grandfather of the Elizabethan lawyer.[15] John Plowden married a Welsh woman, Margaret, daughter of John Blayney, and their only child, a son, was named Humphrey.[16] The date of John Plowden's death is not known but Humphrey must have succeeded his father some

11. Weyman, in *T.S.A.S.*, 4th ser., vi (1916-17), at pp. 194-6; Burton, *History of the Family of Walcot*, 16, 17.

12. Information from Mr. W. F. G. Plowden who, however, is not disposed to place much reliance on the tradition.

13. Skeel, *Council in the Marches*, 61.

14. *cf.* Owen and Blakeway, *History of Shrewsbury*, ii, 335, n. 1.

15. Forrest, *Shrewsbury Burgess Roll*, 236.

16. *B.M.P.*, 10, 11.

time before 1522 as he is referred to as owner of the Plowden estates in a muster taken in September of that year.[17]

If one can rely on a statement made many years later by Edmund Plowden's nephew, Andrew Blunden, it seems that the Plowden estates were in a prosperous condition in Humphrey Plowden's time; at any rate there is no indication that Humphrey was ever in straitened circumstances.[18] However, the house itself seems to have been in a dilapidated state. Humphrey lived in a house at Bishop's Castle which, in all probability, was Blunden Hall, an old house which still exists on the outskirts of Bishop's Castle near the church.[19] At the age of eighteen he married a widow, Elizabeth Wollascott, whose husband, William Wollascott, had died some time earlier leaving her with a small son, also called William; she was the daughter of John Sturry of Down Rossall in the Isle of Rossall, near Shrewsbury.[20]

Humphrey Plowden appears to have been a man of a traditional Catholic cast of mind. He seems to have been affronted by the 'divorce' of Henry VIII from Catherine of Aragon, and during that long drawn out affair he was sympathetic to the cause of the queen and regarded Henry's marriage to Anne Boleyn as invalid and their daughter Elizabeth as illegitimate.[21] Some years later, however, he acted, not very zealously, on behalf of the king; with Edward More he was a collector for Shropshire of the money comprising the 'loan' granted to the king in 1542, but their efforts to collect the loan cannot have been very energetic as no money had been paid over to the crown by the summer of the following year.[22] Humphrey and Elizabeth Plowden had ten children, seven girls and three boys, but the dates of their births are unknown save in the case of Edmund, the subject of this study.[23]

17. *L. & P.*, xvii, p. 509.

18. See *T.S.A.S.*, 2nd ser., ix (1897), 131. Andrew Blunden was writing after the death of his uncle in 1585, and he was not born at the time of which he wrote; but there is no reason to doubt what he said.

19. *B.M.P.*, 11, 13.

20. Norsworthy, in *T.S.A.S.*, lii (1947-8), at p. 179; Grazebrook and Ryland, *Visitation*, p. 448.

21. Norsworthy, in *T.S.A.S.*, lii (1947-8), at p. 180. Miss Norsworthy cited no authority for this statement, but there is no reason to doubt its accuracy.

22. *L. & P.*, xviii, pt. 1, 856 (10 July 1543). The amount of the 'money remaining unpaid' by More and Plowden has been left blank. The statute 35 Hen. VIII, c. 12 (1544) absolved the king from repaying loans then outstanding.

23. *B.M.P.*, 11, 12. The names of Humphrey's children were: Margaret (married Richard Sandford), Jane (married first Richard Blunden, and then Lewis Jones), Elizabeth (married Peter Greenway), John, Edmund, Edward, Anne (married Thomas Higge), Mary (married Charles Needham), and Joyce (married Leonard Meysie). Since Edmund was born two years after his parent's marriage, the other children cannot have been born in the order shown in the pedigree printed in *B.M.P.* where Edmund appears as the sixth child; as he inherited his father's estates (see p. 51, *post*), he must have been the eldest son.

II

EARLY LIFE

Edmund Plowden was born at some time in 1518, most probably at Blunden Hall at Bishop's Castle where his parents were living.[1] He was his father's eldest son and was one of a large family, having two brothers and seven sisters. It has been asserted several times that he was born at Plowden[2] but those statements appear to be based on an ambiguous phrase used by Anthony Wood: 'Edmund Plowden . . . was born of an ancient and genteel family at Plowden in the said county [Shropshire]'.[3] The date of his birth has been given as 1517,[4] but Plowden himself wrote that he entered upon the study of the law 'in the twentieth year of my age, and in the thirtieth year of the reign of the late King Henry VIII [1538]',[5] which fixes the year of his birth as 1518.

Much of his early life is obscure. Nothing is known of his upbringing, and it is not easy to reconcile all the statements made about his education. Plowden himself stated that he began to study law in 1538, and Anthony Wood gave further details which present something of a puzzle. According to Wood, Plowden spent three years at Cambridge studying arts, philosophy and medicine, and afterwards entered one of the Inns of Court; Wood went on to say that 'Soon after, coming to Oxon, he spent four years more in the same studies there, and in November anno 1552 he was admitted to practise chirurgery and physic by the venerable convocation of the said university.'[6] It is just possible to fit that extensive programme of study into the years before 1552 when Plowden was thirty-four years of age, but little time is left for anything else. Yet in 1553 he was elected to parliament and in 1557 he was Autumn Reader of his Inn, showing that by then he was well established in his profession and a senior member of the Inn. At that time it was usual for about fourteen years or more to elapse between admission to the Middle Temple and election as Reader,[7] and during that period the barrister would need to have devoted a great deal of his time to his profession and the obligations of his Inn. Anthony Wood's course of study does not seem to allow sufficient time for all that to happen, and he appears to be the sole authority for the statement that Plowden studied philosophy and medicine at both Oxford and Cambridge.

Charles and Thompson Cooper, writing in 1859 in their first volume of *Athenae Cantabrigienses,* credited Plowden with three years at Cambridge

1. See p.4, *ante.*
2. E.g., Woolrych, *Eminent Serjeants,* i, 103; Cooper, *Athenae Cantabrigienses,* i, 501; Lloyd, *State Worthies,* i, 460; Fuller, *Worthies,* ii, 259.
3. *Athen. Oxon.,* i, 503.
4. *B.M.P.,* 13; Woolrych, *Eminent Serjeants,* i, 103.
5. Plowd., p. iii (Preface).
6. *Athen. Oxon.,* i, 503.
7. See p. 46, *post.*

but they appear to have been doubtful about his four years at Oxford, for they wrote, 'It has been said that subsequently to his studying at Cambridge and the Temple he spent four years at Oxford'; and the source of their information was Anthony Wood. When Thompson Cooper later wrote the article on Plowden for the *Dictionary of National Biography* his doubts appear to have increased, for he cast the whole of the responsibility on Wood: 'Wood asserts that, after studying at Cambridge and in the Temple, Plowden spent four years at Oxford, and in November 1552 was admitted to practice chirurgery by the convocation of that university.'[8] That suggests that Cooper had been unable to find any independent authority to support Wood's assertion. The published lists of members of the two universities include Plowden's name for both Oxford and Cambridge, but in each case the authority given is Anthony Wood, either directly from his *Athenae Oxonienses* or indirectly through the Coopers' *Athenae Cantabrigienses;* the lists do not, therefore, provide any independent confirmation of Wood's assertion.[9] In the *Athenae Oxonienses* Anthony Wood cast his net very wide and it seems very probable that he is here mistaken about Plowden's university career and medical qualifications; he was certainly mistaken in his assertion that Plowden was a serjeant-at-law in 1560.[10]

What is certain is that Plowden began to study law in 1538 when he was twenty years old. It seems likely that he went first to one of the Inns of Chancery, of which there were then ten, where the students learned the elements of jurisprudence and made a preliminary study of ethics and politics. There is no record of the Inn of Chancery to which Plowden went but it seems likely that it was one of the two Inns then attached to and under the control of the Middle Temple (to which Plowden was later admitted), Strand Inn and New Inn; Strand Inn was situated in the Strand, a short distance to the west of St. Clement Danes, and was the largest of all the Inns of Chancery, while New Inn was on the north side of the Strand, near to Clement's Inn.[11]

After spending about a year in an Inn of Chancery Plowden, in the usual way, moved on to an Inn of Court and was admitted to the Middle

8. Cooper, *Athenae Cantabrigienses*, i, 501; *D.N.B.*, s.v. Plowden, Edmund.

9. See Venn, *Alumni Cantabrigienses*, iii, 372; Foster, *Alumni Oxonienses*, iii, 1172; Boase, *Register of University of Oxford*, i, 219. Plowden's name does not appear in Emden, *Biographical Register of the University of Oxford, 1501–1540.*

10. *Athen. Oxon.*, i, 503: 'In 1557 he [Plowden] became autumn or summer reader of the Middle Temple, and three years after Lent Reader, being then a serjeant at, and accounted the oracle of, the law.' The mistake here is a double one: Plowden was never a serjeant (see p. 54, *post*), and no one could be both a serjeant and a reader at one of the Inns of Court at the same time, but a serjeant elect could read (*cf.* Edward Fenner who had been Autumn Reader in 1576 was invited to read again on being chosen to be serjeant-at-law in 1557; *M.T.R.*, i, 216). Plowden was Autumn Reader in 1557, and Lent Reader in 1558 and again in 1561.

11. Strand Inn, also known as Chester Inn, was destroyed in 1549 to make way for the new palace built by the Protector Somerset; see p. 62, *post*. For the Inns of Chancery, see Megarry, *Inns Ancient and Modern*, 27–48, and the authorities there cited.

Temple.[12] It is possible that his choice of Inn was influenced by a friend and neighbour of his family, Sir Thomas Englefield, who owned large estates in Up Rossall near Shrewsbury; Englefield, who had been a bencher of the Middle Temple, subsequently became a judge of the Common Pleas and had died in 1537 shortly before Plowden began his studies.[13] Of the buildings with which he then became familiar only the Temple Church remains. Such buildings as the lawyers had erected for their own accommodation were, presumably, constructed of wood and plaster. The only substantial buildings in the Temple were the halls of the two Inns and the church. The Inner Temple hall stood on the site of its modern successor and continued in use in an increasingly decayed and overcrowded state until it was pulled down between 1868 and 1870 to make way for a new and more commodious building. The Middle Temple hall which Plowden first knew stood on the east side of Middle Temple Lane on ground that is now included partly in Pump Court and partly in Elm Court.[14]

When Plowden entered the Temple there had recently been constructed a wall along the northern bank of the Thames, built, no doubt, to protect the Temple gardens in times of flood. The building of the wall occupied most of the fifteen-twenties and among the contributors to its cost was the Lord Saint Johns who paid £20.[15] The 'Lord Saint Johns' was the Prior of the Order of the Knights of the Hospital of St. John of Jerusalem, the Knights Hospitallers, who succeeded to the property of the Knights Templars after the suppression of the latter order in the fourteenth century. The Knights Templars, who gave their name to the tract of land lying between the Strand and the Thames, had owned it since the reign of Henry II, and by 1185 they had completed their round church which eventually became the church of the two Temple societies. The Knights Hospitallers did not themselves settle in the Temple (they had a house in Clerkenwell) but leased it to various tenants until, in the course of time, the lawyers became established there.[16] Thus, at the time when Edmund Plowden entered the Middle Temple, the Prior of the Hospitallers, popularly known as the Lord of St. John's, was the landlord of the 'New Temple' to whom

12. There is no record of the date of Plowden's admission to the Middle Temple, as the relevant records of the Inn are no longer in existence. It is frequently stated that he was admitted in 1538, which follows Plowden's own statement (see p. 5, *ante*) on the assumption that he started his legal studies at the Middle Temple (e.g., *D.N.B.*; Woolrych, *Eminent Serjeants*, i, 104; Williamson, *Middle Temple Bench Book*, 71; Rope, in *The Month*, n.s., xvi (1956), at p. 102); but if it is assumed, as here, that he went first to an Inn of Chancery, the date of his admission to the Middle Temple would be c. 1539. Professor Abbott's statement (*Law Reporting*, 199) that Plowden 'tells us that he entered the Middle Temple in 1538 at the age of twenty' is inaccurate; Plowden did not mention the Middle Temple.

13. Williamson, *Middle Temple Bench Book*, 57.

14. *W.H.T.*, 139, 229, 669. Sir William Dugdale (*D.O.J.*, 146) supposed that the Inner Temple hall, as it stood in his day (17th cent.), dated from the reign of Edward III, but it probably underwent substantial reconstruction after the damage caused by Wat Tyler and his followers in 1381.

15. *cf. I.T.R.*, i, 74.

16. See generally, *W.H.T.*, Part I.

each of the two societies paid an annual rent of £10.[17] In 1540, however, Henry VIII seized all the property in England and Ireland of the Knights Hospitallers, which was vested by Act of Parliament in the king to use and employ at his own free will and pleasure.[18] Strangely enough, there is no documentary evidence concerning the relationship between the two Temple societies and their new landlord, but it seems that no change took place save that their rents were thereafter paid to the crown.

In Plowden's time the Temple was not closely surrounded by buildings as it is to-day. To the east of the Inner Temple was Whitefriars, the great convent of the Carmelites, while further east, beyond the Bridewell and the mouth of the Fleet river, was Blackfriars, the convent of the Dominicans, in whose great hall parliament sometimes assembled and where, some ten years before Plowden's arrival in the Temple, cardinals Campeggio and Wolsey had sat to hear Henry VIII's divorce suit. The city itself, overflowing its walls, came close to the Temple on the east, only stopping at Temple Bar. The suburban area to the east of Chancery Lane, between Fleet Street and Holborn, was fairly densely built over, but to the west, and north of the Strand, there was for the most part open country; there were then hardly any buildings in Lincoln's Inn Fields and north of Holborn the buildings of Gray's Inn stood almost in isolation. To the west of the Middle Temple were the great mansions built by their noble owners with spacious gardens and walks; they lay between the river and the Strand along which the lawyers travelled on their way from the Temple to Westminster Hall where the courts of common law and the court of chancery sat. Although the Temple was close to the city of London, all the Inns of Court, of which Gray's Inn was the most isolated, enjoyed a pleasant seclusion and were approached from the north and west largely through fields and woods. During his lifetime Plowden was to see much building on those open spaces.[19]

To the west of the Middle Temple, on the river, was Exeter Inn, the London lodging of the bishops of Exeter. In the reign of Edward VI it was acquired by the first Lord Paget and it subsequently came into the possession of two of queen Elizabeth's favourites, first the earl of Leicester, and subsequently the earl of Essex who rebuilt it and renamed it Essex House; it was there that he withstood a short siege during his ill starred rebellion. In the seventeenth century those riverside palaces were losing their popularity so that many of them were sold to speculative builders. In 1674 Essex House was sold to Dr. Nicholas Barbon, the son of Praise-God Barebones, who has a tenuous and fortuitous connection with the subject of this book. Barbon, a doctor of medicine, had given up his practice for the more lucrative calling of speculative builder. The Middle Temple secured from Barbon the garden wall of Essex House, of which a

17. *W.H.T.*, 111.
18. 35 Hen. VIII, c. 24.
19. For the foregoing, see *A to Z of Elizabethan London*, and Brett-James, *The Growth of Stuart London*.

portion can still be seen in Fountain Court, together with the plot of land on which parts of New Court and Garden Court now stand, and a strip of land on the west side of the Temple boundary. After the disastrous fire in 1678 which destroyed a great part of the Temple, Barbon was engaged in much rebuilding there while he was still developing the Essex House estate, and among the buildings in the Temple which he erected were two blocks on the west side of Middle Temple Lane, just south of the present hall. Barbon's buildings in Middle Temple Lane are no longer in existence; they were rebuilt in 1732 and are now known as Plowden Buildings.[20]

The society in which Plowden found himself at the beginning of his professional life was an hierarchical one. Like the other Inns of Court the Middle Temple was governed by a small number of senior members known as Masters of the Bench or, more shortly, 'Benchers'.[21] In the words of an anonymous writer of a description of the Inn at that time, the benchers were 'those utter-barristers which after they have continued in the house by the space of fourteen or fifteen years, are by the elders of the house chosen to read, expound, and declare some statute openly unto all the company of the house, in one of the two principal times of their learning which they call the grand vacation in summer, and during the time of his reading, he hath the name of a reader and after of bencher.'[22] The benchers were thus a self-perpetuating body as they alone had the power to choose those who were to be of their number. It was customary for the benchers to meet formally four times a year in order to exercise their plenary powers in relation to the govenment of the Inn; such a meeting was known in the Inn as a 'Parliament', and the orders made by a Parliament were binding upon all members of the Inn, of whatever rank.[23] The executive officer of the Inn was (and is) the Treasurer who was normally elected from among the benchers.[24]

20. See Brett-James,*Growth of Stuart London*, 324–7; *W.H.T.*, 519–21.
21. The term 'bencher' appears in the records of the Middle Temple for the first time in the minutes of a parliament held on 2 Nov. 1507, which established certain orders for the house: ' . . . that yerely at Hyllary terme the Reader for somer vacacion then next folowyng be chosyn, and that immediately after his eleccion, he be taken and admitted for a Bencher, . . . ' (*M.T.R.*, i, 21). *cf.* Inner Temple, *I.T.R.*, i, 90 (Feb. 1527).
22. An account of the Inn in general terms, written before 1540, is contained in a document entitled 'A Description of the form and manner, how and by what orders and customs the state of the Fellowship of the Middle Temple (one of the Houses of Court) is maintained; and what ways they have to attain unto learning', Br. Lib., Cotton MS Vit. C. ix, art. 34 (ff. 319–323v). The MS has been damaged by fire, but it has been printed in *D.O.J.*, 193–7, and *A.I.T.*, 211–22. For the quotation above, see f. 321 (*D.O.J.*, 194; *A.I.T.*. 214). Reference may also be made to a report, probably written between 1534 and 1540, upon the four Inns of Court, made to Henry VIII by Nicholas Bacon of Gray's Inn, Thomas Denton of the Middle Temple, and Robert Cary; the MS is no longer in existence, but it was printed in Waterhous, *Fortescutus Illustratus*, 543–6, and reprinted by Bland in *Jo. of Soc. of Public Teachers of Law*, n.s., x (1969), 178–94, at pp. 183–94.
23. The meetings of benchers were known in the Inner Temple as a Parliament, in Lincoln's Inn as a Council, and in Gray's Inn as a Pension. All the Inns of Court are unincorporated voluntary societies which have no charters and no founders; their origins are obscure and the source of the powers exercised by the benchers is unknown.
24. Br. Lib., Cotton MS Vit. C. ix, f. 319.

Below the benchers came the utter-barristers, or those who had been
called to the Utter-Bar. When Plowden was admitted to the Inn the term
'utter-barrister' had largely displaced the older term 'apprentice' which
had been used to denote counsel who were not of the degree of serjeant-
at-law. Yet the older term lingered on and Plowden, on the title-page of
his famous *Commentaries* or reports of cases, described himself as 'Un
Apprentice de le Common Ley', while the anonymous advocate of
considerable ability and power who appears in those reports under the
description of 'an apprentice of the Middle Temple' may confidently be
identified with Plowden himself.[25]

The lowest of the ranks in the Inn comprised the students or, as they
were known, the 'inner-barristers'. Not all those who were admitted as
inner-barristers came to the Inns with the intention of practising in the
courts. Although the Inns of Court were primarily societies and schools
for lawyers, the studies pursued there did not exclude the liberal arts and
they were centres of an intense intellectual and social life. Writing in the
previous century Sir John Fortescue had noted that the Inns of Court
attracted young men of good family who neither need nor wished to
devote themselves to a career in the law; they came, he said, to learn the
accomplishments of a gentleman, because 'there is in these greater Inns
[i.e., the Inns of Court] . . . beside the study of the laws, as it were an
university or school of all commendable qualities requisite for noblemen.[26]
There they learn to sing and to exercise themselves in all kinds of harmony.
There also they practice dancing and other noblemen's pastimes as they
use to do which are brought up in the king's house.'[27] Such students,
however, did not arrive in the Inns in substantial numbers until about the
middle of the sixteenth century, when many gentlemen sent their sons
there, not necessarily to prepare them for practice in the law but to educate
them and to ensure that they had a sufficient grounding in the law to

25. The term 'apprentice' is not used in the description of the Middle Temple in the Cotton
MS nor in the Bacon report on the four Inns of Court (see p. 9, *ante*, note). It appears only
rarely in the records of the Middle Temple; once in 1562, when Plowden was Treasurer, when it
was ordered that if Master Mawdeley should die or leave his chamber, the Treasurer might
admit an apprentice or any other thereto (*M.T.R.*, i, 138). The original Latin entry is: 'Et si
contingat predictum Magistrum Mawdeley obire aut relinquere cameram predictam aliquo
modo tunc licebit Thesaur. admittere alterum qui erit apprenticius aut alius quicunque in
eandem cameram a pro suo libito quia est una ex xii cameris pro Magistris de Banco'; M.T.,
B.M.B., D. 47. There were three similar admissions in 1593, 1598 and 1603, where Matthew
Dale, a bencher and father of the persons admitted, is so described (*M.T.R.*, i, 335, 383, 431).
The relevant part of the original Latin entries is 'filius, etc. Mathei Dale apprenticii legis et
Medii Templi London Socii . . . '; M.T., B.M.B., D. 231, 277, 320. The term 'barrister' seems
to have been originally a purely domestic term used in the Inns of Court. The modern term
'barrister-at-law' did not emerge until the end of the 17th cent. See generally, *W.H.T.*, 114–6;
Baker, in *L.Q.R.*, lxxxv (1969), 334–8; Baker, in *Camb. Law Jo.*, xxvii (1969), 204–29; Simpson,
in *Camb. Law Jo.*, xxviii (1970), 241–86.

26. The translation used here is that of John Selden; Fortescue's word was *nobiles* ('In hiis
vero hospiciis maioribus . . . ultra studium legum est quasi gimnasium omnium morum qui
nobiles docent.'), which should now, no doubt, be more accurately rendered by 'gentlemen'.

27. Fortescue, *De Laudibus Legum Angliae* (trans. J. Selden; London, 1616), 110 (ch. xlix).

enable them to manage their estates and to take their places in the commissions of the peace.

Owing to the loss of the relevant records, we do not know either the actual date on which Plowden was admitted to the Middle Temple, or to whose chamber he was admitted or with whom he was bound.[28] Students who were Londoners could live at home while others, if they were unable to obtain lodgings in the Inns, got what accommodation they could in the homes of relatives or in neighbouring lodging houses; in addition, there were officially approved tenements such as Fulwood's Rents and Bentley's Rents near Gray's Inn, and there were nearby taverns such as the Antelope in Holborn and the Black Spread Eagle in Fleet Street.[29] It seems likely that Plowden lodged in the Middle Temple itself.

Once admitted to the Inn Plowden came under the general obligation to 'keep commons' and attend the learning exercises during certain vacations. Keeping commons was regarded as essential to maintain the corporate life of the Inns and was enforced by penalties imposed by the benchers, although it was open to a member of an Inn to purchase, by way of fine, exemption from serving in any of the offices of the society, or from keeping commons or the learning vacations. Such exemptions, however, were rare as the obligation of 'continuance' in commons was fundamental to the life of the Inn.[30] On joining the Society Plowden, like other new members, would have taken his place in Clerks' Commons with the other junior students. Dinner, which was a midday meal, and supper were eaten in common in the hall. The most junior members messed together in Clerks' Commons and waited on others who had passed that stage. Masters' Commons were divided into three groups which messed at separate tables: those who were not utter-barristers, the utter-barristers, and the benchers. Those in Clerks' Commons received smaller portions than those in Masters' Commons, but they paid less, and the juniors did not pay pension money which was charged to those in Masters' Commons.[31]

28. The volume containing the Minutes of Parliament of the Middle Temple from 3 Feb. 1550 is missing.

29. Prest, *Inns of Court*, 13.

30. If a new member paid a fine to be excused all or some of the obligations of membership, he was said to be admitted 'specially'; otherwise a new member was admitted 'generally'.

31. *W.H.T.*, 109, 113, 117. The charge for those in Master's Commons was then £6 10s. p.a., and for those in Clerks's Commons £5 4s.; pension money was 3s. 4d. p.a. The payment of those sums was a constant source of trouble.

III

LEARNING THE LAW

Plowden began his legal studies at a momentous time in the history of England and the development of English law. Only a few years previously Henry VIII had brought about the final breach with Rome after the long drawn out drama of his 'divorce' from Catherine of Aragon, and Plowden may well have shared his father's opinions concerning those events.[1] John Fisher and Thomas More had only recently been executed, and their deaths had left the whole of Europe aghast. And in the law a significant event had occurred with the cessation of the Year Books: 'In 1535, the year in which More was done to death, the Year Books came to an end: in other words, the great stream of law reports that had been flowing for near two centuries and a half, ever since the days of Edward I, becomes discontinuous and then runs dry.'[2]

The method of instruction in the law was mainly oral. Text books were few and expensive and there were no reports of cases save what was contained in the Year Books which were, in general, collections of notes of matters arising during argument and frequently omitted the final judgment. And when Plowden began his studies the Middle Temple had no library: 'They now have no library so that they cannot attain to the knowledge of divers learning but to their great charges by the buying of such books as they lust to study. They had a simple library in which were not many books besides the law and that library, by means that it stood always open and that the learners had not each a key to it, it was [at] last robbed of all the books in it.'[3] For the most part the students learned their law by means of the readings and disputations of various kinds which took place in the Inn. The learning exercises were an effective way of training lawyers and, like the university disputations, were suited to producing in the student 'a dexterity in devising or meeting arguments and a readiness in applying acquired knowledge, of comparatively little value to the student of history or physical science, but indispensable to the advocate and even to the judge.'[4]

In addition to the domestic exercises, the students were expected to attend the courts at Westminster during term time and there listen to and

1. See p. 4, *ante*.
2. Maitland, 'English Law and the Renaissance' in *Select Essays*, i, 192. The continuous series of the Year Books does not extend beyond 1500, but between 1501 and 1535 nine further volumes were printed; see Abbott, *Law Reporting*, 10.
3. Br. Lib., Cotton MS Vit. C. ix, f. 323. The want of a library was not made good until 1641 when Robert Ashley, a bencher, died and bequeathed his extensive collection of books to the Inn; see *W.H.T.*, 381–4. In 1642 an order was made that the books left to the Inn by Ashley should be kept under lock and key until a library were built (*M.T.R.*, i, 917; *D.O.J.*, 193).
4. Rashdall, *Universities of Europe*, i, 255.

EDMUND PLOWDEN 13

make notes of the arguments of counsel and the decisions of the judges.[5] Plowden was assiduous in such study. 'When I first entered upon the study of the law,'he wrote, ' . . . I resolved upon two things, which I then purposed earnestly to pursue. The first was, to be present at, and to give diligent attention to, the debates and questions of law, and particularly to the arguments of those who were men of the greatest note and reputation for learning. The second was, to commit to writing what I heard, and the judgment thereupon, which seemed to me to be much better than to rely upon treacherous memory which often deceives its master. These two resolutions I pursued effectually by a constant attendance at moots and lectures, and at all places in court and chancery, to which I might have access, where matters of law were argued and debated.'[6] The attendance of students at the courts during term time explains why the educational activity in the Inns of Court was confined, for the most part, to the vacations when the learning exercises took place.

According to the Bacon report, 'The whole year amongst them [i.e., the Inns of Court] is divided into three parts; that is to say the learning-vacation,[7] the term-times, and the mean or dead vacation. They have yearly two learning-vacations, that is to say, Lent vacation, which begins the first Monday in Lent, and continueth three weeks and three days, the other vacation is called Summer vacation which beginneth the Monday after Lammas-day[8] and continueth as the other. In these vacations are the greatest conference, and exercises of study that they have in all the year.'[9]

The most formal and ceremonious of the learning exercises were the readings which took place twice a year during the Grand vacations. The readings were thus described in the Bacon report: 'First, the Readers and Ancients[10] appoint the eldest utter-barrister in continuance, as one that they think most suitable for that room, to read amongst them openly in the house, during the Summer vacation, and of this appointment he hath always knowledge about half a year before he shall read, that in the mean time he may provide therefor, and then the first day after vacation, about 8 of the clock, he that is so chosen to read openly in the hall before all the company, shall read some one such Act or Statute as shall please him to ground his whole reading on for all that vacation; and that done, doth declare such inconveniences and mischiefs as were unprovided for, and

5. For the law terms, see Cheney, *Handbook of Dates*, 65–9. The dates of the terms varied, but in the middle of the 16th cent. the terms were approximately as follows: Michaelmas, 6 Oct. to 25 Nov.; Hilary, 20 Jan. to shortly before Lent; Easter, a fortnight after Easter Day to Ascension Day; Trinity, a week after Trinity Monday to 8 July.
6. Plowd. p. iii (Preface).
7. In the Temple it was known as the Grand Vacation. The term 'vacation' denotes those intervals of time which separated the legal terms. The 'mean vacation' was the 'whole time out of the learning vacation and term' (Bacon Rep., 187).
8. Lammas Day was 1 August.
9. Bacon Rep., 185. Each Inn had its own special rules and traditions concerning the learning exercises in term and vacation.
10. I.e., benchers. 'Ancienty' or seniority was of great importance in the Inns. Election as Reader was equivalent to election to the bench of an Inn; the Reader took his place among the benchers following his reading.

now by the same Statute be [amended], and then reciteth certain doubts and questions which he hath devised, that may grow upon the said Statute, and declareth his judgement therein. That done, one of the younger utter-barristers rehearseth one question propounded by the Reader, and doth by way of argument labour to prove the Reader's opinion to be against the law, and after him the rest of the utter barristers and Readers one after another in their ancienties [i.e., in order of seniority] do declare their opinions and judgements in the same, and then the Reader who did put the case endeavoureth himself to confute objections laid against him, and to confirm his own opinion, after whom, the judges and serjeants, if any be present, declare their opinions, and after they have done, the youngest utter-barrister again rehearseth another case, which is ordered as the other was; thus the reading ends for that day: and this manner of reading and disputations continue daily two hours, or thereabouts.'[11] That was a general description intended to comprise all the Inns, and shows the discussions being opened by the younger barristers. No doubt the manner of conducting readings was not entirely the same in each house, and the practice at the Middle Temple was a little different, with the seniors opening the discussions, as appears from the anonymous description of that Inn: 'Furthermore, in the same grand vacations when that one of the elders read and expound a statute such utter-barristers as are of long continuance do stand in a place together wheareat they rehearse some one opinion or saying of him that readeth and by all ways of learning and reason that can be invented do impugn it, and some other do approve it, and all the rest of the house give ear unto their disputations; and at last the Reader doth confute all their sayings and confirmeth his opinion.'[12]

When he delivered his discourses the Reader stood at the 'Cupboard' which, despite its name, was (and is) a table. The Cupboard was the centre of ceremonial observance in the hall and it was from the Cupboard that all matters of importance affecting the members of the Inn were announced.[13] At the time when Plowden was a student it was usual for the Reader to discourse upon a statute, and most readings were on statutes relating to land law which provided the major part of the litigation in the courts; disputes about tenure and the inheritance of landed property provided the common lawyer of the sixteenth century with the bulk of his professional income.[14] As Dr. Prest has observed, 'the value of these

11. Bacon Rep., 186.
12. Br. Lib., Cotton MS Vit. C. ix, f. 320v (*D.O.J.*, 194; *A.I.T.*, 215).
13. The present Cupboard, which has been in use for centuries, is made from wood taken from Sir Francis Drake's ship, the *Golden Hind*; Drake was a member of the Inn and on 4 Aug. 1586 came into hall at dinner time and received the congratulations of those present on his successful return from his voyage of circumnavigation (*M.T.R.*, i, 285). Lincoln's Inn and Gray's Inn also had Cupboards, but not the Inner Temple. A new feature was introduced into the Middle Temple readings during the reign of Elizabeth with the election of Cupboardmen; four senior utter barristers were appointed to 'stand at the Cupboard' in order to assist the Reader; the first recorded appointment of Cupboardmen was on 11 Feb. 1568 (M.T., B.M.B., D. 84). Members of the Middle Temple are still called to the Bar at the Cupboard.
14. Prest, *Inns of Court*. 119–24. *cf*. Co. Litt. 280v.

readings depended on their ingenuity and lucidity as expositions of a statute or branch of law, rather than their place in a traditional canon.'[15]

A less formal method of instruction was provided by the moots which were, in essence, mock trials modelled on the procedure of the court of Common Pleas, in which pleadings were prepared by the mootmen. Moots were described in the Bacon report as follows: 'In those vacations every night after supper and every fasting day immediately after six of the clock, boyer ended,[16] (festival days and their evens only excepted) the Reader with two benchers or one at the least cometh into the hall to the Cupboard and there most commonly one of the utter-barristers propoundeth unto them some doubtful case, the which every of the benchers in their ancienties argue and last of all he that moveth; this done the Readers and benchers sit down on the bench in the end of the hall whereof they take their name, and on a form towards the midst of the hall sitteth down two inner-barristers and on the other side of them on the same form two utter-barristers.[17] And the inner-barristers do in French openly declare unto the benchers (even as the serjeants do at the Bar in the King's Courts to the Judges) some kind of action, the one being as it were retained with the plaintiff in the action and the other with the defendants; after which things done the utter-barristers argue such questions as be disputable within the case (as there must be always one at the least) and this ended the benchers do likewise declare their opinions how they think the law to be in the same questions and this manner of exercise of mooting is daily used during the said vacations.'[18]

In the Middle Temple mooting continued after the two learning vacations for the benefit of the more junior students. Those exercises were described by the anonymous writer on the Middle Temple as follows: 'Also after the term ended and the two grand vacations ended, then the young men that be no utter-barristers do dispute and argue in law French some doubtful question before the utter-barristers who at the last do shew their opinions in English thereunto: and this manner of disputations is called mean vacation moots or chapel moots.'[19]

All moots, of whatever kind, were required to raise at least one point of law for argument, and the responsibility for formulating the moot cases rested with the barristers or students who propounded the case. The production of the cases, which, in the more formal moots, included the production of pleadings, seems to have made considerable demands upon

15. Prest, *Inns of Court*, 120.
16. 'Boyer' was a form of light refreshment served instead of supper.
17. The procedure at the moots is the probable origin of the terms 'inner-barrister' and 'utter-barrister'. Those who argued the moot cases stood at a bench which seems to have represented the bar of the court. The junior students were placed innermost (and so 'inner-barristers') while those who were more advanced in continuance and learning were placed outermost (and so 'utter-barristers'). The status of utter-barrister did not, at that time, entitle a person called to it to audience in the courts; *cf*. W.H.T., 116.
18. Bacon Rep., 186-7.
19. Br. Lib., Cotton MS Vit. C. ix, f. 321 (*D.O.J.*, 195; *A.I.T.*, 216).

the mootmen, and in the following century printers began the publication of collections of moot points for their assistance. The first of such collections is associated with Edmund Plowden himself and was compiled, in all probability, from his readings and other discourses. The collection consists of 376 moot points which at first circulated in manuscript; it did not appear in print until 1620 or thereabouts when it was published under the title of *Les Quaeres del Mounsieur Plowden.*[20]

It was customary in the Middle Temple for the inner-barristers to take part in a less formal exercise after dinner and supper when, sitting in groups of three, they discussed some arguable point of law. The anonymous writer on the Middle Temple described it as follows: 'One of the three putteth forth some doubtful question in the law to the other two of his company and they reason and argue unto it in English; and at last he that putteth forth the question declareth his mind, also showing unto them the judgment or better opinion of his book, when he had the same question: and this do the students observe every day through the year, except festival days.'[21] This 'putting of cases', or 'moving questions', was not merely an exercise for students but was a distinctive characteristic of all lawyers. It was usual, whenever a number of lawyers were gathered together, whether in the precincts of the courts, in their Inns or even in Parliament, for them to pose doubtful points of law to one another, and the resulting discussion must have resembled a miniature moot.

Like his fellow students Plowden spent his first two years as a member of the Middle Temple in Clerks' Commons. During those years attendance at the learning exercises and continuance in commons was compulsory unless excused or pardoned on payment of a fine. The presence of those in Clerks' Commons was also required at the solemn keeping of Christmas which was, in effect, the Inn's school of manners. 'By the old custom of the house all such as are made fellows,[22] unless they be dispensed withal at their admittance, are compelled to be personally present at the two first grand vacations in Lent after their coming; at the two first grand vacations in summer after their coming, the two first Christmases that be solemnly kept after their coming, upon pain of forfeiture of 20s. for every default.'[23]

Special officers were nominated for the solemn keeping of Christmas, and the Bacon report stated that their offices 'for the most part are such as are exercised in the King's Highness's house, and other noblemen, and this is done only to the intent that they should in time come to know

20. For MS versions see, e.g., Br. Lib., Harg. MSS 351, 353, 389, and Br. Lib., Add. MSS 36078, 36081. *S.T.C.* (no. 20048) gives the date of publication of *Les Quaeres del Mounsieur Plowden* as '? 1620'. A translation, under the title *The Quaeries of Edmund Plowden, Esq.*, has been appended to the English versions of Plowden's reports. See also H.B., *Plowdens Quaeries.*
21. Br. Lib., Cotton MS Vit. C. ix, f. 321 (*D.O.J.*, 195; *A.I.T.*, 216).
22. That is, members of the Inn.
23. Br. Lib., Cotton MS Vit. C. ix, f. 321v (*D.O.J.*, 194; *A.I.T.*, 214). Christmas ceased to be a compulsory vacation in the Middle Temple in 1607, but it again became compulsory in 1635 (*M.T.R.*, ii, 478, 481).

how to use themselves.'[24] Thus the Christmas festivities were not mere amusements but were designed to have some educational value. The Christmas officers were appointed by the benchers at the first parliament held in November. At the beginning of the reign of queen Elizabeth, however, the appointments ceased and at a parliament held on 26 November 1560 it was ordered that no solemn Christmas be kept. Thereafter for many years a similar order was made but a cartload of coals and an allowance of 40s. for minstrels were provided for the benefit of those remaining in residence.[25] Christmas was not again solemnly kept until 1596.[26]

After two years a new member of the Inn left Clerks' Commons and moved to Masters' Commons, and thereafter was free to attend the learning exercises or not as he pleased.[27] Nevertheless, for any young man such as Plowden, who aspired to become an utter-barrister and practise in the courts, further attendance at the learning exercises was a practical necessity. It was said of Plowden that in his youth he was 'excessive studious, so that (as we have it by tradition) in three years space he went not once out of the Temple.'[28] That is, no doubt, an exaggeration but it emphasizes the hard work and devotion to learning that were characteristic of Plowden throughout his life, and the young man who became what Sir William Holdsworth described as 'perhaps the most learned lawyer in a century of learned lawyers' must have applied himself to his studies with assiduity.[29]

Having performed the learning exercises as an inner-barrister Plowden was called to the degree of utter-barrister. That was a domestic matter of the Inn and did not, of itself, confer a right of audience in the courts at Westminster; indeed, barristers are still called to the bar of their Inn and not to the bar of any court of law. The judges exercised a strict control over those who appeared before them and from time to time they issued orders prescribing the period of time that must elapse before the right of audience could be exercised. The date of Plowden's call is unknown; even had the relevant records of the Inn survived that information would probably not have been forthcoming as it was not then the practice to record calls to the Bar in the Minutes of Parliament. The anonymous writer on the Middle Temple, however, stated that 'The utter-barristers are they which after they have continued in the house by the space of five or six years and have profited in the study of the law are called by the elders or benchers to plead, argue and dispute some doubtful matter in the law before certain of the same benchers in term time or in the two principal times in the year of their learnings which they call Grand Vacations and

24. Bacon Rep., 188; and see p. 45, *post*.
25. *W.H.T.*, 108, 114, 150, 208; Br. Lib., Cotton MS Vit. C. ix, f. 321v (*D.O.J.*, 194; *A.I.T.*, 215); *M.T.R.*, i, 129. The customs for Christmas at the Inner Temple differed somewhat from those at the Middle Temple.
26. *M.T.R.*, i, 370; 26 Nov. 1596 when it was ordered that 'The feast of Christmas shall be celebrated solemnly, not grandly.'
27. Br. Lib., Cotton MS Vit. C. ix, f. 319v (*D.O.J.*, 193; *A.I.T.*, 212-3).
28. *Athen. Oxon.*, i, 504 (note by Humphrey Wanley).
29. *H.E.L.*, v, 372.

the same manner of argument or disputations is called mooting, and this making of utter-barristers is as a preferment or degree given him for his learning.'[30] It seems probable that the power of calling members of the Inn to the utter bar was vested at that time in the Reader who exercised the power at his reading. That practice was probably due to the fact that the Reader, as the principal instructor in the Inn, was best able to judge which of the students attending his reading and the moots were sufficiently advanced in learning to merit call to the Bar.[31]

On the basis of the practice indicated by the anonymous writer, Plowden would have been called to the degree of utter-barrister sometime about the year 1545 when he was about twenty-seven years of age. That call to the Bar did not confer a right of audience in the courts was emphasized by a royal proclamation in the summer of the following year. The proclamation stated that, with the advice of the Lord Chancellor of England and all the judges of both benches, the king had ordered 'that no person except that he hath read in court[32] shall be admitted nor suffered to be a pleader in any of his highness' honourable courts at Westminster; that is to say, in the Courts of Chancery, King's Bench, Common Pleas, Exchequer, Star Chamber, Duchy Chamber, Augmentations, Sewers, Tenths and First Fruits, and Wards and Liveries, unless he be thereunto admitted and appointed by the said Lord Chancellor and the two Chief Justices with the advice of two of the benchers and ancients of either of the four houses of Court.' The proclamation provided that any person infringing the order should be committed to ward and fined at the king's pleasure.[33]

However, at the end of 1547, in the first year of the reign of Edward VI, a further proclamation provided that those 'now being or that hereafter shall be student, utter-barrister, or utter-barristers in any of the said houses of court, and being fellow in any of the said houses by the space of eight years, shall and may from henceforth lawfully plead and be counsellors and pleaders at or in any court of record within this realm of England and

30. Br. Lib., Cotton MS Vit. C. ix, f. 320 (*D.O.J.*, 194; *A.I.T.*, 213–4); *cf.* Bacon Rep., 185, and *D.O.J.*, 144, 202. The first recorded call to the Bar in the Middle Temple was on 26 June 1574, when the minutes of Parliament included the following entry: 'Item ad hoc Parliamentum Magister Reginaldus Braye et Magister Richardus Moldworth vocati sunt et electi sunt ad gradum de le utter Barre per assensu omnium Magistrorum de Banco' (M.T., B.M.B., D. 112; *cf. M.T.R.*, i, 202).

31. *W.H.T.*, 116, 185–8; Prest, *Inns of Court*, 50–8. That the Readers did not always carry out their duties with regard to call in a satisfactory manner is indicated by the order made by the Middle Temple Parliament on 9 Nov. 1565, that no Reader should promote anyone to be utter-barrister without the assent of Parliament, on pain of a fine of £10, and loss of rank by the person promoted (*M.T.R.*, i, 150). Two years later, however, Readers were again authorized to call (e.g., *M.T.R.*, i, 160, 163, 169, etc.).

32. I.e., had been elected Reader in his Inn of Court.

33. *T.R.P.*, i, 371–2 (proclamation of 28 June 1546).

the marches of the same, the said Court of Common Pleas . . . only excepted.'[34] At the time when that proclamation was issued Plowden had been a 'fellow' of the Middle Temple for eight years and was thus qualified to plead in the superior courts by the terms of the proclamation, and it seems probable, therefore, that he began his professional career in 1548, when he was thirty years of age.

34. *T.R.P.*, i, 408–9 (proclamation of 28 Nov. 1547). The exception of the Court of Common Pleas was because the serjeants-at-law had the exlusive right of audience in that court, a privilege which they retained until 1846 when the court was opened to all members of the Bar by the statute 9 & 10 Vict., c. 54.

IV

RELIGIOUS CHANGE

Although Plowden had been advanced to the degree of utter-barrister, he was not thereby relieved of all obligation to participate in the moots and other exercises of learning. It was a custom of long standing in the Middle Temple that barristers should continue to take part in the learning exercises for some three years after their call, and a tendency towards the end of the century to neglect that obligation caused the benchers to make regulations to enforce it.[1] Plowden must therefore have continued to keep the learning vacations until about 1551.

Save that he was taking his elaborate notes of cases that were eventually turned into his celebrated *Commentaries*, there is little that can be recorded of Plowden's early years in his chosen profession; that, however, is hardly surprising in the case of a man of Plowden's religious cast of mind. He had entered upon his career at the Bar at a time of great political and religious change. His early youth had been passed during the long drawn out proceedings by which Henry VIII eventually obtained from Archbishop Cranmer the annulment of his marriage to Catherine of Aragon which he had failed to extract from the pope; and that struggle for the 'divorce' led to the breach with Rome and the statutory recognition of Henry's ecclesiastical supremacy and his position as 'only supreme head in earth of the Church of England called Anglicana Ecclesia'.[2] Plowden does not seem to have had a very high opinion of Henry VIII, and if a complaint against Plowden made to the Privy Council in the middle of Elizabeth's reign can be relied upon, he referred to him in slighting terms.[3] Henry died on 28 January 1547 and was succeeded by the son, born to him by Jane Seymour, who ascended the throne as Edward VI. Edward was a frail and sickly youth, less than ten years old when he came to the throne, and during his short reign effective power was exercised by two ambitious men, first by the Protector Somerset and then by the duke of Northumberland. Short though his reign was, it was of great importance for the progress of the Reformation in England and for the future of Catholicism to which the Plowden family were adherents. The uneasy religious compromise established by Henry VIII was abandoned during the reign of his son, and the political reformation effected by the father was followed by a religious reformation under the son which soon brought outright Protestantism to England.

When Henry died the Council was dominated by a group of men, including Cranmer, who wished to put their reforming ideas into practice. Henry's will, which provided for a council of regency during the minority of his son, was not much to the taste of those men; they ignored it and

---

1. *cf.* M.T., B.M.B., D. 254.
2. *cf.* 26 Hen. VIII, c. 1 (*Statutes of the Realm*, iii, 492).
3. P.R.O., S.P. 12/144/45; see p. 130, *post*.

proposed instead to appoint a Protector who would be sympathetic to their ideas. That office was something of a novelty, but such guidance as could be found in English constitutional practice indicated that the Protector should be the new king's uncle, Edward Seymour, then earl of Hertford and soon to be created duke of Somerset. It was well known, from the start of the reign, that Seymour was 'well disposed to pious doctrine and [did] abominate the fond inventions of the Papists',[4] and was thus acceptable to the dominant group in the Council. Once established as Protector it did not take him long to gather all power into his own hands. Somerset had opened a correspondence with the reformers in Geneva soon after the accession of Edward VI,[5] and he and Cranmer proposed to take the religious settlement established by Henry VIII much further than that monarch had been prepared to go. Whereas Henry had been content to establish the royal supremacy that brought the church in England, like any other institution, under the government of the king and rendered it independent of any foreign jurisdiction such as that of the pope, Somerset and Cranmer intended to use the royal supremacy during the king's minority to bring about religious alterations of so radical a character that they could not afterwards be reversed.[6]

During the period of Somerset's power doctrinal change proceeded gradually and was effected by a method very similar to that used by Henry VIII, a combination of injunction and statute. The first change came in July when the Injunctions of 1547 were issued.[7] Those injunctions were moderate in tone and followed fairly closely the injunctions of 1536 and 1538, issued by Thomas Cromwell as vice-gerent of Henry VIII. It was not until early in 1549 that the first radical religious change was made, during the session of parliament which lasted from 24 November 1548 to 14 March 1549. In that session parliament gave statutory recognition to the first Prayer Book of Edward VI, and thereby accomplished a revolution in the public worship of the nation. The Act enforced the use of the Prayer Book throughout the kingdom and prohibited all forms of public worship not in accordance with that book.[8] The Prayer Book was markedly Lutheran in tone and the services which it prescribed were in English, written in the beautiful liturgical language in whose composition Cranmer

4. See Richard Hilles to Henry Bullinger, Strassbourg, 26 Jan. 1547 (printed in Robinson, *Original Letters*, i, 255, at p. 256).

5. See *D.N.B.*

6. Bishop Burnet observed that Cranmer 'being now delivered from that too awful subjection that he had been held under by King Henry, resolved to go on more vigorously in purging out abuses' (Burnet, *History of the Reformation*, ii, 25; Pt. 2, Bk. 1). And as Professor Mackie remarked, 'The royal supremacy, bereft of Henry's conscience (which though peculiar was a very real thing), turned to sheer "Erastianism".' (Mackie, *Earlier Tudors*, 511).

7. *T.R.P.*, i, 393–403; Cardwell, *Documentary Annals*, i, 38. The proclamation was dated 31 July 1547.

8. 2 & 3 Edw. VI, c. 1 (*Statutes of the Realm*, iv, 37), the first Act of Uniformity; for the short title, 'The Act of Uniformity', see s. 3 of the Interpretation Measure, 1925 (15 & 16 Geo. V, No. 1).

was so skilled. In the same session an Act was passed which legalized the marriage of priests.[9]

Those religious changes, which made a violent break with the past, did not meet with passive acceptance, and local rebellions broke out in several parts of the country. In June 1549 there was a serious rising by a substantial number of men in the west country, to whom the new English services seemed 'like a Christmas game', and many of those who took up arms demanded to 'have our old service of matins, Mass, evensong and procession in Latin, as it was before'. The royal forces did not have an easy task in suppressing the rebellion. Exeter was besieged by Lord Russel for six weeks and was only relieved on 6 August with the help of German and Italian mercenaries; the rising was not finally crushed for another ten days.[10] There was also a rising in Oxfordshire which was savagely quelled by the marquis of Dorset, the father of Lady Jane Grey, who hanged the rebellious priests from the steeples of their own churches.[11]

A more serious revolt broke out in Norfolk, but although it began near Kenninghall, where the resolutely Catholic princess Mary lived, the motives which inspired it appear to have been agrarian and economic, although Kett's manifesto contained several articles relating to religion. For months previously there had been agrarian unrest and some lawlessness provoked by the oppressive manner in which enclosures had been carried out in the county, and matters came to a head in July when Robert Kett, a well-to-do tanner and landowner, put himself at the head of an assembly at Wymondham. Men rallied to him from many parts of Norfolk, and it was only after some difficulty and a good deal of bloodshed that the revolt was crushed. In December Kett was hanged as a traitor in Norwich castle and his brother William was hanged from the steeple of Wymondham church.[12]

A sharp reaction followed the rebellions. Somerset had already lost valuable support when, earlier in the year, he had acquiesced in the attainder and execution of his brother Thomas. Some of the Council drew the conclusion that a man who did not defend his own brother might not be able to defend himself; the matter was decided for them by the rebellions which resulted in the discrediting of Somerset and the enhancement of the position of John Dudley, viscount of Lisle, who had recently been granted the title of earl of Warwick. In October 1549 the removal of Somerset was effected by a group of councillors, including Sir Thomas Wriothesley, by now created earl of Southampton, and the earl of Arundel, Henry FitzAlan,

9. 2 & 3 Edw. VI, c. 21 (*Statutes of the Realm*, iv, 67).
10. See, generally, Rose-Troup, *The Western Rebellion*; Cornwall, *Revolt of the Peasantry, 1549*.
11. See Woodman, in *Oxoniensia*, xxii (1957), 78–84.
12. See Land, *Kett's Rebellion*; Russell, *Kett's Rebellion*; Cornwall, *Revolt of the Peasantry, 1549*; and Bindoff, *Ket's Rebellion*. cf. Brinkelow, *Complaynt*. Brinkelow was an ex-Franciscan who, although an enthusiast for the destruction of 'popery', was appalled by some of the economic and social results of the change of religion; it seemed to him that those changes had been seized upon by the more fortunately placed as a golden opportunity to enrich themselves at the expense of ordinary men upon whom fell great suffering as the result of enclosures, rack-renting and other economic evils.

who were at first believed to be intent on a Catholic reaction. Their main motive, however, was disenchantment with Somerset's political views; Warwick seized his opportunity and became the natural leader of the council. Warwick was an unscrupulous adventurer and, although he had not hesitated to rely on Catholic support in his bid for power, he determined to champion the Protestant cause and to use his position to create an authoritarian rule which he would exercise in the name of the child king. In 1551 Warwick was created duke of Northumberland, and on 22 January 1552 Somerset was executed.[13]

The abolition of the Protectorate and the assumption of effective power by Northumberland were accompanied by a marked change of policy. Northumberland abandoned the somewhat cautious religious policy of Somerset and greatly increased the pace of the Reformation. Acts were passed for the removal of images and 'superstitious books', for the reform of canon law, and for the composition of an Ordinal for the ordination of priests and the consecration of bishops. At the same time altars were removed from churches and replaced by tables,[14] and Northumberland saw to it that the conservative Catholic bishops either resigned their sees or were deprived of them.[15]

The greatest changes were made in 1552 when parliament passed the second Act of Uniformity which authorized the second Prayer Book of Edward VI.[16] The Act made drastic changes in the first Prayer Book, as well as altering the Ordinal of 1550, and it imposed stringent penalties to ensure that only the services set out in the new Prayer Book were used; not only were the clergy obliged to use those services and forbidden to use any other form, but laymen who absented themselves from the authorized public services or attended other services were made liable to the penalties imposed by the Act. Once the liturgy of the English church had been established, it only remained to define the doctrine which the liturgy expressed, and that was done by the publication of the Forty-Two Articles of Religion in which the royal supremacy was clearly set out and the authority of the pope repudiated.[17] Such, in the barest outline, were the principal religious changes that took place during the short reign of

---

13. In his journal the king, then aged 14, recorded the death of his uncle in the following terms: 'The duke of Somerset had his head cut of apon Towre hill betwene eight and nine a cloke in the morning' (Nicholas, *Literary Remains of Edward VI*, ii, 390).

14. 3 & 4 Edw. VI, cc. 10, 11 & 12 (*Statutes of the Realm*, iv, 110–12); Cardwell, *Documentary Annals*, i, 89.

15. E.g., Edmund Bonner of London was deprived in Oct. 1549 and was succeeded by Nicholas Ridley (translated from Rochester); Stephen Gardiner of Winchester (imprisoned since July 1548) was deprived in Feb. 1551, and was succeeded by John Ponet who had succeeded Ridley at Rochester; John Veysey of Exeter resigned in Aug. 1551 in favour of Miles Coverdale; George Day of Chichester and Nicholas Heath of Worcester were deprived in Oct. 1551 and succeeded by John Scory and John Hooper; Cuthbert Tunstall of Durham was put under house arrest in the spring of 1551 and deprived in Oct. 1552.

16. 5 & 6 Edw. VI, c. 1 (*Statutes of the Realm*, iv, 130).

17. *Articles agreed on by the Bishoppes, in the Synod, 1552*, London, 1553 (*S.T.C.*, no. 10034).

Edward VI.[18] Such fundamental changes, following so rapidly upon the more restrained innovations of Henry VIII, must have left the large majority of Englishmen in a state of bewilderment. The conservatively minded bishops who might have rallied Catholicism against the reformers had been removed, and no word came from the papacy. Almost alone among Catholic churchmen Reginald Pole urged the pope to make efforts to regain what the church had lost in England, but nothing was done.

In the absence of any spiritual guidance either from the English Catholic bishops or from the papacy, conservatively minded Englishmen had to make what they could of the religious changes imposed upon them in the name of a king who was only a boy. Some, like the men of the West Country and Oxfordshire who rose in 1549, objected and made their objection by force of arms, but far more were content to accept, however grudgingly, the changes which government had decreed, especially as some of those changes were enforced by fine and imprisonment. Despite the doubts, regrets and bewilderment, however, it was clear that it behoved anyone who wished to make his way in the world to walk with great circumspection. Unhappily, nothing has come down to us that gives any indication of how the young Plowden viewed the changes or of the manner in which he conducted himself in face of them. The Plowdens were a family that had already given evidence of their dislike of religious change, and Edmund himself remained a notable adherent of the ancient faith throughout his life; it may well be, therefore, that it was during this crucial period of his life that he developed those qualities of prudence and caution that distinguished him in later years.

During much of each year Plowden lived in his chamber in the Temple. There is no record of where that chamber was, but on 21 October 1551 a Parliament of the Middle Temple authorized his transfer to the chamber of a bencher named Orynge who had recently died, and he was succeeded in his former chamber by another barrister named William Browne.[19] It is likewise unknown where he spent those periods of the year during which he was not in London, although it seems almost certain that it was not Plowden Hall. Doubtless he visited his parents at Bishop's Castle, and also his sister Jane who, with her husband Richard Blunden, was then living at their house at Burghfield, near Reading in Berkshire.[20] A neighbour and friend of the Plowdens in Shropshire was Sir Francis Englefield, a man who subsequently figured largely in Plowden's life. Englefield was the son of Sir Thomas Englefield already mentioned, and was some four years younger than Plowden; he had been knighted on the

18. For fuller and more detailed treatment, see Gairdner, *English Church in the sixteenth century,* chs. xiii–xv; Pollard, *England under Protector Somerset*; Pollard, *Cranmer,* chs. 7–10; Constant, *Reformation in England,* vol. 2; Mackie, *Earlier Tudors,* ch. xiv; Hughes, *Reformation,* vol. 2, pt. ii; Dickens, *English Reformation,* chs. 9, 10; Ridley, *Cranmer,* chs. xvii–xxii.
19. *M.T.R.,* i, 81. Very little is known about Orynge, even his christian name being unknown: he became a bencher in 1511, being Autumn Reader in that year and Lent Reader in 1516; see Williamson, *Middle Temple Bench Book,* 55.
20. *B.M.P.,* 11.

accession of Edward VI but, like Plowden, his religious opinions were conservative so that he found the Catholic household of the princess Mary more congenial than the Protestant court of her half-brother Edward VI; in 1551 he was one of the three trusted servants of the princess (the others were Sir Robert Rochester and Sir Edward Waldegrave) who were imprisoned when she refused to dismiss her Catholic chaplains. Englefield owned very large estates in Berkshire, Oxfordshire, Warwickshire, Shropshire and elsewhere to which he had succeeded on the death of his father in 1537.[21] In Berkshire his principal property was the manor of Englefield, some five or six miles west of Reading, and in Shropshire he owned some four hundred acres in the Isle of Up Rossall where, on a smallholding forming part of that estate, another of Plowden's sisters, Margaret, lived with her husband, Richard Sandford, an impoverished member of an old Shropshire family.[22]

It may have been friendship with Englefield that brought him into contact with John Winchcombe, the son of the celebrated 'Jack of Newbury', who, like his father, was the foremost clothing manufacturer of England and a very wealthy man. He had been one of the 'squires' whom Henry VIII had appointed in December 1539 to receive Anne of Cleves on her fateful arrival in England, and in the following February he was rewarded with grants of land at Bucklebury and Thatcham (not far from Englefield) together with other land near Reading, all of which had formerly been owned by Reading Abbey. He had been in the commission of the peace since February 1541 and, besides his business affairs, took some interest in politics; in January 1545 he had been elected to parliament as member for Great Bedwyn in Wiltshire.[23] In 1547, when he was nearly sixty years of age and Plowden had just been called to the Bar, he decided to settle his extensive landed property and in February of the following year he obtained royal licences, by letters patent, to grant various lands to trustees on trust for himself, his wife and children. That transaction was carried out by means of several settlements and for two of them, both concerned with land in Berkshire, the trustees were John Cheyney, Edmund Plowden and Thomas Edwards; by the first he settled his land at Thatcham and by the second his property at Ging and Ardington together with land at East Hendred in the tenure of John Eyston.[24] That was an event of some significance in Plowden's life for he was thus brought, while still under thirty years of age, into close association with one of the leading

21. For Sir Francis Englefield, see *D.N.B.,* and Loomie, *Spanish Elizabethans,* ch. 2. Englefield's father, Sir Thomas Englefield, had been a bencher of the Middle Temple until he was advanced to the degree of serjeant-at-law in 1521; he was promoted to be a judge of the Court of Common Pleas in 1526 (Williamson, *Middle Temple Bench Book,* 57). His grandfather, also named Sir Thomas Englefield, had been a bencher of the Middle Temple and Justice of Chester (*ibid.*, 49).

22. *B.M.P.*, 11; Blakeway, *Isle,* 115, 119. Edmund Plowden was remotely connected with the Englefields: his mother (née Elizabeth Sturry) claimed descent in the female line from Philip de Englefield who, in the 15th cent., acquired the estate at Up Rossall; see Rope, in *The Month,* n.s., xvi (1956), 100, at p. 101.

23. See *D.N.B.* for John Winchcombe and his father, 'Jack of Newbury'.

24. *C.P.R., 1548–1549,* 89.

merchants of the day who had some political influence.[25] His acquisition
in 1550 of the stewardship of Greenham in the parish of Thatcham was
probably due to his connection with John Winchcombe.[26]

The standing in his profession which he had acquired by the end of the
reign of Edward VI shows clearly that from the time of his call to the Bar
he devoted himself assiduously to the practice of the law, and that those
who had legal business to transact soon appreciated the ability and
diligence of the young Plowden. By the time queen Mary came to the
throne Plowden seems to have acquired a lucrative practice and an enviable
reputation for ability.

By then he was making his influence felt in his Inn. His first official
appointment in the Middle Temple was made in the middle of the reign of
Edward VI. The Inns of Chancery had their own exercises of learning
which followed the pattern of those observed in the Inns of Court, save
that in each Inn of Chancery the Reader and those who assisted him were
appointed by the Inn of Court to which the Inn of Chancery was attached.
The Middle Temple, responsible for New Inn and, until 1549, Strand
Inn,[27] appointed every year a Reader for each of those Inns of Chancery,
and the Reader took with him two other members of the Middle Temple
who assisted him in the arguments on the subject-matter of his reading.
In contrast to the Inns of Court, however, the readings in the Inns of
Chancery took place in term time but, as in the Inns of Court, they were
upon a statute.[28] According to Sir William Dugdale, who described the
Middle Temple more than a century later, it was customary for that Inn
to appoint as Reader at New Inn an utter-barrister of about eight or nine
years standing at the Bar;[29] Plowden, however, was appointed to that
office when he had less than half that seniority, a circumstance that gives
some indication of the estimation in which he was already held by his
fellow members of the Middle Temple. There are still in existence some
manuscript notes of the reading which he gave at New Inn during Easter
Term 1550; his subject was chapters 1 and 2 of the second Statute
of Westminster, which are concerned with estates tail and replevin
respectively.[30]

25. In a list of justices of the peace in Wiltshire and Berkshire, compiled in 1564 by the
bishop of Salisbury, John Jewel, with comments on their religious inclinations, there occurs the
entry: 'John Winchcombe of Bucklebury, A furtherer [of the established religion]'; see Bateson,
Collection of Original Letters, 38.

26. See *History of Parliament. The House of Commons, 1509–1588*, vol. 3, p. 112.

27. Strand Inn was demolished in 1549 with other neighbouring buildings to make way for
Somerset House, the mansion which the Lord Protector proposed to build in the Strand; the
present Somerset House, replacing the earlier one, was built in the years 1776–80.

28. *cf.* Br. Lib., Cotton MS Vit. C. ix, f. 321 (*D.O.J.*, 195; *A.I.T.*, 216–7); Bacon Rep., 187.

29. *D.O.J.*, 203.

30. The Statute of Westminster II is dated 1285. For the notes of Plowden's reading, see Br.
Lib., Harg. MS 89, art. 4. The document is headed 'Les Lectures de Edmd. Plo. de Mid. Temp.
Lector de Newe Inne fait sur Lestat. W. ii . . . Termo pasche Ao. 4 Edw. sexti', and is in two
parts: the first part (ff. 38–41v) is divided into 8 'Divisions' which are subdivided into numbered
paragraphs, and concluded with the words, 'Finis Lect. super stat. W. 2. cap: 1'; the second
part (ff. 41v–47), which is similarly arranged in 'Divisions' and numbered paragraphs, is headed
'W. 2. cap. 2'.

By the early summer of 1553 it was clear that the young king was dying. The prospect of the king's death threatened the position of Northumberland, but he made a daring effort to maintain himself in power. In June 1553, by playing on the very real religious susceptibilities of the dying boy, he persuaded him that the survival of Prostestantism in England could only be secured by a change in the succession to the crown and so was able to induce him to devise the crown to the heirs male of Lady Jane Grey, a girl of seventeen who was his first cousin once removed. Henry VIII, it is true, had more than once personally settled the succession to the crown, but his arrangements had largely followed the ordinary rules of descent; he had, for instance, passed over his nieces, Frances and Eleanor,[31] in favour of their heirs male.

Northumberland, however, wished to bring the crown closer to himself. His first scheme was to marry his son to Margaret Clifford, Eleanor's daughter, whose claim to the throne was improved now that her mother was dead. Northumberland soon realized that his scheme had a greater chance of success if his family were to marry into the senior line, that of Frances, represented by Lady Jane Grey, the eldest of the three daughters of Frances. Accordingly he induced the king to alter his 'devise' so as to bequeath the crown, not to 'the Lady Jane's heirs male', but to 'the Lady Jane and her heirs males';[32] and on 21 May 1553 his son Guildford married Lady Jane. When the young king died on 6 July 1553, however, Northumberland's project miscarried. He was disliked and feared even by his political allies, some of whom suspected that he had poisoned the king, and in 1552 he had been forced by lack of money to dispense with the mercenary bands which had been formed in the previous year. Thus it was that when the princess Mary, who did not lack the courage of the Tudors nor their ability to act in a crisis, asserted her right to the crown and carried much of English opinion with her, Northumberland had no armed force to meet the emergency and his *coup d'état* was a fiasco.

Lady Jane was brought to the Tower and proclaimed queen throughout the city but there was little cheering and Northumberland's own adherents were dismayed at the prospect of his son as the queen's husband. It was at that moment of crisis that Northumberland's last and most surprising mistake made its decisive contribution to his spectacular failure. It was essential for the success of his enterprise that the princess Mary should not be at liberty to assert her claim to the throne, but instead of securing her close imprisonment as soon as Edward had died, he had allowed her escape from Hunsdon into East Anglia where she was able to gather considerable

31. They were the daughters of Henry's sister, Mary, who eventually married Charles Brandon, duke of Suffolk; Frances married Henry Grey, duke of Suffolk (executed 1554) and Eleanor married the earl of Cumberland.

32. For king Edward's 'devise', see Inner Temple, Petyt MS 47, f. 317. See also the king's letters patent for the limitation of the crown, of which Ralph Starkey's transcript is in Br. Lib., Harl. MS 35, f. 364. Both those documents are printed in Nichols, *Chronicle of Queen Jane,* 89, 91–100.

popular support. Northumberland's mistake proved fatal. His own supporters in London were wavering and Mary was gaining support in the
country, so that his half-hearted and reluctant march into East Anglia
achieved nothing. His disheartened force was dissolved and when he saw
the large number of 'the common folk' who had turned out for Mary—it
was said that she had some 30,000 men at her disposal—he realized that
his bid for power was over and he retreated to Cambridge.

In Northumberland's absence his support in London had collapsed.
Suffolk tore down with his own hands the cloth of estate above the head
of his daughter, Lady Jane Grey, and, if his own account is to be believed,
he himself proclaimed Mary on Tower Hill; then he went into the City,
leaving his daughter as a prisoner in the Tower. Meanwhile the whole of
London gave itself up to general rejoicing at the news that Mary was
queen.[33]

When the news of those events reached Northumberland at Cambridge
he conceded defeat. On 21 July he was arrested and taken, with his brother
Andrew and three of his sons, to the Tower where his hapless daughter-in-
law was already confined. Mary entered London on 3 August, being met
by a notable gathering of ladies and gentlemen, and among the ladies who
rode out to meet her were the princess Elizabeth and Anne of Cleves.
Among the prisoners whom she released when she entered the Tower were
the old duke of Norfolk who had been saved from execution by the death
of Henry VIII, the duchess of Somerset, and bishop Gardiner who had
been a prisoner since 1548. Subsequently the other Catholic bishops were
released and Bonner emerged from the Marshalsea, Tunstall from the
King's Bench and Heath and Day from the Tower. A Catholic sovereign
once again sat on the throne and the adherents of the ancient faith could
look forward with hope.

Catholic hopes for the future, however, rested on no secure foundations.
The execution of Northumberland, widely execrated as a traitor, had, it is
true, done much damage to the progress of the Reformation in England;
as the modern historian of the Reformation has succinctly put it, 'as
Northumberland had injured the cause of the Reformation by his policies,
so at his execution he continued the work by recanting and by exhorting
the spectators to eschew all heresy. In the words of an eye-witness, "He
edified the people more than if all the Catholics in the land had preached
for ten years." '[34] On the other hand, the new queen lacked the ability of
her half-sister Elizabeth to gauge the temper of ordinary Englishmen, and
she did not possess the temperament and histrionic gifts that enabled
Elizabeth, in her turn, to ride out the many stresses of her long and
remarkable reign. Mary, too, was unable to hide the natural loyalties
which she derived from her Spanish relations, and her boasting of her
Spanish descent was not congenial to the self-conscious nationalism of

33. For the proclamation, dated 19 July 1553, announcing the accession of queen Mary, see
T.R.P., ii, no. 388.
34. Dickens, *English Reformation*, 355.

Tudor England.[35] Her marriage to a Spaniard almost exactly a year after her accession was extremely unpopular and fed the general fear of foreign domination. And it may be that, misled by the ease with which she, a Catholic, had successfully asserted her claim to the throne, she over-estimated popular support for the Catholic religion. Those who had rallied to her support in London and East Anglia (two of the most Prostestant areas in England) had done so because they regarded her as the legitimate heir and because of their hatred of Northumberland; her suport rested on those factors and not on her religion.

35. See the long report of the Venetian ambassador, Giacomo Soranzo, dated 18 Aug. 1554, to the Venetian Senate; *C.S.P.V., 1534-1554,* 532-64, at p. 560.

V

PROFFESSIONAL AND PUBLIC LIFE

When Mary began her reign she regarded it as her duty to restore the Catholic religion and to bring England once more into communion with the Holy See, although she stated publicly that she would use no compulsion. In a proclamation issued a month after her accession she made her intention plain enough: 'First, her majesty, . . . cannot now hide that religion which God and the world knoweth she hath ever professed from her infancy hitherto, which as her majesty is minded to observe and maintain for herself by God's grace during her time, so doth her highness much desire and would be glad the same were of all her subjects quietly and charitably embraced. And yet she doth signify unto all her majesty's said loving subjects that of her most gracious disposition and clemency her highness mindeth not to compel any her said subjects thereunto unto such time as further order by common assent may be taken therein.'[1]

Four Protestant bishops were deprived of their sees in 1553 and five more in March 1554, and three others resigned.[2] Cranmer himself was sent to the Tower in September 1553 on a charge of treason for having supported Lady Jane Grey; in November he was convicted and in the following month was declared a traitor by Act of attainder, but he was not executed and was left in prison for the time being.[3] Other leading Protestant divines, such as Hugh Latimer, Nicholas Ridley and Thomas Becon, were sent to join Cranmer in the Tower, while others, such as Miles Coverdale and the foreigners Bernardino Ochino, Peter Martyr, John à Lasco and Valérien Poullain, together with many of the lesser reformers, went abroad.

Mary's council was an ill assorted group of men. It contained no less than twelve of Edward's councillors, and to them the queen added seven of Henry VIII's councillors, whom she recalled, and twelve of her own personal supporters including Sir Robert Rochester, Sir Francis Englefield, Sir Henry Jerningham and Sir Edward Waldegrave. The council thus constituted was too large for the effective conduct of administration and its notorious lack of unity resulted in a failure to neutralize the substantial group of Protestant members returned to each of Mary's parliaments.

Plowden's friend, Sir Francis Englefield, now in his thirty-first year, was thus able to begin what promised to be a prosperous and distinguished career. In addition to being sworn of the Privy Council he was appointed in the following year, on 1 May 1554, to the lucrative office of Master of

---

1. Proclamation dated 18 Aug. 1553; see *T.R.P.*, ii, no. 390, at pp. 5-6.
2. Miles Coverdale of Exeter, Nicholas Ridley of London, John Scory of Chichester, and Robert Ferrar of St. David's were deprived in 1553; John Bird of Chester, John Harley of Hereford, John Taylor of Lincoln, John Hooper of Worcester and Robert Holgate of York in March 1554. William Barlow of Bath and Wells and John Ponet of Rochester resigned in 1553, and Paul Bush of Bristol in June 1554.
3. Ridley, *Thomas Cranmer*, ch. xxii.

the Court of Wards and Liveries which his father, Sir Thomas Englefield, had held some twenty years earlier;[4] and not long afterwards the queen granted him the manor and the borough and town of Wootton Bassett in Wiltshire.[5]

It was, no doubt, the influence of Englefield that brought Plowden into public life. At the accession of queen Mary he was thirty-five years of age and had a well established and prosperous practice at the Bar where his reputation as a lawyer of ability and a man of integrity stood high. With the change of sovereign, moreover, his religion no longer caused him to confine his energies to the law. In 1553 he was appointed a member of the Council of the Marches of Wales, a body subordinate to the Privy Council, which had extensive judicial and administrative responsibilities in an area that included not only Wales and the Marcher Lordships but also the English counties of Shropshire, Worcestershire, Herefordshire and Gloucestershire.[6] The centre of the council's authority was Ludlow, where its records were kept, but it often met at Bewdley and Shrewsbury; its meeting place at Shrewsbury, now known as the Council House, would have been familiar to Plowden as it was probably the town house then owned by his family.[7]

In connection with that appointment Plowden was included in the new commissions of the peace for Gloucestershire, Herefordshire, Shropshire and Worcestershire, issued on 18 February 1554, in each of which he was named as of the quorum.[8] Among those appointed by one or more of the commissions were Nicholas Heath, recently restored as bishop of Worcester and at that time lord president of the Council in Wales; the recently created earl of Pembroke who had deserted Lady Jane Grey just in time to support Mary; John Whiddon, recently appointed a judge of the King's Bench; Sir Thomas Bromley, a native of Shropshire and recently promoted to be chief justice of the King's Bench; and, in the commission for Worcestershire only, William Sheldon whose daughter Plowden married.

---

4. Letters patent dated 1 May 1554 (*C.P.R., 1553-1554*, 249); Hurstfield, *Queen's Wards*, 212, 243; Hurstfield, in *E.H.R.*, lxviii (1933), 22–36.

5. By letters patent dated 16 Dec. 1554 the queen granted to Englefield in tail male the Great Park of Vastern at Wootton Bassett (*C.P.R., 1553-1554*, 59); he surrendered that grant, together with other property, and, by letters patent dated 4 March 1555 was granted the lordship and manor and the borough and town of Wootton Bassett, the Great and Little Parks of Vastern, and other extensive lands to hold in tail male with remainder in tail male to his brother John (*C.P.R., 1554-1555*, 52). The manor and borough of Wootton and the parks of Vastern had been granted by Henry VII to his queen. Thereafter they formed part of the jointure of several of the wives of Henry VIII: they were granted to Catherine of Aragon in 1509, to Anne of Cleves in 1540, to Catherine Howard in 1541, and to Catherine Parr in 1544. Before the death of Catherine Parr the reversion was granted by Edward VI to the Protector Somerset in whom it became vested in 1550. After Somerset's execution they were granted to Northumberland in 1553, and when he was attainted in 1554 they were forfeited to the crown; see *V.C.H., Wilts.*, ix, 191.

6. Cooper, *Athenae Cantabrigienses*, i, 501. For the Council in Wales, see Skeel, *Council in the Marches of Wales*; Williams, *Council in the Marches of Wales*.

7. See p. 3, *ante*. cf. Clive, *Documents connected with the History of Ludlow*.

8. *C.P.R., 1553-1554*, 19, 23, 25.

Plowden now felt free to indulge a taste for politics which had not been open to him during the previous reign. The queen's first parliament was held in the autumn of 1553.[9] Writs of summons were issued on 14 August and the election which followed gave rise to legal proceedings which Plowden himself reported.[10] Sir Richard Buckley (or, more correctly, Bulkeley) claimed to have been elected as knight of the shire for the county of Anglesey, but the sheriff, Rice Thomas, returned instead the name of William Lewis. Buckley thereupon sued the sheriff, in an action of debt, for the statutory penalty of £100 for making a false return.[11] The judges, by a majority, decided that the action was maintainable, and Buckley obtained judgment for the penalty together with the sum of £6 13s. 4d. as damages for the sheriff's failure to pay the penalty when it became due.[12] The sheriff then sued out a writ of error, in order to challenge the judgment, but there was no further argument as the parties came to terms.

Plowden himself was returned as one of the burgesses for the borough of Wallingford in Berkshire, presumably with the influence of Sir Francis Englefield, the greatest landowner in the county, who was himself elected as one of the knights of the shire for Berkshire.[13] It was probably a little before the election that Plowden acquired a house in Berkshire; at any rate, in January 1555 he was described as of Tidmarsh in that county.[14] Tidmarsh was one of the Berkshire manors owned by the Englefields and presumably he was a tenant of Sir Francis.

The first session of parliament opened with a Votive Mass of the Holy Ghost, a custom which had not been observed for a long time. Unhappily, there is no record of Plowden's activities in the first parliament of the reign, but doubtless, as a common lawyer, he welcomed the passing of the Treason Act of 1553,[15] during the first session, which repealed certain Acts of the previous reign creating treasons (including treasons by words alone), and enacted that only such acts should be treason as were declared so by the Treason Act of 1352.[16]

Early in the second session there was introduced into the house of commons a bill to declare that the marriage of Henry VIII and Catherine of Aragon was valid and that Mary had been born in lawful wedlock,

9. Parliament sat in two sessions, from 5 Oct. to 21 Oct., and from 24 Oct. to 5 Dec., when it was dissolved; see *B.C.*, 536; *Commons Journals*, i, 27–32; *Lords Journals*, i, 447–63.

10. *Buckley* v. *Thomas*, Plowd. 118. The case was decided in the Common Pleas in Trinity Term 1555. There is also a much shorter report in Dyer 113, where the case is listed as Easter Term 1556. It is the only reported case of a disputed election in the 16th cent.

11. See 8 Hen. VI, c. 7, and 23 Hen. VI, c. 15.

12. The judges were Broke, C. J., Saunders and Browne, JJ., with Staunford, J, dissenting. The judgments of Broke and Staunford contain some interesting observations on election procedure.

13. *O.R.*, i, 381: the other member for Wallingford was George Wright, and the second member for the county was William Hyde; the election return was made on 17 Sept. 1553.

14. *cf.* P.R.O., K.B. 27/1180, Rex et regina, rot. 36; 4 Co. Inst. 17. Tidmarsh is some 4 miles west of Reading and about 2 miles south of Pangbourne on the river Thames which forms the border with Oxfordshire.

15. 1 Mary, sess. 1, c. 1 (*Statutes of the Realm*, iv, 198).

16. 25 Edw. III, stat. 5, c. 3.

notwithstanding any sentence or Act of Parliament to the contrary. That bill was necessary because archbishop Cranmer, in his court at Dunstable, had pronounced Henry's marriage with Catherine to be invalid, and that judgment had been confirmed by Act of Parliament thus bastardizing Mary at common law.[17] The bill was read a first time on 26 October and quickly passed all its stages in both houses.[18] And in the same session it must have given the conservative and catholic Plowden considerable satisfaction to vote in favour of the bill which eventually became Mary's first statute of repeals.[19] That Act, which encountered some opposition in the commons, repealed several statutes concerning religion passed in the previous reign, and provided that the forms of divine service and the administration of the sacraments which had been commonly used in the last year of the reign of Henry VIII should be used throughout the country from 20 December 1553, and prohibited the use of any other form of service.[20] The effects of the act were far-reaching: it put an end to Cranmer's reformed liturgy and the First and Second Books of Common Prayer, it withdrew the recognition of a married clergy and it restored the Mass, thus sweeping away the chief results of Cranmer's exertions during the previous reign.

In the summer of 1554 Plowden, as a justice of the peace for Shropshire, was included in a commission of Gaol Delivery to try various cases at the sessions held at Shrewsbury on 9 July 1554.[21] The commissioners were Sir Thomas Bromley, the chief justice of the King's Bench, Serjeant Townsend,[22] William Simmonds, the Queen's Attorney in the Marches of Wales, Plowden and others, and they sat for a week. The sessions were held to deliver certain gaols in Wales and the prisoners were brought to Shropshire because, that county being the next adjoining English county, the statute 26 Henry VIII, c. 6 gave jurisdiction to try them.[23] The first

17. 25 Hen. VIII, c. 22 (1534).

18. *Common Journals*, i, 28, 29. The bill became the Act 1 Mary, sess. 2, c. 1 (*Statutes of the Realm*, iv, 2–1).

19. The bill was introduced into the commons on 31 Oct. when it was read a first time; it had its second reading on 3 Nov., and third reading on 7 Nov., while arguments on the bill took place on 8 Nov. when it passed the commons: *Commons Journals*, i, 29.

20. 1 Mary, sess. 2, c. 2 (*Statutes of the Realm*, iv, 202). The Acts repealed were: 1 Edw. VI, c. 1 (concerning the Sacrament of the Altar); 1 Edw. VI, c. 2 (concerning the election of bishops); 2 & 3 Edw. VI, c. 1 (the first Act of Uniformity); 2 & 3 Edw. VI, c. 21 (concerning the marriage of priests); 3 & 4 Edw. VI, c. 10 (concerning images); 3 & 4 Edw. VI, c. 12 (the consecration of bishops, etc.); 5 & 6 Edw. VI, c. 1 (the second Act of Uniformity); 5 & 6 Edw. VI, c. 3 (the keeping of holidays and fast days); and 5 & 6 Edw. VI, c. 12 (the marriage of priests). Mary's statute did not mention the royal supremacy. In the same session there was also passed the Act of Attainder for the duke of Northumberland (1 Mary, sess. 2, c. 16).

21.See *Matters del Corone auenants a Salop*, Plowd. 97. In his report Plowden refers to the town of Shrewsbury as 'ville de Salop'.

22. In the heading of his report Plowden names 'Sir R. Townsend chiualer Serieant de ley' among the commissioners, but I have been unable to identify him.

23. 26 Hen. VIII, c. 6 (*Statutes of the Realm*, iii, 500); 'An Act that murders and felonies done or committed within any Lordship Marcher in Wales shall be enquired of at the sessions holden within the shire grounds next adjoining, with many good orders for administration of Justice to be had.'

case to be heard was a charge of murder. Several men from Montgomery were indicted for killing one Oliver ap David ap Hoel Vaughan at Berriew in Montgomery; some for inflicting the wounds from which Vaughan died, and Griffith ap David ap John and others, who were present, for aiding and abetting the rest to commit the murder. Those, however, who had inflicted the wounds had fled and only Griffith ap David ap John and the rest were arraigned at the bar. In those circumstances Bromley doubted whether they should be arraigned. He pointed out that, although all of those concerned in the death of Vaughan were principals, those who struck Vaughan and killed him were principals in the first degree, while those present at the bar were only principals in the second degree. Bromley was concerned that those at the bar might be found guilty but afterwards the others might be arraigned and acquitted, and in that case, he said to his fellow commissioners. 'I would know your opinion what should be done.'[24] The matter was debated at some length until all the commissioners were agreed that the prisoners present at the bar might be arraigned. On arraignment they pleaded not guilty but Plowden, who was concerned in his report only with the point of law, did not disclose the outcome of the trial.

It so happened that a certain Morris Gittin was also included in the same indictment as accessory to all of them, that is, both to those present at the bar and to those who were absent. Bromley again raised an objection and questioned whether Gittin could be arraigned. He said to his fellow commissioners, 'You see that he is indicted as accessory to all, but some of the principals are present, and some are absent, who are not attainted, and it is not good to arraign him with the principals now present, as accessory to them only, and we cannot arraign him as accessory to the others that are absent, because they are not attainted nor present to be arraigned with him.'[25] During the debate that followed Bromley sent to his house in Shrewsbury for a law book, and it was eventually decided to pursue 'the same course that the sages before have used', and the whole court was agreed that Gittin should be respited from arraignment until he could be arraigned as accessory to all the principals at once.

At the same sessions there was another murder case in which five men, George Salisbury, John Vane Salisbury and Richard Salisbury and two others named Pigot and Knowsley were charged with murdering the servant of a Doctor Ellis in the county of Denbigh. When they had all pleaded not guilty it was found that there were insufficient jurors present to make up a jury, and accordingly the court awarded a *tales* returnable

24. ' . . . donques ieo voile sacher vr̃e opinions que serroit fait.' (Plowd. 97).
25. 'Vous veies bñ coṁt il est indite coṁ accessorie a touts, mes ascuns de les principals sont present, & ascũs sont absent que ne sont pas attaint, & il nest bone de arraigner luy oue les principals ore present come accessory a eux solement, & coṁ accessory a les auters que sont absent nous ne poiomus luy arraigner, pur ceo que ils ne sont attaint ne present destr̃ arraigñ oue luy.' (Plowd. 98b).

immediately.[26] As it was known that the number of persons in the town qualified to sit as jurors was small, the prisoners were sufficiently acute to realize that the situation might be exploited to their advantage. Each prisoner was allowed to challenge jurors peremptorily (that is, without showing cause for his challenge) twenty times, and a juror so challenged had to be withdrawn. The prisoners, therefore, began their peremptory challenges, being careful not to agree, and they contended that once a peremptory challenge was made it must be accepted whether it were made by all the prisoners or only one. In that way they could muster a hundred peremptory challenges which were more than enough to exhaust the available jurors and bring the trial to a halt. To avoid that result the court was minded to 'sever the panel' so that the same panel might be constituted between the crown and each of the prisoners individually, but they hesitated to do so because the *tales* was issued jointly for all five prisoners. After consulting authorities, Bromley said to the prisoners. 'We perceive your subtlety well enough, which merits but small favour from the court, and therefore tell us if you will agree in your challenges, for if you will not the clerk shall sever the panel.'[27] Eventually the prisoners were persuaded to agree in their challenges and the trial proceeded.

By that time Plowden had a number of professional interests in Oxfordshire and Berkshire, and among his clients was the corporation of the city of Oxford. For instance, the city chamberlain's accounts for the year 1554–5 disclose that two shillings was paid 'for almond butter, wine, and other things given to Mr. Plowden'.[28] The fact that he was attending the Oxford Assizes indicates that he went the Oxford Circuit which covered his own county of Shropshire and the adjoining counties.[29]

Despite his substantial reputation as an advocate, it was not until 1554 that there appeared the first reference to him as an advocate in court. In Michaelmas Term of that year he appeared in the court of Wards and Liveries in a case that he himself reported;[30] the court was presided over

26. If a jury is summoned and found to be insufficient in number, the court may award a *tales de circumstantibus*, which is an order to the sheriff to return so many other duly qualified men that should be present or could be found, as were needed to make up the deficiency in numbers; the jurors so added are called 'talesmen'.
27. 'Nous perceiuomes vostre subtlety assets bñ, le quel merite petite fauor del court, & pur ceo dists a nous si vous voiles agreer in vostre challenges: Car si vous ne voiles, le clerk seuera le panel.' (Plowd. 100).
28. Turner, *Records of the City of Oxford*, 226. And see pp. 45, 140, *post*.
29. Oxfordshire and Berkshire had been transferred from the Western Circuit to the Oxford Circuit which covered the counties of Gloucestershire, Monmouthshire, Herefordshire, Shropshire, Staffordshire, Worcestershire, Berkshire and Oxfordshire; see Cockburn, *History of English Assizes*, 19, 23.
30. *Townsend's Case* (1554), Plowd. 111. The other members of the court, besides the Master, were the council thereof and two judges, Sir William Portman and Edward Saunders. In his report Plowden refers to himself as 'one of the Middle Temple' (un de Middle Temple). Appearing with Plowden were serjeant William Dalison (the law reporter), Gilbert Gerard and Edmund Prideaux; on the other side were serjeant James Dyer (the law reporter and later chief justice of the Common Pleas), serjeant Robert Catlin (later chief justice of the King's Bench), and Gilbert Walpole. There is also a short report of the case in Dyer, 106, pl. 19.

by the Master, Sir Francis Englefield. The case was concerned with the right of the grandchildren of Roger and Amy Townsend to inherit the manor of Akenham and other lands in Suffolk of which Amy Townsend had been seized in tail before her marriage and which was held of the king by knight's service.

It will be seen that Plowden's professional standing was, by the beginning of the new reign, considerable. His increasing financial prosperity is indicated by a substantial purchase of land from the crown which he made in May 1554, in conjunction with a prosperous city merchant, a grocer, named John White. Part of the land was situated in Lydbury North, adjoining the Plowden family lands, and part in Surrey. The grant included the lordship and manor of Lydbury North, which had belonged to the Augustinian Abbey of Wigmore before its suppression in 1538, together with the advowson and vicarage there and a very substantial amount of land, as well as the reversion of a lease (for twenty-one years from 20 March 1553) of some land forming part of the manor. There was also granted the lordship and manor of Frimley in Surrey, which had formerly belonged to the Benedictine Abbey of Chertsey, surrendered in 1537 by the abbot and fourteen monks; and there was included a long list of the lands and liberties in Lydbury North and Frimley belonging to the two manors included in the grant. All the property in Shropshire was to be held by White for his life and then in fee to Plowden to be held by socage tenure; after White's death Plowden became the sole owner and was still in possession of the estate at the time of his own death.[31] The manor of Frimley was granted in fee to White in chief by service of one-fortieth of a knight's fee. For all that substantial property White paid the crown £252 and Plowden £91 7s. The purchase has a further interest as showing that Plowden, staunch Catholic though he was, had no scruples about buying former monastic property.[32]

31. Inq. p. m., dated 13 March 1585 (P.R.O., C. 142/206/13, and Ward 7/21/108) where it was stated that Plowden held the manor of Lydbury North of the queen, as of her castle of Ludlow, by fealty only, in free socage and not in capite.

32. *C.P.R., 1553–1554*, 268. The patent making the grant was dated 19 May 1554, and it stated the yearly value of the manor of Lydbury North to be £3 6s. 1½d., and that of the manor of Frimley to be £10 10s. All the lead, bells and advowsons belonging to the manor of Frimley were excepted from the grant.

VI

PARLIAMENT

Mary's reign began in bitter controversy. She was a spinster, nearly forty years of age, and her marriage was a matter of high importance to her subjects. An unmarried queen regnant was a novelty and many Englishmen feared that Mary's marriage to a foreigner would prove disastrous for England. The succession to the crown was inseparably bound up with the marriage, and the marriage was inextricably linked with the two most important questions of the day, foreign policy and religion. Moreover, the manifest difficulty experienced by the Tudors in producing male heirs reinforced the anxieties of many men at the prospect of another disputed succession.

The queen's marriage was not merely a domestic question for Englishmen alone; it was a matter of great importance to two of the major continental powers. When Edward VI died the houses of Valois and Habsburg were still engrossed in their quarrel, and for very different reasons both the Habsburg emperor, Charles V, and the Valois king, Henry II of France, set great store on achieving an alliance with England. Mary, whose mother was a Spaniard, made no secret of her preference for a Spanish husband, and she looked to the emperor to find one for her; but in English minds the prospect of a foreign marriage raised the spectre of foreign domination. Mary, however, brusquely brushed aside the suggestion that she should marry an Englishman and stubbornly adhered to her resolve to marry Philip of Spain, the emperor's son. When the terms of the marriage treaty were announced by the chancellor, bishop Stephen Gardiner, to an assembly of nobles and gentlemen in the presence chamber at Westminster on 14 January 1554 and to the lord mayor and citizens of London on the following day, the announcement was received with a marked lack of enthusiasm;[1] indeed, some malcontents were already plotting rebellion.

The plotting had begun early, and was enthusiastically encouraged by Antoine de Noailles, the French ambassador, who still hoped to prevent the marriage. Some feeble and inept risings took place in the Welsh Marches and the Midlands but they came to nothing. A much more serious threat was the rising in Kent led by the young and hot-headed Sir Thomas Wyatt. Wyatt was the son of a poet and the boon companion of another, the earl of Surrey. He made his first proclamation in the market place of Maidstone on 25 January 1554, and then moved forward towards London with a substantial body of Kentishmen. At Strood he was confronted by the London militia who spontaneously deserted to him. He was soon in London, but the support in the city on which he had counted did not materialize, and when he failed to gain admittance at Ludgate he retreated

---

1. For the terms of the marriage treaty, see the proclamation of 14 Jan. 1554 (*T.R.P.*, ii, 21-6); and see Nichols, *Chronicle of Queen Jane*, 34, 35.

to Temple Bar where, after a short skirmish, he surrendered on 7 February. The immediate result of the rebellion was the execution of Lady Jane Grey and her husband; they were brought from the Tower and beheaded on Tower Hill on 12 February 1554. Some 480 of Wyatt's followers were convicted, but only ninety were executed and almost all of them were poor people. Wyatt was executed in April, as was Suffolk and his brother Lord Thomas Grey. Wyatt's conviction for treason involved the forfeiture of his considerable property and the subsequent fate of that property was to be the professional concern of Plowden some twenty years later.[2]

Meanwhile parliament had assembled. Writs had been issued on 17 February 1554 for a parliament to meet at Oxford, but on 15 March it was prorogued to Westminster where it eventually met on 2 April. Plowden did not sit in that parliament which had been summoned, so Gardiner as lord chancellor declared, 'for corroboration of true religion and touching the Queen's Highness' most noble marriage.'[3] An Act confirming the marriage treaty was passed without opposition; at the same time, in order to ensure that there should be no Spanish interference in English affairs, another Act was passed which declared that the regal power of the realm was vested in the queen as fully and absolutely as ever it was in any of her progenitors, and that she should not cease to rule when she took a husband.[4]

Bills of a religious nature were also considered in that parliament. A bill to revive the statutes against Lollardy and another to revive the Henrician Act of Six Articles passed the commons, together with a third for extirpating heresies, but none of them passed the lords. Their failure to do so sprang directly from the quarrel between the lay peers, led by Lord Paget, and the bishops, led by Gardiner, a quarrel which represented one of the many causes of division in Mary's council; while the bishops were anxious to revive the heresy laws (and eventually got their way), Paget and his faction were equally determined to frustrate any attempts by the church to recover ecclesiastical lands that had come into lay hands.[5] The parliament was dissolved on 5 May 1554, when the royal assent was given to the Acts for the queen's marriage and her royal power, together

2 For Wyatt's rebellion, see the graphic contemporary narrative in Nichols, *Chronicle of Queen Jane*, 36 et seqq. (and Apps. VII & VIII); Proctor, *Historie of Wyate's rebellion*; and Wiatt, in *Renaisance News*, xx (1962), 128-33 (deals with a contemporary account by John Mychell). The best modern accounts are Loades, *Popular Subversion*, chs. v-vii, and Loades, *Two Tudor Conspiracies*; see also Kennedy, in *E.H.R.*, xxxviii (1923), 251-8.

3. *B.C.*, 536; *Commons Journals*, i, 33. For the proclamation proroguing parliament from Oxford to Westminster, see *T.R.P.*, ii, 40.

4. The Act confirming the marriage treaty is 1 Mary, sess. 3, c. 2 (*Statutes of the Realm*, iv, 222-6), and that concerning the queen's regal power is 1 Mary, sess. 3, c. 1 (*Statutes of the Realm*, iv, 222). The latter statute is of constitutional importance because it finally disposed of the idea that a woman could not succeed to the throne of England in her own right; *cf.* Tanner, *Constitutional Documents*, 123.

5. *Commons Journals*, i, 33-6; *Lords Journals*, i, 458-63; Dickens, *English Reformation*, 360.

with certain other statutes.[6] The marriage took place in Winchester Cathedral on 25 July 1554.[7]

On 3 October writs were issued for a new parliament summoned to assemble at Westminster on 12 November.[8] The queen appears to have made no attempt to influence the two earlier elections, but the situation had greatly changed by the autumn of 1554. The upsurge of loyalty engendered by Northumberland's attempted *coup d'état* had largely spent itself, Wyatt had rebelled and the Spanish marriage had taken place. In those unpromising circumstances the queen determined that there should be no further delay in the reconciliation of her country with Rome; what she was set upon was the undoing not only of all that had been done during the reign of Edward VI but of all that had been done since the fall of Wolsey.[9] A little before the election letters were sent in the queen's name to all the sheriffs requiring them to 'admonish' the electors to 'choose knights, citizens, and burgesses, . . . as the old laws require, and of the wise, grave and Catholic sort'; and the letter went on to declare that the queen's chief intention was to bring about the advancement of the true honour of God, 'without alteration of any particular man's possessions', a reference to the question of the ultimate possession of former ecclesiastical land which was then causing anxiety to many landowners.[10] To that parliament Plowden was elected as one of the burgesses for Reading, his fellow burgess being John Bourne;[11] the influence of Sir Francis Englefield is once more discernible, as he was steward of Reading.

The most urgent task of the new parliament was to regularize the position of the papal legate, Reginald Pole, since he had been attainted of treason in 1539 and the Act of Attainder was still in force.[12] A bill for that purpose was introduced into the house of lords on 17 November and it

6. *Lords Journals*, i, 463.

7. For a description of Philip's arrival and marriage, see Elder, *Copie of a letter* (1555; *S.T.C.*, no. 7552), reprinted in Nichols, *Chronicle of Queen Jane*, App. x. *cf.* Hilton, in *Hants. Arch. Soc. Proc.*, xiv (1938), 46–63.

8. *B.C.*, 536. *cf.* Burnet, *History of the Reformation*, ii, 291: 'In the Writ of Summons, the Title of *Supream Head of the Church* was left out, though it was still by Law united to the other Royal Titles: And therefore it was urged, in the beginning of Queen Elizabeth's reign, as a good reason for annulling that Parliament, since it was not called by a lawful writ.' See also Strype, *Ecclesiastical Memorials*, III, i, 246. Note the proclamation, dated 25 July 1554, announcing the regnal style of Philip and Mary, in which the title of Supreme Head does not appear (*T.R.P.*, ii, 45).

9. *cf.* Hughes, *Reformation*, ii, 186.

10. For the text of the queen's letter, see Strype, *Ecclesiastical Memorials*, II, i, 245–6. See also Neale, *Elizabethan House of Commons*, 286–7.

11. *O.R.*, i, 389. The knights of the shire for Berkshire were Sir Francis Englefield and Sir Richard Briggs. The Speaker was Clement Heigham, then a bencher of Lincoln's Inn and a Privy Councillor; he was knighted on 27 Jan. 1555, and appointed chief baron of the Exchequer on 2 Mar. 1558; see Foss, *Judges of England*, v, 511–3.

12. See 31 Hen. VIII, c. 15. Pole had been specifically excluded from Edward VI's Act of general pardon (1 Edw. VI, c. 15). Before parliament assembled a proclamation had been issued on 10 Nov. ordering obedience to Pole; see *T.R.P.*, ii, 48.

passed all its stages in both houses within three days. On 22 November the king and queen personally appeared in the parliament chamber at about three o'clock in the afternoon and gave the royal assent to the bill, 'and so made a perfect Act.'[13] Within the ensuing week the reconciliation of England with the Catholic Church was brought about. Pole himself had arrived in England on 20 November with wide powers as papal legate to arrange for the reconciliation of England, and was received by Mary seven days later.[14] On 28 November both houses of parliament assembled in the presence of the king and queen to hear an address by Pole in which he explained the purpose of his return to England;[15] and on the following day each house separately voted the proposed text of a petition for reconciliation.[16] On 30 November, St. Andrew's Day, there was again a joint session of both houses in the presence of the king and queen. The lord chancellor, Stephen Gardiner, read the petition and begged the king and queen to present it to the legate. That was done and, after his ecclesiastical faculties had been read aloud, the legate addressed the assembly. Then, while all those present knelt, he absolved England from all ecclesiastical censures incurred by consents to heresy and schism and declared that the nation was restored to the unity of the Catholic Church.[17]

Thereafter parliament turned to the legislation needed to carry out the bargain already made with the papacy. That was effected by the second statute of repeals,[18] a lengthy measure which repealed all the statutes against the papal authority passed since the year 1528 with one important exception: the statutes dissolving the monasteries were not repealed and special provision was made to protect the holders of ecclesiastical lands, the price which had to be paid to secure the agreement of the landowners to the reconciliation with Rome. An Act was passed for the punishment of traitorous words against the queen, and the treason laws were extended to include Philip as well as the queen.[19]

In addition to those important matters there was one bill that was said to have involved Plowden in the displeasure of the queen. An attempt had been made in the previous parliament, of which Plowden was not a member, to revive the laws against heresy, but although those bills had passed the commons they had failed to pass the lords.[20] A further bill for the same purpose now had a different fate. On 12 December a bill to revive

13. *Lords Journals*, i, 467, 468; *Commons Journals*, i, 37, 38.
14. Pole's papal commission, *Si ullo unquam*, was dated 5 Aug. 1553 (printed in *T.—D.*, ii, p. cviii). The delay in his arrival in England was due to the emperor, Charles V, who wished to postpone his arrival until Mary had married Philip. Among those who went to Brussels to conduct Pole to England was William Cecil.
15. Pole's address was printed in Elder, *Copie of a letter* (reprinted in Nichols, *Chronicle of Queen Jane*, 154 et seq.
16. The petition was printed in Elder, *Copie of a letter* (reprinted in Nichols, *Chronicle of Queen Jane*, 160-1).
17. *cf.* Nichols, *Chronicle of Queen Jane*, 160; Foxe, *Acts and Monuments*, vi, 572.
18. 1 & 2 Phil. & Mary, c. 8 (*Statutes of the Realm*, iv, 246).
19. 1 & 2 Phil. & Mary, cc. 9 & 10 (*Statutes of the Realm*, iv, 254, 255).
20. See p. 38, *ante*.

three Acts for the punishment of heresy[21] was introduced into the house
of commons and read a first time; the bill had its second reading on the
following day and on 14 December it was read a third time and sent to the
lords on 15 December. In the lords it had passed all its stages by
18 December.[22] Early in January 1555, about a month after the bill had
passed the commons, over one hundred members of that house absented
themselves from parliament without having obtained leave to do so; among
them was Edmund Plowden.[23] The reason for their absence is obscure.
According to John Strype, they were absent because 'it went against the
grain' with them 'to lay upon the nation the old Roman yoke again, and
to receive the Pope's authority into the realm'.[24] It seems unlikely that
Plowden (and probably many of the others) would have objected to the
revival of the pope's authority in England, and even had they done so it is
curious that they should have waited for nearly a month before making
their protest; yet Strype's opinion was followed by Miss Strickland who
believed that it was the decision to revive the laws against heresy and a
regard for toleration that induced Plowden and the others to leave the
house by way of protest.[25] Another explanation was provided by William
Cobbett who regarded the withdrawal of the seceding members as 'a
voluntary secession of some members of the Commons, who actually left
the house, when they saw the majority inclined to sacrifice everything to
the ministry'.[26] Neither of those explanations seems to be satisfactory, but
they have been ingeniously combined by the late Richard O'Sullivan who
suggested that, in the view of the seceding members (especially, one may
add, in the view of Edmund Plowden), 'the coercion of conscience was
repugnant to the genius of the Common Law.'[27]

Whatever may have been the true reason for the withdrawal of the
seceding members, their action brought down upon them the disapproval
of the queen. It had long been a recognized obligation of an elected
member of parliament to give his full attendance from the beginning to
the end of a parliamentary session unless he had been given leave to be
absent, and that obligation was, theoretically at least, enforced by the

21. The Acts to be revived were 5 Ric. II, stat. 2, c. 5 (1382), 2 Hen. IV, c. 15 (1401; the
statute *De Haeretico comburendo*), and 2 Hen. V, stat. 1, c. 7 (1414); the statutes of 1382 and
1414 had been repealed by 1 Edw. VI, c. 12, and the statute of 1401 by 25 Hen. VIII, c. 14.
The importance of the anti-heresy Acts was that they provided a specific legal procedure which
linked the sentence pronounced in the ecclesiastical court with an execution by officers of the
crown. The bill became the Act 1 & 2 Phil. & Mary, c. 6, which was repealed by 1 Eliz. I, c. 1,
s. 6.
22. *Common Journals*, i, 39; *Lords Journals*, i, 477, 478.
23. *History of Parliament. The House of Commons 1509–1588*, vol. 1, pp. 17–19. The actual
number was 106. Earlier writers gave the number as 39 which was the number of the first batch
of members against whom proceedings were started; see Strype, *Ecclesiastical Memorials*, III,
i, 262; Cobbett, *Parliamentary History*, i, 625. For the legal proceedings, in which groups of
members were successively indicted, see 4 Co. Inst. 17–21.
24. Strype, *Ecclesiastical Memorials*, III, i, 262.
25. Strickland, *Lives of the Queens of England*, iii, 544, cf.B.M.P., 19.
26. Cobbett, *Parliamentary History*, i, 625.
27. O'Sullivan, *Edmund Plowden*, 11.

crown. Members, however, did not always fulfill their obligation and the
maintenance of attendance was a constant problem; there was, too, a
marked tendency for country members to leave London for their homes
before the end of a session. In an attempt to deal with the problem
parliament had enacted a statute in 1515 which prohibited the departure
of an elected member before the end of a parliament under pain of loss of
wages, unless he had the 'licence of the Speaker and Commons in the same
parliament assembled'; but although the statute thus placed the duty of
licensing absences upon the Speaker and the house of commons, leave of
absence continued to be granted by the crown until the accession of queen
Elizabeth I.[28] Plowden and his fellow members had not obtained leave of
absence.

On 16 January 1555 the royal assent was given to the bills passed during
the session and parliament was dissolved.[29] That was only a few days after
the members had absented themselves, and it is possible that their premature
departure was only one more instance of country members returning home
a little before the end of a session. The dissolution of parliament, however,
did not mean that their absence without leave was to be overlooked. The
attorney-general, Edward Griffin, received instructions to begin proceedings
against them, and in the following Easter Term, on 4 May 1555, he
appeared in the King's Bench at Westminster to prefer an information
against Plowden and the others. The information charged them with
departing from parliament without licence, contrary to the inhibition of
the king and queen at the beginning of the parliament.[30] As a result they
were summoned by the sheriff to appear and reply to the charge. According
to Coke, six of those charged 'being timorous burgesses *ad redimendam
vexationem* submitted themselves to their fines, but whether they paid any,
or very small, we have not yet found.'[31]

Plowden adopted a more uncompromising stance. On the appointed
day, Friday 8 November 1555, he appeared in the King's Bench by his
attorney, Andrew Tusser, a fellow member of parliament, and, in the
words of Coke, 'took a traverse full of pregnancy'. A traverse is a denial
of the facts alleged against a party and puts the opposing party to proof
of those facts. Plowden denied that he had been absent from parliament

28. 6 Hen. VIII, c. 16 (*Statutes of the Realm*, iii, 134). See Pollard, *Evolution of Parliament*,
161; Neale, *Elizabethan House of Commons*, 413. The wages of members of parliament were
paid by their constituencies, but as constituencies ceased to pay wages the deterrent value of the
penalty declined.

29. *Lords Journals*, i, 491.

30. For the record of the proceedings, on the Coram Rege Roll, see P.R.O., K.B. 27/1180,
Rex et Regina, rot. 36. Coke printed a version (see 4 Co. Inst. 17–19) which is not verballly
identical with that on the Coram Rege Roll. *cf.* Strype, *Ecclesiastical Memorials*, III, i, 263. On
the record Plowden is described as 'Edmundus Plowden de Tydmershe in Comitatu Berk,
armiger'.

31. 4 Co. Inst. 17.

as alleged, and pleaded that he had remained continually from the beginning to the end of the parliament.[32] That plea was indeed 'full of pregnancy' for the crown would have been hard put to it to prove his alleged absence from parliament in a period when no daily record of attendances was kept, and the roll of members was called only occasionally. After the plea the attorney-general asked the court to fix 20 January 1556 as the day for imparlance, and that was done.[33] The difficulties in the way of the crown seem to have been appreciated by the attorney-general; no further steps were taken in the proceedings, and eventually the information abated on the death of the queen. There was, moreover, a constitutional objection. Sir Edward Coke, in his *Institutes*, strongly disapproved of proceedings being brought before one of the common law courts for offences in parliament, because 'matters of Parliament (as hath been often said) are not to be ruled by the common law' but by parliament itself according to its laws and customs.[34]

Whatever may be the true explanation of the incident, it is clear that it did not affect Plowden's parliamentary career. A new parliament was summoned on 3 September 1555 and on 8 October Plowden and Richard Brunning were elected burgesses for Wootton Bassett in Wiltshire, a borough which the queen had granted to Sir Francis Englefield some months earlier. The parliament assembled on 21 October and continued until 9 December, but whatever part Plowden played in that short parliament has not been recorded.[35] Once again the Englefield influence is apparent, but in this election Plowden may also have had the assistance of the earl of Pembroke, a substantial Wiltshire magnate, who later showed considerable favour to Plowden.[36] During queen Mary's reign he was an intimate of Philip of Spain but after Elizabeth's accession he became a supporter of Cecil and the Protestant party.

---

32. ' . . . dicit quod ipse ad dictum parliamentum in Informacione predicta specificatum interfuit et presens fuit, Ac in eodem parliamento continue remansit videlicet A principio ipsius parliamenti usque ad Finem eiusdem . . . '; P.R.O., K.B. 27/1800, Rex et Regina, rot. 36.

33. 'Imparlance is said to be, when the court gives a party leave to answer at another time, without the assent of the other party; and in this sense, it signified time to reply, rejoin, surrejoin, &c. But the more common signification of imparlance was time to plead'; see Tidd, *New Practice*, 226.

34. 4 Co. Inst. 17; *cf.* Strype, *Ecclesiastical Memorials*, III, i, 264. Coke added an acid comment on the whole affair: 'Thus you may observe, that the poor Commons, Members of the Parliament, *in diebus illis*, had no great joy to continue in Parliament, but departed.' (4 Co. Inst. 21).

35. *B.C.*, 536; *O.R.*, i, 395. Sir Francis Englefield and William Hyde were returned as members for the county of Berkshire; *O.R.*, i, 392. For the grant to Englefield, see p. 31, *ante*, note 5.

36. See p. 100, *post*. The earl, then about forty-nine years of age, was William Herbert who, in 1551, became the first earl of the Herbert line of the second creation of the earldom of Pembroke. He took part in the trial of Protector Somerset and subsequently obtained his Wiltshire estates. See *D.N.B.* Pembroke was one of those who, with Plowden, were appointed to various commissions of the peace; see p. 31, *ante*.

VII

THE MIDDLE TEMPLE AND THE BAR

It was, doubtless, the increase in the volume of his professional work that led Plowden to contemplate changing his chamber in the Inn. For such a move he required the leave of the treasurer but there was, it seems, no suitable chamber immediately available. On 31 January 1555 the admission 'in expectancy' of William Barker to Plowden's chamber was authorized, 'and he will enjoy his place there when Mr. Plowden is promoted from the same'; at the same time the admission to Plowden's chamber of Edward Martin 'as expectant with Mr. Barker' was authorized at the special instance of Plowden and Barker.[1] A suitable chamber did not become available until the summer of 1556 when Edmund Mordaunt died and Plowden was admitted to his chamber; the arrangement fell through, however, the entry being struck out, and in the following November Edmund Sture was admitted to Mordaunt's chamber.[2] Whether Plowden eventually changed his chamber at that time cannot now be determined as the relevant records of the Inn contain no further entry relating to the matter.

Plowden's standing and ability were recognized not only by litigants and others needing the services of a barrister, but also by those needing a mediator to assist in the settlement of disputes. For instance, in 1555 he and Richard Weston, a bencher of the Middle Temple,[3] were instrumental as arbitrators in resolving the differences between two widows engaged in litigation concerning their respective rights to the manor of Abbots Aston in Buckinghamshire. The action was one of ejectment by which Jane Dormer, the widow of Sir Robert Dormer, sought to recover possession of the manor from Elizabeth Clarke whose intestate husband had inherited a lease of it from his father, Sir John Clarke.[4] The action began in Hilary Term 1555 but in the following Michaelmas Term, at the end of the argument, the parties came to terms through the mediation of Plowden and Weston, and Lady Dormer paid £230 to Mrs. Clarke.[5] The monks of Westminster Abbey, restored in 1556, were also anxious to have the benefit

1. *M.T.R.*, i, 99. The dates when William Barker and Edward Martin were admitted to the Middle Temple are unknown, as the relevant volume of the Middle Temple records is missing; see *M.R.A.R.*, i, 13, 16.
2. *M.T.R.*, i, 106, 108. Edmund Sture, who was probably the son of Henry Sture of Bradley, Devon., was a bencher of the Inn, having been Autumn Reader in 1549; he was Lent Reader in 1557 and died in 1559 (Williams, *Middle Temple Bench Book*, 68).
3. Richard Weston was admitted to the Middle Temple on 5 Feb. 1515, was Autumn Reader in 1554, and was appointed solicitor-general in 1557 and a judge of the Common Pleas in 1559; he died in 1572. See Foss, *Judges of England*, v, 412-3; Williamson, *Middle Temple Bench Book*, 70; *D.N.B.*
4. See *Dormer* v. *Clarke* (1555), Dyer 110. Ejectment was a 'mixed' action at common law to recover the possession of land (a real action) and damages and costs for the wrongful withholding of the land (a personal action).
5. 'Et tandem partes concord per Plowden et Weston de medio Templo, mediatores. Et Mistres Clark aver 230P. del dame'; Dyer 111.

44

of his legal learning and wisdom, and for that purpose gave him an annual retainer; on 14 October 1558 the abbey granted him for life the annual sum of £4 in return for his giving advice to the abbot and his successors. The arrangement, however, did not last long as the abbey was once again suppressed in 1560.[6]

His practice on the Oxford Circuit frequently took him to Oxford to attend the Assizes there. Early in 1556 he was one of the lawyers who were entertained to supper by the mayor of Oxford, and the fact that the meal consisted entirely of fish (pickerel, roach, eels and 'a chine of fresh salmon') together with wine, bread and beer, suggests that the entertainment took place in Lent. Plowden's fellow guests were all old friends from the Middle Temple, serjeant Francis Morgan, Thomas Denton and Reginald Corbet: Plowden and Corbet were each presented with a pair of gloves.[7] The corporation of Oxford was also making use of his services. In the autumn of 1556, when the corporation was in dispute about some land at Cripley Mead, near Port Meadow, Plowden and Francis Morgan were arbitrators, with John Pollard, the recorder of Oxford, as umpire.[8]

Plowden's position at the Bar was reflected in his rise in the more domestic affairs of his Inn. He first occupied an important office there late in 1556. As already noted,[9] it was then customary for the Inn to keep the Christmas festival in a solemn manner, unless for some special reason the benchers decided that Christmas should not be solemnly kept. When the Middle Temple kept Christmas solemnly the benchers nominated special officers for the occasion: the Steward, the Marshal, the Butler, the Master of the Revels, the Constable of the Tower and the Marshal's Constable. All those offices, save that of Steward, were filled by junior members of the Inn who had not yet attained the status of utter-barrister; the duties of the Steward for Christmas, on the other hand, were discharged by a barrister of some standing, and as the member appointed was usually chosen later to serve as Reader in the following Summer, the office of Steward for Christmas was one of importance in the Inn.[10]

The appointment of the officers for Christmas was normally made at a Parliament held in the preceding November and it was usual to appoint more than one person to fill each of the Christmas offices, in case of

6. *H.M.C.*, 10th Rep., App., pt. iv, p. 409; the original grant is preserved at Plowden Hall.
7. Turner, *Records of the City of Oxford*, 260. Francis Morgan had been Autumn Reader in 1546 and Lent Reader in 1552, and was Treasurer in 1553 and 1554. He was promoted serjeant-at-law in 1555 and a judge of the King's Bench in 1558, the year of his death. Thomas Denton's admission to the Middle Temple is not recorded, but he was Treasurer in 1556 and 1557; he married Margaret, daughter of Lord Mordaunt and widow of Edmund Fetiplace of Shifford, Berks., who was a Berkshire neighbour of Plowden. He was one of the authors of the report on the four Inns of Court made to Henry VIII (see p. 9, *ante*, note 22). For Reginald Corbet, see p. 53, *post*. See Williamson, *Middle Temple Bench Book*, 65, 66. Morgan had, of course, left the Middle Temple when he became a serjeant.
8. Turner, *Records of the City of Oxford*, 257.
9. See pp. 16–7, *ante*.
10. *W.H.T.*, 108, 109, 114.

default for some reason. At a Parliament held on 4 November 1556 those appointed to the office of Steward were three barristers named Willimott, Gilbert and Bellingham and, in their default, Edmund Plowden. At the same parliament Edmund Sture, who had been Autumn Reader in 1549, was chosen as Lent Reader for 1557, and Thomas Denton, who was one of Plowden's fellow guests entertained by the mayor of Oxford earlier in the year, was chosen as Treasurer of the Inn.[11]

Plowden's appointment as Steward for Christmas led naturally to the more important office of Reader. At a Parliament held on 12 May 1557, when he was only thirty-nine years of age, he was chosen Autumn Reader for that year, and at a subsequent Parliament, on 25 June, Edmund Sture was chosen to be his assistant.[12] Those appointments were in accordance with the custom of chosing as Autumn Reader a member of the Inn who had not read before, and as Lent Reader one who had already done so.[13]

Something has already been said of the educational duties of a Reader who was required to give a reading (or a series of discourses) on a legal topic extending over a period of at least three weeks.[14] Failure to take up the duties of Reader entailed a fine which was often substantial; thus Leonard Arscott and John Hunt were each fined £40 in October 1555 for failure to read, and in February 1557 Robert Cary was fined £10.[15] Unfortunately, there does not appear to be any note or record of Plowden's reading and its subject is unknown but, if his later published writings are any guide, his discourses were doubtless distinguished by great learning, lucidity and orderly presentation.

There were, however, other incidents to the office of Reader which were of a social nature. No doubt because the office he occupied was one of honour it was customary for the Reader, during his period of office, to extend hospitality to other members of the Inn. For that purpose he kept a special table in Hall and from time to time he supplemented the usual fare at other tables with extra dishes, later known as 'exceedings', which were provided at his cost. Moreover, during the reading there was provided a special entertainment, known as the Reader's Feast, to which the Reader was entitled to invite guests who were not members of the Inn. Originally the cost of the Feast appears to have been borne by the Inn, although it seems to have been customary for the Reader to give the necessary instructions for providing the fare.[16]

---

11. *M.T.R.*, i, 107.
12. *M.T.R.*, i, 110, 111.
13. The custom gave rise to the description of Readers as 'single' and 'double', which came into use in the 16th cent. At the present day the Reader is chosen from among the benchers who have already been elected. The office of Reader is now purely an honorary one, and does not involve the Reader in giving a series of legal discourses.
14. The customary days on which the Reader delivered his discourses in Hall were Monday, Wednesday and Friday.
15. *M.T.R.*, i, 102, 109.
16. *W.H.T.*, 131, 179.

The popularity of such gratuitous entertainment must have provided a powerful stimulus to extravagance and early in the sixteenth century the benchers had become concerned at the cost of the Feast which had reached such proportions as to become a burden on the Inn and the Reader. Venison was consumed in large quantities, especially at the Autumn Feast, and in 1513 the benchers attempted to reduce the cost by limiting the number of bucks for which they were prepared to pay. On 4 July of that year a Parliament agreed 'that for as much as the house of the Middle Temple is and hath been, and also is likely for to be greatly charged by reason that the Reader that shall read in the Summer vacation causeth many bucks in to the said Temple, to the great costs and charges of the company of the said Temple; therefore it is agreed by the said company, that if there be sent twelve bucks [they shall be] to the charge of the said company; and as many bucks as shall be sent to the said Temple above the number of twelve bucks to be to the charge of the Reader for the time being.'[17] In 1556 the allowance of bucks was increased to fifteen,[18] but in the following year, at the Parliament which appointed Edmund Sture as Plowden's assistant, the number of guests at the Reader's table was limited to three.[19]

Plowden's substantial practice enabled him to face that heavy expenditure without flinching. Others, however, were not so fortunate and preferred to pay a fine rather than shoulder the costs inherent in the office of Reader. The prospective burden of the Readership increased with the passage of time so that the imposition of fines on reluctant readers did little to decrease the number of those who declined to read. Eventually, in 1566 a new system was introduced to relieve the burden on the Reader. Parliament then decided that in the term preceding each reading a steward should be chosen to provide the Reader's Feast and bear a part of the cost; early in 1567 two stewards were nominated for that purpose, and that was the practice of the Inn for the next ten years.[20]

One consequence of the financial burden of the Readership was that those senior members of the Inn who declined to read were excluded from the bench table, but no provision was made for them until the end of 1595 when a Parliament made an order, recorded in Latin, which provided that those Masters of the Utter Bar who had passed their time of reading and had not read should thereafter dine and sup at a special table, on the north side of the hall, to be called 'Mensa Seniorum Magistrorum de le Utter

17. M.T., B.M.B., A. 21 (*M.T.R.*, i, 42). The benchers, on 8 May 1551, found it necessary to reiterate that a Reader should only be allowed 12 bucks during his Reading, and that if he brought any more he should pay for them himself (M.T., B.M.B., D. 2; *M.T.R.*, i, 80).
18. *M.T.R.*, i, 107 (4 Nov. 1556); the original entry has been corrected by substituting 'xv' for 'xx'.
19. *M.T.R.*, i, 112.
20. *M.T.R.*, i, 155, 158. On 20 May 1569 a Parliament ordered that the Reader's guests should not exceed three in number, that the steward should not invite any guests, and that the cost of the Feast should not exceed £10 (*M.T.R.*, i. 168).

Bar—Anglice, the Auncientes table.'[21] There were, however, certain privileges enjoyed by a newly appointed Reader. He was entitled to admit one new member to the Inn, and he had a right to occupy one of the special chambers set apart for the use of benchers.[22]

The Parliament held on 3 November 1557 chose George Freville as Lent Reader for the following year but he stood down and on 8 February 1558, with Freville's consent, Plowden was chosen as Lent Reader with John Southcote, a bencher, as his assistant; Plowden was allowed 26s. 8d. towards the cost of the bucks for the Reader's Feast.[23] Once again, however, there does not appear to be any extant note of his reading and the subject of his discourses is consequently unknown.

Plowden's professional eminence brought him further public office, this time with the Duchy of Lancaster. The duchy was one of the greatest of the special franchises which at one time had been numerous in England. Only a few, however, had survived into the Tudor period, and of those the most important were the palatinates of Lancaster, Chester and Durham. The holder of a county palatinate had royal power within his county. He could pardon treasons, murders and felonies, and appoint judges and justices of the peace; all writs and indictments ran in his name, and offences were stated to be done against his peace and not *contra pacem domini nostri*.[24] The county of Lancaster had been erected into a county palatine by Edward III who conferred it upon his cousin, Henry duke of Lancaster, for life only, so that when Henry died in 1362 the county palatine became extinct. In 1377, however with the consent of parliament, it was revived in favour of Edward III's son, John of Gaunt, who had married the daughter and heiress of Henry duke of Lancaster, and was himself created duke of Lancaster in 1362. The original grant to John of Gaunt had been for life, but in 1390 the dukedom and the palatinate were granted to him and his heirs male. When John of Gaunt's son, Henry of Lancaster, succeeded to

21. M.T., B.M.D., D. 252 (*M.T.R.*, i, 358; 21 Nov. 1595). The order also provided that other Masters of the Utter Bar and fellows might sit at the Ancients' Table until it was full. An author writing in the time of Charles I referred to the Ancients' Table as follows: 'It is no disgrace for any man to be removed hither for by reason of the great and excessive charge of Readinges many men of great learninge and competent practise and others of less learninge but great estates have refused to Read and are heare placed' (M.T., Brerewood MS, f. 14; the MS was used by Sir William Dugdale in his *Origines Juridiciales*). The Ancients' Table later fell into disuse, but was revived in 1876; it is now placed in the centre of the Hall, just below the bench table, and accommodates eight senior members of the Inn who are not benchers.

22. See *W.H.T.*, 134. The first mention of special chambers for benchers occurs in the minutes of the Parliament held on 14 June 1553 where there is a list, in French, of 17 chambers identified as the benchers' chambers and described by the names of their occupants; such chambers were only to be granted by a Parliament (M.T., B.M.B., D. 13; *M.T.R.*, i, 93).

23. *M.T.R.*, i, 113, 115. Freville was appointed Reader for Lent 1559 (*M.T.R.*, i, 118); he was appointed recorder of Cambridge in 1553 and a baron of the Exchequer in 1559 although he had not been advanced to the degree of serjeant-at-law; he died in 1579 (Foss, *Judges of England*, v, 488; *D.N.B.*). Southcote, who was born in 1511, became serjeant-at-law in 1559 and a judge of the King's Bench in 1563; he died in 1585 (*D.N.B.*).

24. *cf.* 4 Co. Inst., ch. 36.

the throne of England in 1399, on the deposition of Richard II, he kept his family estate, including the county palatine separate from the estates of the crown. The duchy of Lancaster, however, together with the county palatine as parcel of the duchy, were united with the crown by Edward IV, but they were restored to their original position by Henry VII and they have remained so ever since.[25]

As part of its *jura regalia* the duchy had a complete judicial system. There was a Court of Pleas, and a Chancery Court (which still exists) presided over by the vice-chancellor of the duchy, and there was power to issue commissions of Assize, Oyer and Terminer, and Gaol Delivery. In addition there was the Court of Duchy Chamber, presided over by the chancellor of the duchy, which sat at Westminster; the court exercised an equitable jurisdiction in cases concerning lands that were parcel of the duchy, whether situated within the county palatine or not. Although the Court of Duchy Chamber was quite distinct from the palatine court of chancery, the chancellor, sitting in the former court, seems to have acquired power to hear appeals from the latter.[26]

The duchy estates were not confined to the county palatine of Lancaster; there were many other estates, scattered over the whole of England, which had been considerably increased by the additions made to them over the years.[27] To manage the duchy property and to exercise its *jura regalia* there was a chancellor and a council, supported and assisted by the holders of a number of offices. The office of chancellor was in reality two offices, chancellor of the duchy and chancellor of the county palatine, which, until the middle of the fifteenth century, had been held separately; the holder of the combined office presided (and still presides) over the duchy council whose principal duty was to superintend the officers of the duchy in their management of all its estates, franchises and privileges. For administrative reasons the duchy was divided into the North Parts and the South Parts, each with its appropriate officers, the division between them being the River Trent.

Over the years the establishment of offices had varied; some offices had disappeared and others had been created. The chamberlain, once the most important of the officers, had disappeared by the end of the fourteenth century. The chief stewards, one for each Part, had been the next to go. The last of the chief stewards of the South Parts was the earl of Sussex[28]

25. For the early history of the duchy, see Somerville, *History of the Duchy of Lancaster*; and see also *Case of the Dutchy of Lancaster*, Plowd. 212. *cf.* Lapsley, *County Palatine of Durham*.

26. The Judicature Act of 1873 merged the Lancaster Court of Pleas in the High Court and prohibited the issue of commissions of Assize, etc. (36 & 37 Vict., c. 66, ss. 16, 99). The separate commission of the peace was not abolished by the Act of 1873 and justices of the peace continue to be appointed by the chancellor of the duchy. The Court of Duchy Chamber has not been abolished but it has not sat since 1835. The palatine court of chancery is still in existence and exercises a jurisdiction co-ordinate with that of the High Court.

27. The principal accretions were the estates inherited by Henry V from his mother, and the additions made by Henry VIII and Mary.

28. Sir Robert Radcliffe (1483–1542), first earl of Sussex, first viscount Fitzwalter and second baron Fitzwalter.

who had been appointed in 1540, but when he died two years later the office was not filled. There was a chief steward of the North Parts for a little longer. Lord Willoughby of Parham was appointed to the North Parts as successor to Sir Thomas Heneage[29] who had died in 1553, and he held the office until his death in 1574, but no successor was appointed.[30]

Despite the disappearance of the chief stewards, it was necessary to retain the offices of deputy chief stewards because of the need to hold courts and deal with other legal matters concerning the duchy. It was to the office of deputy chief steward of the South Parts that Plowden was appointed on 22 August 1557. His appointment was to serve the office *durante bene placito*, but on 26 September 1558 he was re-appointed for life, and he retained the office until he died.[31]

When Plowden was appointed the chancellor of the duchy was Sir Robert Rochester who had been appointed in 1553, soon after queen Mary's accession; he died, however, on 28 November 1557 and was succeeded by his nephew, Sir Edward Waldegrave, appointed on 22 January 1558.[32] Rochester, Waldegrave and Sir Francis Englefield were members of queen Mary's council and it seems likely, therefore, that, once again, Englefield's influence had a part in procuring Plowden's appointment.

Waldegrave did not remain chancellor of the duchy for long. Soon after Mary's death he was deprived of all his employments, and on 24 January 1559 Sir Ambrose Cave was appointed to replace him as chancellor. Waldegrave was committed to the Tower on 20 April 1561 at the time of the anti-Catholic activity occasioned by the projected visit of the papal envoy, Girolamo Martinengo, and he died there on 1 September of that year.[33]

Soon after his appointment with the duchy of Lancaster Plowden suffered a severe personal loss; his father died on 10 March 1558 and was buried at Bishop's Castle.[34] Plowden's mother did not long survive her

---

29. Sir Thomas Heneage had been gentleman usher to Wolsey and of the privy chamber; he was knighted in 1537. His nephew, also Sir Thomas Heneage, was appointed chancellor of the duchy in 1590; *D.N.B.*

30. Somerville, *History of Duchy of Lancaster*, i, 332.

31. Somerville, *History of Duchy of Lancaster*, i, 432. The names of the deputy chief stewards, South Parts, immediately before and after Plowden's tenure of the office, are of interest and give some indication of his standing: 1528 William Roper (son-in-law of Sir Thomas More); 1532 Richard Rich (later baron Rich and lord chancellor); 1537 Edmund Mordaunt (son-in-law of Rich); 1543 John Pollard (serjeant-at-law and speaker of the house of commons; his brother Anthony and Plowden married sisters); 1557 Edmund Plowden; 1585 Edward Flowerdew (a baron of the Exchequer in 1584); 1586 William Fleetwood (Recorder of London); 1594 Francis Bacon (later Lord Verulam, Viscount St. Albans and lord chancellor). See Somerville, op. cit., 431–2.

32. *B.C.*, 140

33. *B.C.*, 140; *C.R.S.*, vol. 1, pp. 49, 51, 55; and see Cecil's letter to Sir Nicholas Throckmorton, ambassador at Paris, dated 8 May 1561; P.R.O., S.P. 70/18/103.

34. His will (P.C.C. 20 Noodes) was proved on 6 May 1558. A brass tablet, commemorating Humphrey Plowden, his wife and children, was erected in the church at Bishop's Castle; it has been removed and is now in the private chapel at Plowden Hall. The Latin inscription on the tablet is printed in *T.S.A.S.*, 2nd ser., ix (1897), 119, and an English version (shortened and not entirely accurate) is given in *B.M.P.*, 11.

husband; she died on 30 March 1559.[35] On the death of his father Plowden inherited the family estate, and on 23 February 1559 a licence was issued for him to enter upon his lands as from the date of his father's death.[36] As already noted, Plowden Hall was in such a state of dilapidation that his parents had lived elsewhere. The house which Plowden inherited seems to have been largely medieval in construction, its principal features being an aisled hall and a solar wing which display an interesting combination of base-crucks, aisled construction and crown-post roof. On becoming owner of the house, Plowden took in hand its restoration and it is very likely that he was responsible for the addition of the large box-framed north wing which was built in the sixteenth century and is the dominating feature of the house as it is to-day.[37] When Plowden's younger brother, Edward, made his will in April 1575 he described himself as 'of Plowden', so that he may have gone to live at Plowden Hall once it had been made habitable.[38]

It seems probable that it was towards the end of Mary's reign, or at the beginning of the next, that Plowden married, but unfortunately no record of the marriage has yet been found. His bride was Katherine Sheldon, a daughter of William Sheldon of Beoley in Worcestershire.[39] William Sheldon came of a Catholic family that had amassed great wealth and which possessed extensive landed property. The Sheldons were an industrious and business-like family whose members were, for the most part, careful to remain aloof from public affairs, especially in times of tension or conflict. Their caution may have been due to the lesson learned when an earlier William Sheldon had fought for Richard III at Bosworth; although he survived, his estates were confiscated by the victorious Henry VII and were not restored to his family until after his death in 1517. His younger brother Ralph, who succeeded him, devoted much time and industry to increasing the family estates. As early as 1505 he had been leasing land from the Abbot of Pershore, but his greatest contributions came with the dissolution of the monasteries when he was able to make considerable additions to his property, a process that caused him no qualms of conscience. It was Ralph's eldest son William who became Plowden's father-in-law.

William Sheldon seems to have inherited the drive and acquisitiveness of his father, to which he added a pronounced business ability of his own.

---

35. See *B.M.P.*, 12.

36. *C.P.R., 1558-1560*, 76.

37. See Moran, in *T.S.A.S.*, n.s., lix (1973-4) 264-71. A stable range was added to the house in the 18th cent; Pevsner, *Buildings of England: Shropshire*, 299. There are two priest-holes and an 'escaping place' at Plowden Hall; it is unlikely that they were constructed before 1580 and may have been contrived even later (for a description, see Squiers, *Secret Hiding-Places*, 173-4; and *cf.* Hodgetts, in *R.H.*, xi (1971-2), 279-298).

38. P.C.C. 39 Carew.

39. The marriage is not recorded in the parish registers of Beoley which begin in 1538. That fact does not, however, exclude the possibility that Plowden was married at Beoley as there are gaps in the early part of the register where entries (sometimes for a whole year) have not been made by the incumbent, and some of the entries (temp. Hen. VIII) are out of order. The marriage does not appear in Bernaud, *Sixteenth Century Marriages*.

His marriage to Mary Willington brought him substantial property in Warwickshire and he bought much other land in Gloucestershire, Hereford-shire and Shropshire. It was William Sheldon who introduced tapestry weaving into this country and he established the small factories which produced the celebrated Sheldon tapestries. William Sheldon, who died in 1570, remained a staunch Catholic throughout his life, as did his son Ralph who succeeded him, and with their support Beoley became a Catholic stronghold. Ralph Sheldon had added to the parish church of Beoley a chantry chapel dedicated to the Blessed Virgin which remained in Sheldon hands and there, it is said, Mass was celebrated until nearly the end of Elizabeth's reign.[40]

40. For the Sheldons, see Barnard, *The Sheldons*; Minney, in *Worcestershire Recusant*, v (1965), 1–17; Davidson, in *Worcestershire Recusant*, xii (1968), 1–7; Davidson, in *Worcestershire Recusant*, xiv (1969), 15–21. See also Humphreys, *Elizabethan Sheldon Tapestries*.

VIII

RELIGIOUS CHANGE AGAIN

In the autumn of 1558 Plowden was one of those appointed, on 10 September, to hold the inquisition *post mortem* following the death of a Shropshire man, Griffyn Hynton. The appointment itself is of no significance, but it is of interest on account of the position of those appointed with him: they were Sir Adam Mytton, Reginald Corbet, Richard Onslow and one other.[1] Mytton came of a well known Shropshire family that later produced Squire John Mytton, the celebrated sportsman and eccentric who was appointed high sheriff of Shropshire and Merionethshire and, after running through a fortune, died in 1834 of delirium tremens in the King's Bench prison at the age of thirty-eight. Corbet came of an ancient Shropshire family and was one of Plowden's fellow benchers at the Middle Temple; he had been Lent Reader in 1551, and recorder of Shrewsbury from about 1555 to 1559 when he was advanced to the degree of serjeant-at-law and soon afterwards elevated to the King's Bench. Onslow was another lawyer; he was a barrister of the Inner Temple who, in 1563, was appointed Recorder of London, and in the course of a long parliamentary career was speaker of the house of commons from 1566 to 1571.[2]

When Plowden and his fellow commissioners were holding their inquest on the property of Griffin Hynton, it had become clear that the queen's reign was nearing its end. In August she experienced a slight indisposition and moved from Hampton Court to Westminster; she died early on 17 November, while Mass was being celebrated at her bedside.

At the time of queen Mary's last illness, death and promotion had reduced the number of serjeants-at-law to one, William Bendlowes, a Catholic and an old friend of Plowden. That circumstance caused a good deal of inconvenience and accordingly the queen, on the advice of her council, appointed new serjeants. On 24 October 1558 writs were issued to eleven barristers informing them that they had been so appointed and ordering them to prepare to take up that estate and grade within three weeks from the coming Easter on pain of forfeiting £1,000. Plowden was one of those who received a writ, his fellows being Thomas Carus, Reginald Corbet, John Walsh and John Southcote, all members of the Middle Temple who subsequently became judges, together with Thomas Gawdy, George Wall, Richard Harpur, Ranulph Cholmeley, Gilbert Gerard and

---

1. *C.P.R., 1557-1558*, 454. An inquisition *post mortem* was held on the death of any landowner who was believed to hold land of the sovereign *in capite*. The inquest was held either by the escheator *virtute officii* or by commissioners specially appointed.
2. Williamson, *Middle Temple Bench Book*, 68; *D.N.B.*; Neale, *Elizabethan House of Commons*, 356.

John Birch.[3] But when the queen died less than a month later the writs immediately abated. Elizabeth called new serjeants in the following December, but no writs were then issued to Plowden, Gawdy and Gerard; William Simmonds and Nicholas Powtrell were advanced in their stead.[4] Thus, for nearly six months, Bendlowes was the only serjeant until the newcomers assumed the coif in Easter Term 1559.[5] It seems likely that Gerard's name was omitted from the list of new serjeants because the new government wanted an uncompromising Protestant as attorney-general, an office to which he was appointed in January 1559. Gawdy's name was probably omitted at his own request; he was created a serjeant in 1567 and elevated to the bench in 1574. Plowden's name was almost certainly omitted because of his religion.[6]

The new queen's refusal to call Plowden to the degree of serjeant-at-law must have caused him great disappointment and, as it turned out, it closed to him any further advancement in the profession of which he was so distinguished an ornament. Since it was only from among the serjeants that the judges of the common law courts were chosen, Plowden was effectively barred from sitting on the bench; there can be little doubt that, had he ever held judicial office, his influence upon the common law would have been immense.[7] To that disappointment was added another. It is probable that Plowden's first child, a son, was born in the early part of 1559; the boy was christened Humphrey, after his grandfather, but he did not long survive and died in infancy.[8]

The omission of Plowden's name from the list of new serjeants had another result that was, as things turned out, of immense benefit to the Middle Temple. When a barrister became a serjeant he was required to leave the Inn of Court to which he belonged and to migrate to Serjeants' Inn,[9] his departure from his old Inn being marked by a feast and the gift of a gold ring. Had Plowden become a serjeant he would have been compelled to leave the Middle Temple and much of lasting value that he

---

3. *C.P.R., 1557-1558*, 457; Baker, *Order of Serjeants at Law*, 134, 170. Carus became a judge of the King's Bench in 1566 and Corbet in 1559; Walsh became a judge of the Common Pleas in 1563 (Williamson, *Middle Temple Bench Book*, 68, 70, 71); for Southcote, see p. 48, note 23. Of the remainder Gawdy became a judge of the King's Bench in 1574, and Harpur a judge of the Common Pleas in 1567; Gerard was appointed attorney-general in 1559 and Master of the Rolls in 1581.

4. *C.P.R., 1558-1560*, 65.

5. cf. Foss, *Judges of England*, v, 414, 415. For Bendlowes, see *D.N.B.*, Abbot, *Law Reporting*, ch. 3; Nolan, in *Essex Recusant*, v (1963), 105-13.

6. cf. Foss, *Judges of England*, v, 489, 492. Gerard remained attorney-general for 22 years and was then appointed Master of the Rolls.

7. See, generally, Pulling, *Order of the Coif*. The Order was never formally abolished; it merely died out when new serjeants ceased to be appointed in the 19th cent. The last surviving serjeant was Lord Lindley who died in 1921.

8. *B.M.P.*, 16. No record of either the birth or death of the child has yet been found.

9. In the 16th cent. there were, in fact, two Serjeants' Inns, one on the south side of Fleet Street, at the north-east corner of the Inner Temple (the site is approximately that of the present building at 49 Fleet St.), and the other at the southern end of Chancery Lane (the site is that of the present 5 Chancery Lane, the offices of the Royal Insurance Group); the Fleet St. Inn seems to have been the main Inn. See Megarry, *Inns Ancient and Modern*, 23-6.

did for his Inn would have remained undone. As it was, he remained for the rest of his life in the Middle Temple as a figure of great influence.

From then onwards he was the dominating figure in the Middle Temple and a man of enormous prestige in the profession of the law. Indeed so great was his reputation that his name was embodied in the popular aphorism, 'The case is altered, quoth Plowden.' There is more than one story to account for the origin of the phrase. One is that Plowden, when defending a man for hearing Mass, elicited the fact that the service had been performed, not by a priest, but by a layman masquerading as a priest for the purpose of informing against the worshippers; thereupon Plowden is supposed to have said, 'The case is altered; no priest, no Mass.'[10] That explanation is not a particularly convincing one; a more plausible explanation is that Plowden was once asked what legal remedy there was against a man who allowed his pigs to stray on to the land of his questioner. 'There is a very good remedy', he began, but when told that the pigs were his own, he promptly replied, 'Nay then, the case is altered'. If there is no truth in that version, it is at least the kind of tale that would have appealed to his colleagues in the Inns of Court.[11] The phrase, 'The case is altered' was later used by Thomas Lodge and Robert Greene in their *Looking Glass for London* and by Thomas Dekker in *The Batchelars Banquet*,[12] and Ben Jonson adopted it as the title for his comedy *The Case is altered*;[13] according to John Nichols, it even formed part of the dying words of queen Elizabeth: 'My lord, I am tied with a chain of iron about my feet . . . I am tied, tied, and the case is altered with me.'[14] It may be that it was no more than a popular catch-phrase of the time that was fathered upon Plowden.

The new reign, however, brought Plowden not only professional disappointment but religious perplexity; once more the established religion was to be changed. The progress of the Reformation in England had been interrupted by the five years' reign of the Catholic queen Mary, but immediately after queen Elizabeth had succeeded her half-sister, parliament laid the statutory foundations of the new religion. Those foundations were the Act of Supremacy and the Act of Uniformity which received the royal assent on 8 May 1559.[15] Section 9 of the Act of Supremacy provided that

10. See e.g., Cooper, *Athenae Cantabrigienses*, i, 502; O'Sullivan, *Edmund Plowden*, 14; *D.N.B.*; Fuller, *Worthies of England*, ii, 254.

11. *Stevenson's Book of Proverbs*, 291.

12. Lodge and Greene, *A Looking Glasse for London and England* (1594), Act ii, scene 2: 'Faith, sir, the case is altered; you told me it before in another manner; the law is quite against you.' Dekker, *The Batchelars Banquet* (1603): 'Then is their long warre come to an end, and the case (as Ploydon sayth) cleane altered.'

13. Jonson, *The Case is Altered* (1609), Act v, scene 6: 'I have betrayed myself with my own tongue; the case is altered.'

14. Nicholls, *Progresses of Queen Elizabeth*, iii., 612.

15. 1 Eliz. I, c. 1 (Act of Supremacy), and 1 Eliz. I, c. 2 (Act of Uniformity). For the parliamentary history of those Acts, see *Neale I*, 51–84. Immediately after the Act of Uniformity came into force on 24 June 1559, the queen issued her Injunctions of 1559, printed in Cardwell, *Documentary Annals*, i, 178, in *G.& H.*, 417, and in *T.R.P.*, ii, no. 460 (although strictly not a royal proclamation).

all ecclesiastical persons and 'all and every temporal officer, judge, justicer, mayor and other lay or temporal officer and minister' and certain other persons should take an oath, the form of which was set out in the section, that acknowledged the queen's ecclesiastical supremacy and renounced all foreign jurisdiction and authority including that of the pope. The penalty for refusing the oath was deprivation of office and disqualification for life from holding office.

Counsel who did not hold any of the specified offices were not at first affected by the Act of Supremacy since the requirement to take the oath did not apply to barristers. And it had remarkably little effect upon the judges to whom it did apply. The immediate judicial changes that were made took place before the Act of Supremacy had received the royal assent, and they were confined, virtually, to changes among the chief justices. Sir Clement Heigham, chief baron of the Exchequer, was removed (or resigned) and was replaced by the Catholic Sir Edward Saunders who had been chief justice of the King's Bench. Saunders was replaced as chief justice by Sir Robert Catlin, a puisne judge of the Common Pleas; and in the Common Pleas Anthony Browne, the chief justice and a notorious Catholic, was replaced by one of his puisnes, Sir James Dyer, but he remained in the court in the place vacated by Dyer. The attorney-general, Edward Griffin, was removed from his office and replaced by Gilbert Gerard, but the solicitor-general, Richard Weston, although displaced by William Roswell, was promoted to the degree of serjeant-at-law and he then succeeded Robert Catlin as a puisne judge of the Common Pleas.[16] A substantial proportion of the judges affected by the changes had formerly been benchers of the Middle Temple and were old friends of Plowden.[17]

Although the Act of Supremacy may not have had any great effect on the lawyers and those connected with the law,[18] the Act of Uniformity was a different matter; the latter Act directly affected all members of the Inns of Court since it applied to every one of the queen's subjects. The Act of Uniformity restored the Book of Common Prayer of 1552,[19] with some cautious modifications, and made its use compulsory in all churches from 24 June 1559, while the use of any other rite or ceremony was prohibited under penalty. The Act also required the queen's subjects 'to resort to their parish church or chapel accustomed' on every Sunday and Holy Day, 'and then and there to abide orderly and soberly during the time of the Common Prayer', upon pain of a fine of twelve pence for each failure to do so.

The general change to the new form of service was slow, but it was accepted by all but a few of the clergy, most of whom conformed. In that way Catholicism in England was almost deprived of its means of life, and it seems to have been the expectation of the government that the catholic

16. See Parmiter, *Elizabethan Popish Recusancy in the Inns of Court*, 3–4.
17. The former members of the Inn, with the dates of their elevation to the bench of the Inn, were: Saunders (1539), Catlin (1547), Dyer (1552), Browne (1553), Weston (1554).
18. *cf. A.P.C.*, xxiii, 253–61; Lambard, *Eirenarcha*, 62.
19. See p.23, *ante*.

religion would disappear from England as the older generation died out. The Catholic bishops had been removed from their sees very early in the reign because of their refusal to take the oath of supremacy, and there was no recognized leader among the catholic laity. Although, by 1563, the Roman Inquisition and a committee of the Council of Trent had condemned as unlawful the attendance of Catholics at heretical services and sermons, their decrees were little known outside the south-eastern area of Lancashire. The Catholics were, therefore, without any form of effective leadership, and in the critical years during the early part of Elizabeth's reign they were without real guidance on the vexed question of attending the services of the new church.[20]

From the beginning of the reign a number of Catholics left the country because they could no longer practice their religion there, while others who remained in England steadfastly refused to attend the new services, despite the penalties.[21] There were, however, many others who, in the absence of any authoritative guidance, were prepared to attend their parish churches on the days prescribed by law. Such advice on the question of church attendance as was available to Catholics in England in the early years of the reign was conflicting and the problem of whether and to what extent Catholics might conform to the law was still being debated in the fifteen eighties. The uncertainty on this matter brought into existence an unknown number of 'church papists' who, although they were Catholics at heart, complied with the minimum requirements of the law as to church attendance in order to avoid fines for recusancy.[22] Father Robert Persons, S.J., remarked on that phenomenon in the course of a letter which he wrote to the rector of the English College in Rome some twenty years after Elizabeth came to the throne: 'at the beginning of the reign of this queen, when the danger of this schism was not very well realized, for ten consecutive years practically all Catholics without distinction used to go to their churches.'[23] During those ten years Plowden, like many of his co-religionists, saw no reason why he should not comply with the law and he regularly attended the prescribed services. In 1564 the bishop of Salisbury, when reporting on the religious reliability of the justices of the peace for Berkshire, said that Plowden was 'as it is supposed, a hinderer [of the established religion]'; but he does not appear to have communicated, since the Act of Uniformity provided no penalty for failure to do so.[24]

20. *cf.* Hughes, *Reformation*, iii, 247-52.
21. One of those who left the country was William Rastell, a zealous Catholic and a nephew of Sir Thomas More. He had been appointed a judge of the King's Bench by queen Mary in 1558, and he remained on the bench until at least Michaelmas Term 1562, when he was one of the judges concerned in *The Case of the Dutchy of Lancaster*, Plowd. 212; he resigned soon afterwards for religious reasons and went abroad to spend the remainder of his life in Louvain (see Foss, *Judges of England*, v, 535-6).
22. See, e.g., Hughes, *Reformation*, iii, 245-60.
23. Fr. R. Persons, S.J., to Fr. Alphonsus Agazzari, S.J., London, 17 Nov. 1580 (printed in *C.R.S.*, vol. 39, p. 46; the quotation, which is taken from a translation, is at p. 58).
24. Jewel to the Privy Council, 9 Nov. 1564, printed in Bateson, *Collection of Original Letters*, 37-9. And see p. 106, *post*.

For the Catholic Plowden, watching the development of the religious changes in the first years of Elizabeth's reign, the prospect must have looked dark indeed, and he could derive little comfort from the experience of his friend Sir Francis Englefield. Englefield, it will be recalled, had been one of Mary's councillors and held the office of Master of the Court of Wards and Liveries,[25] but with queen Mary's death his fortunes suffered a severe set-back. His disapproval of the reformers was well known and he made no secret of his lack of enthusiasm for the direction in which the religious affairs of the country were moving under their influence. For a few weeks after the accession of Elizabeth he continued to transact public business and to offer advice,[26] but before the end of the year the first serious blow fell; on 26 December 1558 he was ordered to deliver up his seals of office as Master of the Court of Wards. His response to that order, that he obeyed only at the queen's command 'and not to relinquish his interest therein', was little more than an empty gesture, and on 21 January of the following year he was ordered to surrender to the marquis of Winchester, the Treasurer, all the books and records of the court that were still in his possession.[27]

Englefield realized that there was little prospect of his being able to practice his religion undisturbed and early in 1559 he decided to leave England for the continent.[28] In April, before his departure, he obtained the queen's licence to quit the realm for two years; the licence was subject to the condition that he should not resort into the territories or company of the queen's enemies.[29] On 4 May 1559 he executed a deed (which may well have been settled by Plowden) for the benefit of his sister-in-law Margaret Fitton who had married his younger brother John.[30] Apart from its principal purpose of augmenting the jointure of Margaret, the deed provided that if Sir Francis should die without lawful male issue and John and Margaret had male issue then living, the manor of Englefield and all

25. See p. 30, ante.
26. See, e.g., C.S.P.D., 1547–1580, 116.
27. A.P.C., vii, 29, 30, 47; Hurstfield, Queen's Wards, 244-5. On 12 Jan. 1559 the office was granted to Sir Thomas Parry and on 10 Jan. 1561, after Parry's death, to Sir William Cecil (C.P.R., 1558–1560, 60; C.P.R., 1560–1563, 44, 45).
28. See C.R.S., vol. 2, p. 62.
29. Englefield's licence was dated 12 April 1559 (see C.P.R., 1558–1560, 54); it provided that after one year he might be recalled by letters of the queen, her ambassadors or six of the Privy Council, and permitted him to take with him 8 servants, 8 horses, 600 oz. of plate, 100 marks in money and other necessaries. Art 42 of Magna Carta (1215) declared that, except in time of war and provided that no breach of allegiance were committed, all persons, save those under sentence of imprisonment or outlawry, might enter or leave the realm at any time either by land or sea; and art. 41 declared that all foreign merchants, unless publicly prohibited, might do so with impunity to themselves or their goods. However, the statute 5 Ric. II, stat. 1, c. 2 of 1381 (repealed by 14 Jac. I, c. 1, s. 22) restrained all persons except the great lords from leaving the realm without royal licence; see also 13 Ric. II, stat. 1, c. 20 of 1389 (repealed by the Statute Law Revision and Civil Procedure Act, 1881, s. 3). See also 3 Co. Inst. 178-81 (ch. 84).
30. Margaret Fitton's father, Sir Edward Fitton of Gawsworth, Cheshire, was a conformist, but one of his sons, Francis became a Catholic priest; see Wark, Elizabethan Recusancy in Cheshire, 1, 15, 19, 175, 181.

other lands of Sir Francis should descend to John Englefield if he were
alive or to his heirs male if he were dead.[31] Four days later there was
drawn up an account of the rents, annuities and other payments to be paid
out of the revenues of his wife's lands during his absence, and he also
arranged for his brother to take charge of his more southerly estates, and
it seems that Plowden, who had received much assistance from Englefield
in the past, agreed to administer his Shropshire property.[32] Having thus
disposed of his affairs in England he went abroad, leaving his wife at
home.

It may well have been that, in the course of Englefield's disposal of his
affairs, he granted to Plowden a lease or some interest in Shiplake rectory
with the mansion house and lands. Englefield held a long lease of the
rectory and lands which had formerly belonged to the Augustinian Abbey
at Missenden and, on the suppression of the abbey, had passed to the dean
and chapter of the Free Chapel of St. George in Windsor Castle. At any
rate, Plowden was living there in June 1562, and Shiplake appears to have
become his residence when he was not in London.[33]

Although the religious situation at the beginning of the reign caused
such men as Plowden some gloomy forebodings, his professional affairs
were a cause of satisfaction. He was now an influential bencher of his Inn.
On 28 April 1559, when George Nicholls was appointed Autumn Reader,
Plowden was chosen as his assistant; those appointments were again made
on 6 June.[34] On 27 November of the same year he was one of the two
auditors chosen to audit the accounts of William Hone at the end of his
term of office as Treasurer of the Inn.[35] The next two years were a period
of importance in Plowden's life. On 3 November 1560 he was again chosen
as Reader, this time for Lent of the coming year; in the following February
Hone was appointed his assistant. Later, at a Parliament held on 17 May
1561 he was chosen as assistant to Thomas Farmer, the Autumn Reader
for that year, who had been elected Steward for Christmas in 1559 but
fined for failing to exercise that office.[36] Then in the summer of 1561 he

31. See *Sir Francis Englefield's Case* (1591), Poph. 18, at pp. 20, 21, where the substance of
the deed is set out. The report refers to 'the Lady Anne then the wife of the said Sir Francis',
presumably an error for 'Catherine'; Englefield married Catherine Fettiplace, daughter of Sir
Thomas Fettiplace of Compton Beauchamp, Berks. The deed is summarized in Parmiter, in
R.H., xiii (1975-6), 159, at pp. 160-61.

32. P.R.O., S.P. 12/33/48 (i). See also Blakeway, *Sheriffs of Shropshire*, 222. Fr. Loomie
(*Spanish Elizabethans*, 17) gave the date of the deed as 8 May 1559, which is the date of the
account of the rents, annuities, etc. to be paid out of the revenues of his wife; the date of the
deed is given as 4 May 1559 in s. 7 of 35 Eliz. I, c. 5, and in *Sir Francis Englefield's Case*
(1591), Poph. 18, at p. 20.

33. See p. 64, *post*. In 1574, after the forfeiture to the crown of Englefield's estates, Plowden
obtained a grant of the queen's interest in Shiplake rectory; see P.R.O., E 310/22/119, m. 42,
and p. 103, *post*.

34. *M.T.R.*, i, 121, 123. On 28 April 1559 Plowden's brother-in-law, Ralph Sheldon, was
admitted to the chamber of John Mawdeley, a very senior bencher who had been Treasurer in
1551 and 1552 (*M.T.R.*, i, 121; Williamson, *Middle Temple Bench Book*, 61).

35. *M.T.R.*, i, 125. Hone had been chosen Treasurer at a Parliament held on 3 Nov. 1558
(*M.T.R.*, i, 118).

36. *M.T.R.*, i, 126, 128, 130, 131.

was elected to the highest office in the Inn; at a Parliament held on 20 June
he was chosen Treasurer, and William Bavande, a member of the Inn, was
appointed Under Treasurer to assist him.[37] The summer of 1561 also saw
the birth of his second child, a daughter, who was born at her maternal
grandparents' house in Beoley and was christened Anne in the parish
church there on 11 June 1561.[38]

37. *M.T.R.*, i, 131; Williamson, *Middle Temple Bench Book*, 136. Bavande was admitted to
the Inn on 14 Aug. 1557 (*R.A.M.T.*, i, 23).

38. See Beoley Parish Records, vol. 1 (Worcs. R.O., microfilm). *B.M.P.*, 16, erroneously
gives the date as 11 Jan. 1561.

IX

TREASURER

Plowden assumed office as Treasurer towards the end of June 1561. The Treasurer was (and is) the chief executive officer of the Inn, and his office imposed on him a number of responsibilities and entitled him to certain privileges. At the present day it is the practice for the Treasurer to remain in office for one year only, but before the end of the sixteenth century there was no rule limiting the period during which a Treasurer might hold office. Thus Edmund Plowden was Treasurer for six years, and his successor, Thomas Andrews, held the office for three years. Matthew Smith and Edward Ameredith were each Treasurer for six years, Sir John Popham and Myles Sandys for eight; it was not until 1597 that the benchers resolved that a Treasurer should not remain in office for more than one year.[1] To-day no one is eligible for the office of Treasurer who is not already a bencher, but in Plowden's time that was not the case. During the sixteenth century there were several Treasurers who had not been Readers: Sir Amyas Paulet (1521 and 1522), Thomas Andrews (1567-9), Edward Ameredith (1574-9); and Matthew Smith (1570-3) was not even an utter-barrister, having been exempted from taking up that degree.[2]

Admissions to the Inn and to chambers were normally granted by the Treasurer, save in the case of bench chambers which were under the control of Parliament. The Treasurer received all the admission fines, paid the wages of the Inn's servants and other outgoings, and generally controlled the finances of the house for which he rendered an account at the end of his term of office, which was audited by two senior members.[3] The Treasurer had a dispensing power with regard to admissions, which he exercised at his discretion; there are several entries of admissions where the newcomer was excused a fine or paid only a reduced one. It was the duty of the Treasurer to preside at Parliaments at which he took first place; but the wording of some minutes recording the election of a Treasurer, which added that the person elected should have a voice in Parliament, seems to imply that the Treasurer was normally prohibited from voting on a contested matter. The practice, however, was changed

---

1. M.T., B.M.B., D. 264 (*M.T.R.*, i, 371; 11 Feb. 1597): 'Quilibet qui Magistrorum erit summus Thesaurarius hujus hospicii Medii Templi non remanebit diutius quam per tempore unius anni.'

2. For Matthew Smith's exemption, see p. 66, *post*.

3. For a description of the duties of the Treasurer in the reign of Henry VIII, see Br. Lib., Cotton MS Vit. C. ix, f. 319 (*D.O.J.*, 193; *A.I.T.*, 211). At that time there was no Under Treasurer as an established officer of the Inn.

62   EDMUND PLOWDEN

when John Popham, the solicitor-general, was elected Treasurer in 1580.[4] The Treasurer did not, however, take first place at the bench table where precedence was determined by official or social status.[5]

Among the problems facing Plowden when he assumed the office of Treasurer was the resolution of a dispute with the Inner Temple over Lyon's Inn. The origins of the dispute went back to the reign of Edward VI when, in 1549, Protector Somerset pulled down Strand Inn to make way for the building of his new palace of Somerset House.[6] The destruction of Strand Inn left the Middle Temple with only one Inn of Chancery, New Inn, under their control, whereas the Inner Temple had jurisdiction over three such Inns, Clifford's Inn, Clement's Inn and Lyon's Inn. The benchers of the Middle Temple regarded that situation as inequitable and they determined to improve their position by obtaining the transfer to themselves of Lyon's Inn. The year 1561 was deemed to be an appropriate time to put the scheme into effect. A secret approach was made in Trinity Term to the Lord Keeper, Sir Nicholas Bacon, to induce him to exercise his authority over the Inns by making an order severing Lyon's Inn from the Inner Temple and annexing it to the Middle Temple, a proceeding which the benchers of the Inner Temple regarded as 'so wrongfully and unneighbourly practised against us'. In making their approach the benchers obtained the support of the two chief justices, Sir Robert Catlin of the King's Bench and Sir James Dyer of the Common Pleas, both of whom had been benchers of the Middle Temple and were old friends of Plowden.

In the following Michaelmas Term Bacon called the benchers of the Inner Temple before him when Catlin and Dyer vigorously put forward the case for the Middle Temple. The benchers of the Inner Temple were now thoroughly alarmed, 'considering the earnestness of the said chief justices, and they both and the most part of all the other justices of both the benches, and of the barons of the Exchequer now being, had been of the fellowship of the said Middle Temple'.[7] In their difficulties the Inner Temple turned to the queen's favourite, Sir Robert Dudley, and enlisted his help.[8] That astute move won them a victory. Dudley persuaded the queen to intervene, and she ordered Bacon not to meddle further in the

4. *cf.* Williamson, *Middle Temple Bench Book*, pp. xxiv, xxv. The minute recording Popham's election concluded with the words, 'et vox ei conceditur simulatque omnibus aliis hujus domus lectoribus qui in illud officium morabuntur imposterum in tam ampli modo ut si thesaurii non essent' (M.T., B.M.B., D. 142; *cf. M.T.R.*, i, 239). Popham's position was a curious one. He became a bencher in 1568 but left the Inn on being created a serjeant in 1578. On his appointment as solicitor-general in the following year he was exonerated from the degree of serjeant and returned to the Middle Temple.

5. It was not until 1774 that the Treasurer was accorded first place both in Parliament and in Hall; see M.T., B.M.B., K. 483.

6. See p. 6, *ante.*

7. Of the eight common law judges and the four barons of the Exchequer, nine had been members of the Middle Temple: Catlin, C. J., and Corbet, J., in the King's Bench; Dyer, C. J., and Humphrey Browne, Anthony Browne and Weston, JJ., in the Common Pleas; and Saunders, C. B., and Luke and Freville, BB., in the Exchequer.

8. Robert Dudley was then a Knight of the Garter, a privy councillor and master of the horse; he was not created earl of Leicester until 1564.

matter but to allow the jurisdiction of the Inner Temple over Lyon's Inn to continue. There is a long account of the incident in the Parliament books of the Inner Temple, under the date 16 November 1561, from which the foregoing quotations have been taken, but the records of the Middle Temple contain no mention of the matter.[9] The grateful benchers of the Inner Temple passed an ordinance declaring that no member of their Society should ever hold a retainer as counsel against Dudley in any suit in which he might be engaged. They also elected Dudley a governor of their Christmas celebration that year and in those festivities they enrolled him a member of their house.[10]

Almost as soon as he assumed the office of Treasurer Plowden became immersed in a project that was to occupy much of his time for several years to come; that project was the building of a new hall for the members of the Inn, to replace the old hall which stood on the east side of Middle Temple Lane. The reasons which prompted the benchers' decision to abandon the old hall and build a new one are unknown, but they must have been substantial to have induced them to erect so costly a building with little or nothing in the way of endowments behind them, at a time when the financial position of the Inn was far from prosperous, and the Inn was no more than a tenant at will of the crown.[11] It is a surprising fact that, despite the importance of the project and of the financial burden that it would place upon the Inn, the contemporary minutes of the Parliament of the Middle Temple contain no reference to any consideration of the project and there is no recorded resolution authorizing the commencement of building. The Inn, moreover, does not possess any accounts relating to the period in question, and all we have are occasional allusions in the minutes of Parliament to the building of the hall. Such allusions, however, make it possible to establish approximate dates when building began and when it was completed, and they also enable us to gain some idea of how part of the money needed was raised, but in the absence of building accounts the total cost to the Inn remains unknown.

Whatever the circumstances surrounding the decision to build a new hall may have been, it seems probable that it was taken before Plowden became Treasurer, but as a bencher he was doubtless concerned in the preceding discussions. As soon as he became Treasurer he appears to have taken charge of the project with enthusiasm, and the chief credit for building the hall has always been given to him.[12] On 22 June 1562 Plowden wrote from his home at Shiplake to Sir John Thynne to ask for the

9. See *I.T.R.*, i, 215-9.

10. See *I.T.R.*, i, 218. A vivid description of the Christmas revels on that occasion, when Dudley held his court as the 'Mightye Palaphilos Prince of Sophie hyghe Constable Marshal of ye Knightes Templers, Patrone of thonorable Ordre of Pegasus', is given by Gerard Legh, *Accidens of Armory*, 205 et seq.; there is also an account in *D.O.J.*, 150 et seq.

11. Some ten years earlier Gray's Inn had carried out improvements to their hall; in 1553 the interior was newly wainscoted, and between 1556 and 1561 extensive re-edification was carried out at a cost of between £800 and £900 (see *G.I.P.B.*, i, 496-8).

12. *cf.* The inscription at the top of the south window in the south bay at the west end of the hall, for which see p. 120, *post*.

services of one, Lewis, a craftsman employed by Thynne at Longleat, of whose workmanship the benchers held so high an opinion that they wished to put him in charge of the building of their new hall. The letter is as follows:

After my hearty commendations, Lewis your servant, bearer hereof, being sent for to be employed on the queen's highness' works is, by the mediation of my masters and fellows of the Middle Temple, appointed and assigned to the building of a new hall in the said house, being the queen's highness' house and work, and I being Treasurer at this time do most heartily in the behalf of all our house, and they your acquaintance will hereafter particularly desire you, we may have your favour for your man in this behalf, and that you will signify unto him your good contention herein, and that you will not withdraw your goodwill from him in any point by means hereof, wherefor I am the more earnest to request for that your counsel be of the said house. And although some of the house (as I myself) be against you in some things, yet hereafter this your gentleness shall occasion me and my fellows to give to you our friendly furtherance in your matters hereafter to be attempted or begun. This upon desert hereafter, being bold to write to you and to crave your gentleness, hoping to receive the effect of my desire, bid you at this present heartily to farewell. From Shiplake the 23rd of June 1562.

your friend to use or command
Edmunde Plowden.[13]

A few months later there occurred the first reference in the minutes of Parliament to the building of the new hall, which indicates that the benchers were hard pressed for money to carry out their undertaking: on 24 November 1562 it was ordered that, until the new hall had been completed, each member of the Inn should bear the cost of repairs to his own chamber on pain of forfeiture, but those who paid rent should receive an allowance from the Treasurer.[14] It is much to be regretted that no documents now remain which would indicate how the cost of the building was met,[15] but it may be supposed that the raising of the substantial sum needed was, in the main, the result of Plowden's personal efforts; indeed,

13. The letter is the property of the Marquis of Bath and is preserved at Longleat; a transcript is printed in Williamson, *Middle Temple Bench Book*, 335, with a photographic reproduction of the original letter. It is the only known extant letter written by Plowden. The phrases 'the quenes highnes workes' and 'the quenes highnes house and worke' refer to the fact that, after the confiscation of the property of the Order of St. John of Jerusalem in 1540 (see p. 8, *ante*), the Temple became the property of the crown which remained the landlord of the two Societies in the Temple (who were only tenants at will) until 1608 when James I, by letters patent, granted the property to the two Societies; see *W.H.T.*, 260-70.

14. *M.T.R.*, i, 137.

15. It is the belief of the present writer that the relevant documents were kept by Plowden in his own chamber where they remained throughout his life. By his will he left to his clerks his unpaid fees and 'my bookes of receipte alsoe to thend it maye be truly considered what shalbe behinde of my Fees at my deathe' (P.C.C. 54 Brudenell; P.R.O., Prob 11/68/429). If the books of receipt acquired by the clerks after his death included not only his fee books but all account books, then the absence of the accounts for the building of the hall can be easily explained.

the fact that, after he ceased to be Treasurer, he remained as 'proctor and promoter' for the building of the new hall perhaps indicates the value that his fellow benchers placed upon his ability to raise the money needed. Altogether he devoted some twelve years to the building and beautifying of the hall. For nearly a year, however, the work must have been suspended, as there is a note added to the minutes of the Parliament held on 26 June 1563 recording that from that date until 26 April 1564 nothing was done in the Inn on account of the pestilence.[16]

William Fleetwood had been appointed Autumn Reader in 1563, but, because of the pestilence, he did not read until the autumn of the following year.[17] He thus became a bencher, but Plowden could scarcely have found him a congenial companion at the bench table. He was a resolute Protestant and at the time when he was appointed Reader his reputation as a keen reformer was growing fast; in April 1561 he had been one of those appointed to examine a number of Catholics imprisoned in the Marshalsea. He was, moreover, a man of considerable severity, as is shown by a letter written to Lord Burghley in 1577, six years after his appointment as Recorder of London; describing the previous Newgate Sessions, at which he presided; he said that 'there were executed eighteen at Tyburn, and one Barlow . . . was pressed. They were all notable cut-purses and horse-stealers. It was the quietest session that ever I was at.'[18]

Apart from organizing the work of construction and of obtaining materials and the services of suitable craftsmen, Plowden's most urgent task was the raising of the necessary money, as the resources of the Inn were wholly insufficient to bear the considerable cost. In order to do so he seems to have recruited a number of members of the Inn to act as collectors. For example, when Robert Brickett, who had once been steward of the Inn, was admitted to a new chamber in the summer of 1565, the usual fine was not exacted from him 'because he has worked hard in collecting money for the new Hall.'[19] Some gifts were also received from members of the Inn; thus when William and Henry Brunker were admitted to another chamber, only a reduced fine was taken from them 'because they paid £10 for their admission and the building of the new Hall.'[20] Such methods, however, were not enough, and at an early stage in the undertaking a levy was made on all members of the Inn, but the order of Parliament authorizing the levy is not recorded. Thus, on 21 May 1563 Parliament ordered that Henry Wasse, James Cressey and Timothy

16. M.T., B.M.B., D. 53 (cf. M.T.R., i, 142). The year 1563 saw one of the major epidemics of bubonic plague in London; see Hirst, *Conquest of Plague*, 53. The terms were first adjourned from Michaelmas to the octave of St. Hilary at Westminster, and thence to Hertford Castle (*T.R.P.*, ii, 236, 238).
17. *M.T.R.*, i, 140, 141, 142.
18. See, generally, Harris, in *R.H.*, vii (1963-4), 106-22. For Fleetwood's letter (6 Oct. 1577), see Wright, *Queen Elizabeth and her Times*, ii, 66, at p. 69. Fleetwood was appointed Recorder of London in 1571.
19. *M.T.R.*, i, 148; cf. p. 186 (1572).
20. *M.T.R.*, i, 157; cf. p. 173 (1570).

Mockett should lose their chambers for not paying their contributions to the new hall on the days appointed and proclaimed from the Cupboard;[21] and on 24 May 1566 it was ordered that all persons who owed money for rent of chambers, vacations, and the building of the new hall should, unless they paid by the following Sunday, be expelled from their chambers and put out of commons until they paid.[22] Further steps to raise money from the members of the Inn had to be taken a year or two later; on 3 November 1568, after Plowden had ceased to be Treasurer, a Parliament ordered that all members of the Inn summoned for any assessment for building the new hall or any other matter, and not coming or refusing to be assessed, should be assessed by the benchers at their pleasure and pay the sum assessed without delay.[23] A further expedient was tried in 1571 when, on 8 February, Parliament increased the pension money charge for three years; pension money had hitherto been 3s. 4d. per annum, but under the new scale benchers paid 10s. a term, utter-barristers, common attorneys and officers of any of the superior courts, 6s. 8d., and other masters 3s. 4d.[24] The increases were maintained by further orders made in 1574, 1575 and 1577.[25]

Another method employed to finance the building of the hall was the obtaining of loans from members of the Inn. For example, in 1563 Matthew Smith, a papist, lent £60 and Richard Palmer £40, while George Nicholls had lent £10 which was repaid in 1565.[26] Voluntary loans, however, were not apparently very numerous, perhaps because potential lenders held back owing to doubts about the ability of the Inn to repay them. In 1570 a Parliament ordered that any member lending money to the Inn or being surety for money lent for the building of the new hall, should be repaid with the first money coming to the hall, in order of date.[27] That order, however, was not sufficient to overcome the reluctance of members to lend money and early in the following year a system of forced loans was introduced. On 8 February 1581 it was ordered that each bencher should lend to the Treasurer £3, each utter-barrister, common attorney and officer of any of the superior courts 40s., and others of the fellowship 20s.; such loans were to be made as soon as possible before Ascension Day (24 May),

21. *M.T.R.*, i, 140. On 26 June a Parliament ordered that the forfeiture of Wasse's chamber should be of no effect as the cause of non-payment had been approved; on the same day William Boughton was admitted to Cressey's chamber (*M.T.R.*, i, 141).

22. *M.T.R.*, i, 153.

23. *M.T.R.*, i, 153.

24. *M.T.R.*, i, 176. Pension money was an annual charge payable by all those in commons.

25. *M.T.R.*, i, 197, 206, 215. One of the few records of payments made by the Inn is appended to the minutes of the Parliament held on 2 July 1565, where it is stated that £33 15s. 8d. 'of the House money' was employed by Mr. Plowden on the building of the hall (*M.T.R.*, i, 148).

26. *M.T.R.*, i, 141, 142, 151; Smith and Palmer had each been fined £10 for refusing to be called to the Bar, but in consideration of their loan their fines were released and it was agreed that they should 'never be compelled to take up office of utter barrister, nor any other office.' Nicholls' loan was repaid by Plowden out of money received for special admissions (*M.T.R.*, i, 151).

27. *M.T.R.*, i, 171 (5 May 1570).

and it was stated that they should be repaid as soon as possible after the new buildings were finished and other debts paid.[28]

That so costly an undertaking should have been successfully concluded without financial disaster is remarkable, and many members of the Inn must have subscribed generously to the building of their new hall. Many years after the hall was completed such generosity was remembered in a practical way; thus, when John Hippisley was admitted to the Inn in November 1594 he was excused the payment of a fine on admission 'because his grandfather was a Master of the Bench and a benefactor towards the building of the new hall.'[29] Since the Societies in the Temple were at that time only tenants at will of the crown, it is remarkable that the benchers of the Middle Temple should have even considered the erection of so splendid a building as the new hall proved to be. On the ancient maxim of the common law, *quidquid plantatur solo, solo cedit*, the new hall would have become part of the freehold as soon as it was built and the queen might, at any time, have deprived the Inn of its use by terminating the tenancy of the Temple premises. It seems clear that the benchers never doubted the goodwill of the queen and her friendship towards them.

While Plowden was Treasurer there was admitted to the Inn a man who subsequently played a part in Plowden's life. He was Thomas Pagitt who, on 14 November 1562, was admitted 'generally, by assent of the Masters of the Bench.'[30] He was the son of Richard Pagitt of Cranford in Northamptonshire and, like Plowden, was a Catholic. He later served the Inn successively as Under Treasurer, Reader and Treasurer.[31] Plowden, as Treasurer, also saw the admission of two of his nephews. Humfrey Sandford and Andrew Blunden. Sandford was the son of Plowden's eldest sister Margaret, who had married Richard Sandford, and he was admitted to the Middle Temple on 4 November 1564; he was admitted 'generally, with assent of the Masters of the Bench', and on his admission to the chamber of William Babthorpe and Edward Holt in the buildings recently erected, no fine was imposed on him.[32] Andrew Blunden was the son of another of Plowden's sisters, Jane, who had married Richard Blunden of Bishop's Castle, not far from Plowden Hall; he was born at Bishop's Castle but later his parents came to live at Burghfield in Berkshire. He was admitted to the Inn on 19 October 1566 when his father was already dead.[33] He performed many services for his uncle whom he greatly admired, and was called to the Bar in 1585, a few months before Plowden's death.

Plowden's Treasurership was marked by the birth of three more children. At some time, probably in 1562, his first surviving son was born, whom he

28. *M.T.R.*, i, 176.
29. *M.T.R.*, i, 347. His grandfather, John Hippisley, was Autumn Reader in 1567 and died c. 1570; see Williamson, *Middle Temple Bench Book*, 75.
30. *M.T.R.*, i, 137; *R.A.M.T., i, 27*.
31. Williamson, *Middle Temple Bench Book*, 83.
32. *M.T.R.*, i, 144; *R.A.M.T.*, i, 28.
33. *M.T.R.*, i, 155; *R.A.M.T.*, i, 31.

christened Edmund.[34] Another daughter, Mary, was born, probably in 1563,[35] and a second son, Francis, was born in 1564 or 1565.[36]

On 11 February 1562 a new commission of the peace for Berkshire was issued. Plowden was among those named in the commission and he was one of those declared to be of the quorum. A further commission was issued on 1 June 1564 which included all those in the commission of 1562 together with two others.[37] And on 1 February 1564 he was included in a commission of oyer and terminer for the counties of Oxfordshire, Berkshire, Worcestershire, Gloucestershire, Shropshire, Herefordshire, Monmouhtshire and Staffordshire.[38] He was also named in several of the commissions of sewers.[39] The commissioners of sewers were figures of importance with considerable powers. Before the Tudors, they had been appointed at the pleasure of the crown. The Statute of Sewers of 1532,[40] however, extended their powers and provided that they should be appointed at the discretion and on the nomination of the Lord Chancellor, the Lord Treasurer, and the two chief justices; their appointments were to continue for ten years unless revoked by a new commission. The duties of the commissioners, which were limited to the counties for which they were appointed, were to supervise the repair of sea-banks and sea-walls and the cleansing of rivers, streams, ditches and the like. They had power to make laws and ordinances to enable them to carry out such repairs, and to assess

34. No record of the birth of Edmund has yet been found, but in the Inquisition post mortem taken on 13 March 1585, after Plowden's death (P.R.O., C.142/206/13) Edmund jr. is stated to be his heir, aged 22 years and more ('etatis viginti duorum et amplius'); such statements are, however, not very reliable indications of age.

35. No record of the birth of Mary has yet been found, but in his will, made on 2 Jan. 1582, Plowden made certain provision for her if she 'shall lyve vntill her age of Twentye yeares'. It has been assumed that she was then about 19 years of age.

36. No record has yet been found of the birth of Francis. His tombstone at Shiplake records that he died on 11 Nov. 1652, at the age of 90, which puts his date of birth in 1562 or 1563. On the other hand, in the Inquisition post mortem taken on 3 April 1588, after the death of his brother Edmund (P.R.O., C.142/221/123), Francis is stated to be the heir, aged 22 years and more ('etatis xxij annorum et amplius') which suggests 1565 or 1566. Barbara Plowden (*B.M.P.*, 16) mentioned another child, Margaret; if, as is stated, she was twice married, she would probably have survived her father. In his will, however, Plowden made provision for all his children (except Humphrey who died in infancy), but he made no mention of Margaret; it seems likely that Barbara Plowden has here confused the parentage of 'Margaret'.

37. *C.P.R., 1560–1563*, 397; *C.P.R., 1563–1566*, 20. Those in the commission of 1562 were: Sir Nicholas Bacon*, lord keeper; marquis of Winchester*, lord treasurer; earl of Arundel*, steward of the household; Sir John Mason*, treasurer of the chamber; Sir Edward Saunders*, chief baron of the Exchequer; serjeant Thomas Carus*; Sir Thomas Benger; Sir Edward Unton*; Sir Henry Neville*; Robert Keilwey*; Thomas Weldon*; Thomas Hoby; William Hyde; Alexander Fettiplace; Edmund Plowden*; John Fettiplace; Richard Ward; John Yate; Roger Young*; John Winchcombe*; William Dunche*; Griffin Curtiss*; Thomas Stafford*; those marked with an asterisk were of the quorum. The extra two included in the commission of 1564 were John Cheyne and John Dauncey.

38. *C.P.R., 1563–1566*, no. 223. Among those named in the commission was Plowden's father-in-law, William Sheldon.

39. *C.P.R., 1563–1566*, no. 215 (3 June 1564); *C.P.R., 1569–1572*, nos. 1861, 1863 (14 May 1567; 20 March 1568), and no. 1873 (21 Oct. 1570).

40. 23 Hen. VIII, c.5.

and levy a rate to defray the costs. They also had jurisdiction to order the sale of land owned by any person who made default in paying the rate, and they had their own courts which were regarded as courts of record and were subject to the control of the King's Bench.

Plowden's professional earnings were by now considerable, and during his last years as Treasurer of the Inn he began to lay out his money in land as many another successful lawyer did; it was a process that lasted intermittently for some ten years. In January 1565 he acquired an interest in some land in Oxfordshire, when he and William Chauncey, a Northamptonshire gentleman and a member of the Middle Temple, acquired from John Bury and his wife their interest in Culham manor, together with other land in Culham and Nuneham Courtney.[41] Late in the following year he acquired a substantial amount of land near Burghfield where his sister Jane was living; in October 1566 he bought Wokefield Farm from Sylvester Cowper who had bought it, with other property, some years earlier from Sir Richard Rede.[42]

Added to all his other activities, Plowden's period of office as Treasurer must have severely taxed even his considerable energy, and it is possible that after six years he asked his fellow benchers to appoint a successor. At any rate, whether at Plowden's own request or for some other reason, Thomas Andrews was chosen as Treasurer on 9 May 1567 but Plowden's energetic work in connection with the new hall was evidently so highly prized by the benchers that they were unwilling to relieve him of those onerous duties, and the minute recording the election of Andrews as Treasurer concluded with the words, 'Mr. Plowden nevertheless remaining proctor and promotor for the building of the new hall and for making collections.'[43] Richard Wrenche, who seems to have been butler of the Inn before his admission as a member in 1565, was appointed Under Treasurer at the same time.[44]

41. See pardon of alienation, 11 Jan. 1565 (*C.P.R., 1563–1566*, no. 1268).
42. Licence for Sylvester Cowper to alienate, 28 Oct. 1566 (*C.P.R., 1563–1566*, no. 2256); *V.C.H., Berks.*, iii, 425. Wokefield is in the parish of Stratfield Mortimer which is immediately south of that of Burghfield.
43. M.T., B.M.B., D. 77; the original minute is in Latin '. . . M ro Plowden remanente procuratore et promotore nihilominus ad novam aulam edificandam et ad Collectiones Colligendas' (*cf. M.T.R.*, i, 159). There is no earlier minute recording Plowden's appointment as proctor and promotor for the new hall, so presumably it was an ad hoc appointment specially made to meet the exigencies of the occasion.
44. *M.T.R.*, i, 159; Williamson, *Middle Temple Bench Book*, 316.

X

IN COURT

Early in Elizabeth's reign Plowden found himself in professional conflict with the crown in a matter involving the royal prerogative. At the end of her reign queen Mary had taken in hand the improvement of the Customs, and Plowden was professionally involved in the protests that followed at the beginning of her half-sister's reign. The 'ancient customs' on wool, wool-fells and leather, and 'tonnage and poundage', together with the taxes on each tun of imported wine and each pound of imported or exported merchandize except the staple commodities had been levied for centuries, but there were other Customs or 'imposts' which were imposed by virtue of the royal prerogative to regulate trade. The principal purpose of those 'imposts' was not the raising of revenue but the protection of native merchants against foreign competition, and so long as imposts were used in that way they were not unpopular.

Stimulated by Henry VII, there had been a substantial growth of trade which was, of course, reflected in a steady increase of the Customs revenue. Soon after the accession of Edward VI, however, the Customs revenue began to decline. The decline was not the result of falling-off of trade, but was due to a combination of several factors concerned with the administration of the Customs. The most important of those factors, and the main cause of the decline of the Customs revenue, was the obsolete level of official valuations. Although the growth of commerce consisted chiefly in the exchange of cloth, beer and wine, the duties on those goods were too low to yield a buoyant Customs revenue that increased with the increase of trade. Customs duties were collected on the valuations set out in the national rate books of 1536 and 1545, but those were little more than the valuations fixed by the London rate book of 1507, so that by the end of queen Mary's reign they were half a century out of date.[1]

Because of the rise in prices which occurred during the sixteenth century the difference between the valuations of goods set out in the rate book and the actual price of goods became progressively greater and by the middle of the century it was substantial; the adverse effect of the process on the Customs revenue was thus considerable. That was recognized by a commission appointed in the reign of Edward VI to inquire into the Customs and, in consequence, during Mary's reign a committee of the Privy Council proposed that the old rates should be replaced by new ones that reflected the true values of the goods concerned. The proposal was adopted by the queen and a new book of rates with up-to-date valuations was issued on 28 May 1558 accompanied by a privy seal that imposed on cloth a new duty referred to as the impost.[2] In the previous month the

1. The rate book of 1507 was issued on 15 July 1507; a transcript made in 1732 is in Br. Lib., Add. MS 16577, which is printed in Gras, *Early English Customs,* App. C (pp. 694–706). *cf.* Cobb, in *Guildhall Miscellany,* iv (1971), 1–13.
2. See Dietz, *English Government Finance,* 206–8.

council had imposed similar imposts on French wines, imported French dry goods and exported beer.[3] The new rate book and new duties, which resulted in a substantial increase of revenue, was one of Mary's great contributions to the rehabilitation of the public finances, the benefits of which were reaped by her successor.

The new rates appear to have been accepted by the foreign merchants without protest, although they were now required to pay a duty that was substantially higher than that paid by denizens. English merchants, however, voiced considerable dissatisfaction with the new imposts, and their complaints came before the judges very early in the reign of queen Elizabeth in legal proceedings that are difficult to unravel as the surviving reports are incomplete.[4] It was the new impost on cloth that was at the heart of their complaints, and in Dyer's *Reports* there is printed, under the heading Hilary Term 1559, a Memorandum which began by stating that 'lately in the time of Queen Mary a new impost or imposition was put upon cloth as a custom more than the ancient custom granted by parliament . . . And now the merchants of London found great grievance, and made exclamations and suit to the queen to be unburdened of this impost, because it was not granted by parliament, but assessed by queen Mary of her absolute power. And on account of this doubt there were divers assemblies and conferences by the justices and others.'[5]

Plowden developed an argument that appears to have been hostile to the claim of the crown to increase or impose Customs by virtue of the royal prerogative alone, but the manuscript recording the argument does not indicate when or in what capacity Plowden put it forward.[6] The argument began by considering the statutes and common law relating to the freedom of merchants to go out of the kingdom with their merchandize, and reached the conclusion that 'by all the laws it is adjudged that the merchants of England, by law of the realm, may freely pass out of the land in their persons with their merchandize to any place being of the amity of the king, any restraints to the contrary notwithstanding'. He then returned to the 'second and chiefest question' which concerned the imposition of customs duties. He observed that, at common law, 'the king had no custom of his merchants of England for wares carried out nor yet brought in. And first for wares brought into the realm, our English merchants at this day pay no custom, nor yet any time heretofore hath done. And of wares outward or carried out of the realm, there was no

---

3. *A.P.C.*, vi, 305 (17 April 1558).
4. *cf.* Hall, in *L.Q.R.*, lxix (1953), at pp. 209, 210.
5. Dyer, 165, 165b: 'Memorandum que nuper en le tēps del Roigne Mary, un novel Impost ou Imposition fuit myse sur drapes, come un Custome, plus que l'auncient custome graunt per Parliament, . . . Et oze les Marchants de London trovont graund grief et font exclamation et suit al Roigne destre unburthened de cest impost, pur ceo q̃ ne fuit graunt per Parliament, mes assesse per le Roigne Mary de son absolute power, Et pur cett doubt fueront divers assemblies et conferēces per les Justices et auts.'
6. A note of the argument is in Br. Lib., Harg. MS 27, ff. 84–85v; it is endorsed, 'Mr. Plowdens argument 1 Eliz.'

custom paid by the common law until the same was granted by certain statutes as hereafter shall be rehearsed.' He then considered several statutes the choice of which Hubert Hall regarded as 'little more than an expression of the great common lawyer's well-known jealousy of the equitable jurisdiction of the Crown.'[7] In particular, Plowden quoted at length one passed in the reign of Edward I[8] by which, he said, 'it doth appear amongst other things how that the custom of wool and skins [wool-fells] and leather was first granted by parliament. And how that rules and precedents[9] shall not be any title to the king otherwise than is expressed by parliament.' No judgment is recorded, but that does not necessarily mean that none was delivered.

That case was only one of several concerning the royal claim to restrain trade and impose customs that came before the judges at that time, but the cloth case appears to have been the only one in which Plowden was involved.[10] Plowden's argument in the cloth case, however, was sufficiently well thought of by those opposed to the royal claims to be referred to when the vexed question of impositions came to a head with *Bate's Case* in 1606 and the well known parliamentary debates of 1610.[11]

In Easter Term 1560 Plowden appeared in the Exchequer for Rowland Morgan who had been sued for debt by Sir Thomas Stradling, represented by Roger Manwood.[12] The plaintiff's declaration in the Exchequer was founded on the statute 7 Edw. VI, c. 1, which enacted that receivers should not extort fees upon pain of forfeiting 6s 8d. for every penny extorted. The plaintiff, by letters patent of Henry VIII, held the office of bedel and collector of the rents of certain royal manors in Glamorgan, for which he was entitled to an annual fee of £13 6s. 8d. It was alleged that in 1556 the defendant, who was receiver of the rents, when paying the fee due to the

7. Hall, *History of the Custom-Revenue,* i, 131. The contention of the common lawyers was not that aliens should be arbitrarily taxed for the good of England, but that denizens should be taxed in the same way as aliens.

8. 25 Edw. I, Confirmatio Cartarum, c. 5 (*Statutes of the Realm,* i, 123).

9. In the MS, 'rowles and presidents'.

10. See Hall, *L.Q.R.,* lxix (1953), at pp. 206–12. Plowden's name has, however, been linked with one of those cases, which was concerned with the importation of malmsey wine; manuscript reports of that case are to be found in Br. Lib., Harg. MS 27, ff. 92, 92v, and Harg. MS 132, ff. 66v, 67, and in Exeter Coll. MS 128, ff. 149–150v. The report in Harg. MS 27 bears the following marginal note: The part of this leaf from hence is of Plowden but is of the hand writing of C. J. Hyde & relative to the matter. Plowden's name, however, has been substituted in a different hand for another name which has been obliterated. It is the only report to link Plowden with the case, and it is unlikely that he took part in it.

11. In the course of a lengthy argument in the house of commons in 1610 on unparliamentary taxation, William Hakewill, a barrister of Lincoln's Inn, referred to 'Plowden's argument against it in Mr. Tate's hand' (see Hakewill, *Libertie of the Subject,* 95), and that almost certainly refers to the argument noted in Harg. MS 27 (see note [6]). For *Bate's Case,* see Hall, in *L.Q.R.,* lxix (1953), 200–18, and Hall, in *Bull. of John Rylands and Lib,* xxxv (1952–3), 405–27.

12. *Stradling* v. *Morgan* (1560), Plowd. 199. This is one of the many cases in his reports in which Plowden refers to himself as 'an Apprentice of the Middle Temple' (un Apprentice del Middle Temple). In 1560 Manwood was recorder of Sandwich; he was advanced to the degree of serjeant-at-law in 1567, appointed a puisne judge of the Common Pleas in 1572 and promoted to be chief baron in 1578.

plaintiff, extortionately retained 4s. 4d. at the rate of 4d. for every £1 of the fee; that was done at Cardiff. Thereupon the plaintiff claimed the sum of £17 6s. 8d. under the statute, a sum calculated at the rate of 6s. 8d. for every penny extorted; to that claim the defendant pleaded that he did not receive the sum of 4s. 4d. contrary to the statute. That issue was tried at *Nisi Prius* at Hereford because Cardiff was in Wales where an English sheriff had no jurisdiction. The jury found a verdict for the plaintiff, and upon that verdict the plaintiff subsequently asked for judgment in the Exchequer.

The case is of interest for several reasons. It is an early instance of the exercise of the Exchequer jurisdiction in matters originating in Wales; it provided an interesting argument on the jurisdiction of the court; and Plowden's argument is an important part of his considerable contribution to the doctrine of the interpretation of statutes. Plowden argued that the plaintiff was not entitled to judgment. The first point that was argued was a point of pleading, and concerned the meaning of the declaration. Plowden's argument, which was accepted by all the barons, was that the declaration must be taken as alleging that the defendant was receiver to a person other than the king. The next point that was argued was whether the statute 7 Edw. VI, c. 1, extended to receivers who were not receivers to the king; once again the court accepted Plowden's argument that receivers to persons other than the king were 'out of the purview and penalty of the said statute.'[13] For those reasons the declaration was insufficient.

The next point was whether, assuming the declaration to be good, the plaintiff might sue for the statutory penalty elsewhere than in Wales, as the defendant had received the 4s. 4d. in Cardiff. Plowden argued that although the statute 27 Hen. VIII, c. 26, annexed and united Wales to England and so appeared to provide means by which any personal action, for a cause arising in Wales, might be sued in the Common Pleas in England, yet the statute had divided Wales into twelve counties, and by the statute 34 & 35 Hen. VIII, c. 26, four judges were appointed for Wales, one for every three counties, who by statute had jurisdiction to hold pleas of all things within their shires, known as the courts of Great Sessions; accordingly, the defendant could not be sued elsewhere than in Wales. Although that argument was accepted by Baron Freville, the other members of the court disagreed and held that the terms of the statutes of Henry VIII did not exclude the jurisdiction of the English courts.

The last and most important point concerned the jurisdiction of the court itself, in the circumstances of the case. Plowden argued that where, as in the instant case, a statute provided for the recovery of a penalty in any of the king's courts of record, an action by original writ in the Exchequer was, nevertheless, not maintainable despite the words of the

---

13. '. . . ceo fuit . . . tenus per touts les Barons, que . . . receiuors ou ministers accomptant de common persons & lour deputies, queux receiuont argent ou auter profit pur payment de fees &c. sont hors del purview & penaltie del dict statute.' (Plowd., 199, at p. 203).

statute, unless the plaintiff were an officer of the court or a debtor to the king, because such an action was a common plea, and the Exchequer was not a court for common pleas but a court for the king's business only. That argument was accepted by the puisne barons but Saunders, the chief baron, took a different view. Founding on Glanvil he argued that any common plea could be heard in the Exchequer; it was not, he asserted, statutory restraint that had caused the court to cease to hear common pleas but the multitude of the king's business which occupied most of the court's time. Accordingly, Plowden was successful and, notwithstanding the verdict for the plaintiff, judgment was given for the defendant.

About 1560 Plowden was consulted by the corporation of Burford in Oxfordshire, one of several curious survivals from the Middle Ages. Almost from Norman times there had existed in England a number of unincorporated groups which habitually acted as if they were corporations, and in the course of time some concession was made by the lawyers to the actual facts of English life by the recognition of the rule that a corporation might come into existence by prescription. One such was the corporation of Burford. Burford derived its wealth from the wool trade and one of the earliest merchants' guilds was established there between 1088 and 1107. The guild administered the substantial property which in the course of time had been given to pious uses and, since there was no resident lord of the manor until the seventeenth century, the guild habitually exercised many of the powers that strictly belonged to the lord, such as holding the manorial court or, as it became, the borough court. In that way the guild became, by prescription, a corporation that acted as the municipal authority of Burford; a charter of Henry II recognized their privileges and customs as having existed in the time of Henry I.

Since a large part of the corporation's activities consisted of the administration of the extensive charitable property, it suffered a severe setback when, in 1547, it was deprived of that property by the Act of Edward VI which dissolved chantries and confiscated that part of the property of guilds and corporations which were devoted to superstitious uses.[14] With most of its property gone, the corporation had to look elsewhere for work to do; and they appear to have looked principally to extending the business carried on in the borough court. For that purpose they caused their charters to be subjected to a close scrutiny to discover what powers they had, and they sought legal advice as to the meaning and scope of certain terms in the charter granted to them in the first year of the queen's reign; Plowden was among those whose advice was sought, and in 1561 the corporation paid ten shillings to 'Mr. Plowden at London for perusing our charter'.[15]

In Easter Term 1561 Plowden, with serjeant Ranulph Cholmeley and others, was concerned in a case relating to the validity of a bequest to Corpus Christi College, Oxford, made by the college's recently deceased

14. 1 Edw. VI, c. 14 (*Statutes of the Realm,* iv, 24).
15. Gretton, *Burford Records,* 411, 414-5; *H.M.C., Various Coll.,* i, 56 (where the date appears to be in error); Gretton, *Burford Past and Present,* 74-5.

president in his will. The case illustrates the difficulty that lawyers then
had of wholly separating a corporation from incidents in the life of the
natural man who was its head. The conclusion they reached was that, since
at the time when the bequest would take effect the college was without its
head, the corporation that was the college was imperfect and could not
therefore take the property which its erstwhile president had wished it to
receive.[16]

In February of the same year Plowden was appointed arbitrator to
decide a dispute between the dean and canons of St. George's, Windsor,
and Roger Quatermayne of Chalgrove in Oxfordshire. The canons of
Windsor claimed the payment of certain tithes in Chalgrove known as
'Becco herlewyn or Beckharvest tithes', and the portion in question had
been farmed by the canons to William Standish of Oxford. As Quatermayne
was the tenant of the dean and chapter of Christ Church, Oxford, who
asserted a right to the tithes, they also became involved in the dispute and
in May they too agreed to arbitration. Plowden's task was to decide how
far the tithes 'do extend and be leviable, that is to say whether the dean
and canons of Windsor and the farmers of the said portion ought to have
the tithes remaining and grown out of all and singular the demesnes in
Chalgrove aforesaid'. The agreements under which the parties had submitted their dispute to arbitration and bound themselves to abide by the
arbitrator's decision, provided that Plowden should give his decision in
writing before 6 July 1561, but he did not do so until 27 February of the
following year. His decision set out the various titles claimed by the parties
and, as the title of the canons of Windsor seemed to him to be the clearest,
he decided that they were entitled to the tithes in question. Having
dismissed the claim of Christ Church, he ordered that the canons of
Windsor and Standish should have the tithes.[17]

At the very beginning of Michaelmas Term 1561 Plowden was one of
the thirteen distinguished lawyers who assembled in Serjeants' Inn, Fleet
Street, on the orders of the queen; the others were the chief justice of the
Common Pleas, Sir James Dyer, and the chief baron, Sir Edward Saunders;
two judges of the King's Bench, Reginald Corbet and William Rastell;
two judges of the Common Pleas, Anthony Browne and Richard Weston;
George Freville, a baron of the Exchequer; two serjeants-at-law, Thomas
Carus and Nicholas Powtrell; the attorney-general, Gilbert Gerard, and
the solicitor-general, William Roswell; and John Caryll, the attorney-
general for the duchy of Lancaster. They assembled on 30 November 1561,
by the queen's command, 'to confer together in order to understand the
law in a certain case which was depending in the [court of Duchy Chamber]
between the queen on the one part, and divers of her subjects severally on
the other part, wherein the queen required their resolution upon the matter

16. See Br. Lib., Harg. MS 6, f. 14; *cf*. Harg. MS 4, f. 178v, and 4 Leon. 223.
17. See Bodl. MS ch. Oxon. a. 11, no. 142b; Ch. Ch. Arch., MS Estates 67, f. 1, MS D.P.
xi.a.1, f. 10, and MS 1.c.2. The tithes in question were tithes of corn, hay, wool and lambs.

in law.'[18] The question on which their advice was sought was the validity
of a lease, under seal of the duchy of Lancaster, of certain lands belonging
to the duchy granted by Edward VI, to commence after the end of a
former lease which had not expired. All of those assembled, except Roswell
('who had but little time to consider the matter'), agreed that such leases
were good and were not voidable by reason of the nonage of the young
king. On the following day, the feast of St. Andrew, they went to the
house of Sir Robert Catlin, the chief justice of the King's Bench, who
agreed with their opinion. Next day they went to York Place to report
their resolution to Sir Nicholas Bacon, the lord keeper, and Sir Ambrose
Cave, the chancellor of the duchy, in order that the queen might be
informed.

　Plowden's report of the case is long and detailed and those taking part
in the conference must have derived considerable assistance from the
specialized knowledge of the constitution and practice of the duchy
acquired by Plowden as deputy chief steward and one of the counsel of
the court.[19] Sir Robert Somerville observed that the 'most valuable of the
few references to Duchy practice are the notes of the "great case of the
Duchy" in 1561 made by Edmund Plowden. The case involved a good
deal of research, and the statements there made, together with Coke's
additional information and supplemented by a few later references such as
the passage on the Duchy in Blackstone's *Commentaries on the Laws of
England,* formed practically the only authoritative account of the Duchy
available until the nineteenth century. The phrases of Plowden's report
occur again and again in the law books.'[20]

　The effect of the nonage of Edward VI made it necessary for the
conference to consider the constitutional position of the king as understood
in the sixteenth century. The problem which confronted the English lawyers
of the late fifteenth and the sixteenth centuries was to evolve a doctrine
that provided for the inescapable fact that the king was a mortal man but
which, at the same time, could be accommodated to the requirement, both
of state and of law, that the crown should be impersonal and immortal.
That problem, which involved giving legal expression to the constitutional
position of a king who was the head of the state but not possessed of
uncontrolled power within it was not easy to solve and had for long vexed
the minds of Tudor lawyers. The problem was not made easier by the
difficulty of reconciling older legal doctrine relating to the position of a
king, which came from a time when the law was still dominated to some
extent by feudal ideas, with the new position which the king was coming
to adopt in the state.

　18. *Case of the Dutchy of Lancaster* (1561), Plowd. 212: 'pur conferer ensemble, pur
intelligence de ley, en un case que fuit dependant en le dit Court entre le Roigne un party, &
diuers ses subiects seueralment del auter party: en le quel le Roigne require lour resolucion de le
ley.' There are other reports concerning the case at Dyer, 222; Brooke's *Abridgement,* tit.
'Age', no. 52; and Br. Lib., Harg. MS 4, f. 128.
　19. He so described himself in his report of the case; see Plowd., 212; 'Plowden apprentice
que fuit un de counsel de le dit Court'.
　20. Somerville, *History of the Duchy of Lancaster,* i, p. xiii.

The main line along which the lawyers sought to resolve the problem lay in the elaboration of the few references in the medieval law books which suggested the existence of a distinction between the natural and the political capacity of the king. That distinction came to be formulated in the doctrine of the king's 'two bodies', the body natural and the body politic. It was in Plowden's report of the *Case of the Dutchy of Lancaster* that the doctrine received its most elaborate formulation but when, in the winter of 1566, he wrote his *Treatise* on the succession to the crown which has remained in manuscript ever since, he discussed the theory at even greater length.[21] The doctrine of the king's two bodies, which was thus being developed, made a strong appeal to Tudor lawyers,[22] and its formulation by Plowden in the *Case of the Dutchy of Lancaster* seems to have provided the basis of Francis Bacon's summary of the relevant law in *Calvin's Case*.[23]

A few years later Plowden's commanding position as a lawyer was demonstrated in a striking manner. The case in question concerned the title to certain manors in Glamorgan and had been originated by bill in Chancery; it was argued before the two chief justices, Sir Robert Catlin and Sir James Dyer, in 1561 at Serjeants' Inn in Fleet Street. In Trinity Term two utter-barristers, Robert Bell who subsequently became chief baron of the Exchequer, and Thomas Bromley who was later lord chancellor, argued the case for the defendants; later, on 19 October 1564, Plowden argued for the plaintiffs and Christopher Wray, then an utter-barrister but later to become chief justice of the King's Bench, appeared for the defendants. No report of the case has been published but, so highly was Plowden's argument esteemed by his fellow lawyers, that an extensive note of part of it, 'made by an uncertain author', was later printed by Richard Tottel 'at the request of certain students, who thought it to contain matter of much use, and worthy to be made public'.[24] The report was printed soon after the publication of the second part of Plowden's *Commentaries* and has been included in every subsequent edition.[25]

In 1564 Plowden was concerned, on behalf of the former bishop of London, Edmund Bonner, in a case that raised interesting constitutional questions. Bonner was the first of the Marian bishops to lose his see for refusal of the oath of supremacy, having been deprived on 30 May 1559. He remained at liberty for nearly a year, but on 20 April 1560 he was committed to the Marshalsea in Southwark, which was within the diocese

21. See p. 91, *post*.
22. For example, it appeared soon afterwards in another case reported by Plowden in which he did not appear; see *Willion* v. *Berkly* (1562), Plowd. 223, at p. 224.
23. See Bacon, *Works*, vii, 667, 668. *Calvin's Case* (1608) is reported at 7 Co. Rep. 19; 2 St Tr. 559; Moore 790; Jenk. 306 (the case of the *Post Nati*). For the history of the development of the legal conception of the constitutional position of the sovereign, see *H.E.L.*, iv, 190–217. For a learned but diffuse treatment of the theory of the king's two bodies, only part of which is here relevant, see Kantorowicz, *King's Two Bodies*.
24. *Bassett and Morgan* v. *Manxel*, Plowd., App., 1–15 (separate pagination at the end of the reports).
25. Beale, *Bibliography of Early English Law Books*, nos. R 486, R486a, R489b.

and jurisdiction of the bishop of Winchester, Robert Horne, who had been consecrated by archbishop Parker in February 1561. In 1563 parliament enacted 'An Acte for thassurance of the Quenes Maiesties Royall power over all Estates and Subjectes within her Highnes Dominions',[26] which, among other things, sharply increased the penalties for refusal of the oath of supremacy; a first refusal now involved the penalties of praemunire, and a second refusal was to be treated as high treason.

Bonner, who was widely detested, had already refused the oath once and the Act of 1563, providing a traitor's death for those who refused it a second time, seemed to the more zealous of the reformers to provide them with a means for getting their revenge on an old enemy. It seems that the sharp increase in the penalties provided by the Act of 1563 was not altogether to the liking of the queen who, through Cecil, instructed Parker to forbid each of the bishops of his province to tender the oath a second time without his written authority. Edmund Grindal, then occupying Bonner's old see of London, and Robert Horne, the new bishop of Winchester, proposed, with the agreement of Parker, to put the new Act into execution against Bonner and, with a good deal of secrecy, Parker authorized Horne to tender the oath to Bonner for the second time. Although Parker was acting strictly within the queen's instructions, he and Grindal appear to have been uneasy about what they had done and they were careful to prevent all news of their activities from reaching the queen until the oath had been actually tendered.

Bonner was brought from the Marshalsea on 26 April 1564 and taken to the town house of the bishop of Winchester in the parish of St. Saviour's, Southwark, where Horne tendered the oath to him; he refused to swear, and his refusal was thereupon certified into the King's Bench, as the Act of 1563 required, as a preliminary step towards criminal proceedings.[27] His refusal of the oath was followed by an indictment and, with his life in danger, he secured the assistance of Plowden, Christopher Wray and William Lovelace.[28] The indictment charged him with an offence under the statute of 1563 in having refused for the second time to take the oath of supremacy when lawfully required to do so, and the grand jury found a true bill in Easter Term 1564. On 3 October he was brought before the court of King's Bench and pleaded not guilty; on that occasion Bonner was not represented by counsel, but the attorney-general, Gilbert Gerard, appeared to prosecute.[29]

---

26. 5 Eliz. I, c. 1, (*Statutes of the Realm,* iv, 402–5). The Act was repealed by the Religious Disabilities Act, 1846, s. 1.

27. For the certificate, see P.R.O., K.B. 12/1210, Rex, m. 11.

28. For a full account of the prosecution of Bonner, and for a consideration of the constitutional questions raised, see Parmiter, *R.H.,* xi (1971–2), 215–36. Wray and Lovelace became serjeants in 1567 (Foss, *Judges of England,* v, 414) and Wray was appointed a judge of the King's Bench in 1572 and chief justice in 1574 (Foss, op. cit., v, 406).

29. For the indictment, see P.R.O., K.B. 9/608, pt. 1, m. 41; and for the official record of the proceedings, see P.R.O., K.B. 27/1212, Rex, m. 13 (Coram Rege Roll), and K.B. 29/199, m. 34 (Controlment Roll).

The defence put forward by Bonner rested on two main contentions. It was asserted, first, that the Act of Supremacy, which imposed the oath and prescribed its form, was not a statute at all because it had not received the necessary consents in parliament, with the result that the oath lacked any statutory authority. The second contention was that, by the Act of 1563, the oath could be lawfully tendered to Bonner only by the bishop of the diocese in which he was, and because there were defects in the consecration of Horne he was no bishop, with the result that the oath had not been lawfully tendered. Bonner's refusal of the oath had been widely expected, but the grounds for his refusal were both unexpected and disconcerting.[30]

The argument relating to the Act of Supremacy concerned the constitutional position of the lords spiritual in the house of lords. The modern constitutional doctrine is that the lords spiritual and the lords temporal sit and vote together as one house, and that the house of lords, as one of the three units (kings, lords and commons) whose consent is necessary to the passage of legislation, gives or withholds its consent as one house, and not as a combination of two separate parts. In the middle years of the sixteenth century, however, the development of constitutional doctrine had not reached that point, and it was then possible to argue that the lords spiritual and the lords temporal must each give their consent separately. On that basis the Act of Supremacy had not received the consents necessary to constitute it an Act of Parliament because, when it was eventually passed, although all the lords temporal save viscount Montague voted for it, all the lords spiritual, together with Montague, voted against it.[31]

It was, however, the second argument that caused the government a good deal of perturbation. The heart of the argument is to be found in the use of the Ordinal of Edward VI and in the provisions of the Appointment of Bishops Act, 1533.[32] The Ordinal was not part of the Prayer Book of 1552 which had been authorized anew by the Act of Uniformity of 1559, with the result that the authorization there given to the modified Prayer Book itself did not extend to the Ordinal, a difficulty of which Cecil was well aware. It was, therefore, open to argument that the consecration of Horne, at which the Ordinal had been used, was invalid at law for want of form.

The Appointment of Bishops Act, 1533, required that the sovereign should, by letters patent, signify the election of the bishop elect to one archbishop and two bishops, or to four bishops, who were then required

---

30. Bonner held the degrees of bachelor of canon law and doctor of civil law. There is in existence a long memorandum, in Bonner's handwriting, in which he set out a number of objections to the proceedings begun against him; see Br. Lib., Harl. MS 421, ff. 4–6 (the document is mutilated; a printed version is in Strype, *Annals*, I, i, 4–7).

31. For a consideration of the argument, see Parmiter, in *R.H.*, xi (1971–2), pp. 220–3.

32. 25 Hen. VIII, c.20 (*Statutes of the Realm*, iii, 462–4); the short title, 'The Appointment of Bishops Act, 1533' was given to the Act by the Statute Law Revision Act, 1948. The Act had been repealed in Mary's reign by 1 & 2 Phil. & Mary, c. 8, but was revived by s. 2 of the Act of Supremacy of 1559.

to confirm the election and consecrate the elect. Now the archbishop of Canterbury, Matthew Parker, had, on 15 February 1561, confirmed the election of Robert Horne to the see of Winchester and on the following day, with Thomas Young of St. David's (then elect of York), Edmund Grindal of London, and Thomas Bentham of Coventry and Lichfield as assistants, had consecrated him. A question, however, surrounded the validity of Parker's own consecration. Because of the wholesale deprivation of the Marian bishops at the beginning of Elizabeth's reign, following their refusal of the oath of supremacy, there had been created a situation in which, to use Cecil's words in commenting on the difficulties of making Parker an archbishop, 'There is no archbishop nor four bishops now to be had.' The difficulty was overcome by including among the consecrators several Marian exiles who had no English sees; and in order to remedy any defects there might be in the proceedings, there was included in the letters patent a unique clause by which the queen, out of the plentitude of her supreme ecclesiastical authority, made good and supplied all defects in her mandate which arose or might arise out of the special facts of the situation. In the event the queen's commission contained no diocesan bishops and in order to keep the questionable validity of Parker's consecration from public knowledge, it took place early in the morning and was cloaked in considerable secrecy that was maintained for many years. If Parker's own consecration did not comply with the provisions of the Act of 1533 he was no archbishop and in that case, since the required number of bishops had not taken part in the consecration of Horne, Horne was no bishop either.[33] In thay way Bonner called in question the validity of the whole of the Elizabethan episcopate.

After Bonner had pleaded to the indictment certain preliminary questions arose. Since the indictment was founded upon a certificate which the statute required to be entered of record in the King's Bench, the indictment declared the venue to be the county of Middlesex because that was where the court of King's Bench sat. At common law, however, the normal venue was the county in which the offence charged was alleged to have been committed, and in Bonner's case that was the county of Surrey because it was in Southwark that he had refused the oath. The question arose, therefore, whether Bonner should be tried by a Middlesex jury or a Surrey jury; the judges of the King's Bench decided that he should be tried by men of the county of Surrey and the sheriff was directed accordingly and ordered to empanel a jury for 18 November.[34]

---

33. For a consideration of the argument, see Parmiter, in *R.H.,* xi (1971–2), pp. 216–7, 223–5.

34. See P.R.O., K.B. 27/1212, Rex, m. 13; and *Bonner's Case* (1564), Dyer 234: 'Et fuit tenus que le trial ne sera per homines de comitatu Middlesex, sed per homines de comitatu Surrey, de visneto de Southwarke'. *cf.* 3 Co. Inst. 34: '. . . and the question upon the statute of Eliz. was, if Bonner should appear and plead not guilty, by what county he should be tried, whether by a jury of Middlesex where the indictment was, or by a jury of Surrey, where the offence was committed; and resolved that he should be tried by a jury of Surrey; for the statute of 5 Eliz. extendeth to the indictment only, and leaveth the trial to the common law.'

There was another and much more important point that 'was much debated among all the justices at lord Catlin's chambers', and presumably Plowden and his fellow counsel took part in that debate. Bonner had pleaded not guilty, and the question arose whether, upon that plea, it was open to him to raise the issue that Horne was not a lawful bishop when he tendered the oath, and to adduce evidence in support of his contention. The judges eventually decided unanimously that Bonner might raise that issue and adduce such evidence, and that the question should be tried by the jury.[35]

The decision seems to have caused the government a good deal of anxiety, for they were now faced with the prospect of a public trial of the validity of the consecration of Horne and, by implication, of that of all the Elizabethan bishops. Cecil had been well aware of the inherent legal defects of Parker's consecration, and as the government had been at pains to keep the matter secret a public trial would be exceedingly embarrassing. The government dared not now risk bringing Bonner to trial. By the continuance made in October, notice of trial had been given for 18 November 1564 and on that date the attorney-general appeared to prosecute and Bonner appeared *in propria persona sua*. The sheriff returned the names of twelve jurors but they were not sworn and the court made a continuance to the quindene of Easter 1565. Thereafter the case was adjourned from term to term, by a series of continuances, while the government tried to solve the problem with which Bonner had faced them.[36]

In reality there was only one means by which they could extricate themselves from their predicament: legislation. A bill for that purpose was introduced into the house of commons in October 1566 and after some amendments received the royal assent on 2 January 1567. That Act provided that all episcopal consecrations which had been held according to the queen's letters patent should be valid, and all bishops so consecrated were declared to be good and perfect bishops notwithstanding any statute law, canon or other thing to the contrary. The Act also provided that no person should be molested on account of any certificate of any bishop which had been entered of record prior to the end of the session in which the bill was passed, and it was expressly provided that any tender of the oath of supremacy made by any bishop before the end of the session should be void and of no account.[37] The Act removed the foundation of the case against Bonner because the tender of the oath to him by Horne

---

35. *Bonner's Case* (1564), Dyer 234: 'Et fuit mult debate inter onmes Justices, in camera domini Catlyne, si Bonner poit donner en evidence sur cest issue, scilicet quod ipse non est inde culpabilis, que le dit Evesque de Winton non fuit Episcopus tempore oblationis sacramenti. Et resolve per omnes, que si le veritie & matter soit tiel en fait, il a ceo sera bien receive sur cet issue, et le Jurie ceo triera.'

36. P.R.O., K.B. 27/1212, Rex, m. 13.

37. 8 Eliz. I, c. 1 (*Statutes of the Realm*, iv, 484–6). For the reasons why the latter provisions were included, see Parmiter, in *R.H.*, xi (1971–2), pp. 228–9). The Act was repealed by the Statute Law Revision Act, 1863.

was now declared to be void and of no effect. In that curious way the prosecution of Bonner eventually fizzled out. Bonner, however, was not released from prison; presumably he was considered too dangerous to be set at liberty, and he remained in the Marshalsea until his death in 1569. Bonner and his counsel had struck a not inconsiderable blow at the statutory foundations of the Elizabethan settlement which had, in consequence, to be hastily shored up by further legislation.

It is a striking testimony to the high regard in which Plowden was held as a lawyer that soon after this devastating work on behalf of a former Catholic bishop, his services were sought by a puritanically minded privy councillor and an Anglican dean. In December 1565 he was retained by the earl of Leicester who granted him the yearly sum of £5, issuing out of the castle and manor of Kenilworth, in consideration of his counsel;[38] and in the following year he appeared at the bar of the house of commons on behalf of the dean of Westminster, Gabriel Goodman, who had been Cecil's chaplain. On 2 October 1566, immediately after the election of the Speaker, Richard Onslow, a bill to abolish sanctuaries for debtors was introduced into the house of commons and received its first reading three days later. On 7 October the bill was read a second time and ordered to be engrossed but that order was stayed after representations had been made by the dean for exempting the sanctuary of Westminster from the provisions of the bill on the ground that the bill was prejudicial to the liberties and privileges of Westminster Abbey; it was also ordered that the dean should attend the house with his counsel on the following Friday, 10 October, to show cause why the sanctuary should be exempted. However, on Thursday the time was extended to 16 October when Plowden appeared at the bar of the house accompanied by a civilian lawyer named Ford. Goodman himself addressed the house and was followed by Plowden and Ford, after which the bill was committed to the Master of the Rolls and others to consider and report upon the submissions made. Plowden does not appear to have been successful for when, on 31 October, the house considered the report, it was agreed that the bill should be engrossed. The bill, however, did not pass the commons; when it came up for third reading on 4 December, it was rejected by sixty votes in its favour and seventy-seven against.[39]

In 1565 Plowden appeared in a case that is of interest for several reasons. The case, *Sharington* v. *Strotton*,[40] was heard on demurrer in the King's Bench in Michaelmas Term 1565, but judgement was not given until the following Trinity Term. The case arose on a bill of trespass and William Fleetwood and Christopher Wray appeared for the plaintiffs, and Thomas

38. *H.M.C., 10th Rep., pt. 4*, p. 409; *T.S.A.S.*, ser. 1, xi, 411. The deed by which Leicester made his grant to Plowden is still preserved at Plowden Hall.

39. D'Ewes, *Journals of all the Parliaments*, 119, 121–24, 126, 132; *Commons Journals*, i, 73, 74, 76, 79. See also Strype, *Annals*, I, i, 228–9. The accounts of the case given by Cooper (*Athenae Cantabrigienses*, i, 501), O'Sullivan (*Edmund Plowden*, 17), and Abbott (*Law Reporting*, 203) are misleading.

40. Plowd. 298.

Bromley and Plowden ('an Apprentice of the Middle Temple') for the defendants. The case turned upon the validity of a use (or, in modern terms, a trust) created by a covenant or agreement under seal, and counsel for the plaintiffs argued that, as there was no consideration, the agreement was insufficient to raise a use. By the sixteenth century the doctrine of consideration had come to be the most distinctive feature of the English law of contract, but it was not then fully developed and the status of instruments under seal had not been settled. Lawyers were, however, taking the view that contracts under seal could be brought into line with the general rule requiring consideration by saying that the seal 'imported consideration'; and an early example of that view being put forward in court is provided by Plowden's argument in the instant case.[41] That, however, was not Plowden's main argument which he developed from Aristotle's treatment of the natural law in his *Politics*. The conclusion to which his argument led was that natural love and affection provided sufficient consideration to raise a use. That argument was accepted and judgment was given for the defendants.[42] Plowden's elaborate argument, derived from Aristotle's *Politics,* displays in a remarkable way, the breadth of his learning.[43]

41. See *Sharington* v. *Strotton* (1565), Plowd. 298, at p. 309.
42. In *Callard* v. *Callard* (1597), decided after Plowden's death, the Exchequer Chamber reversed the judgment of the King's Bench and held that, in order to raise a use, a contract in consideration of natural love and affection must be made under seal; the case in the King's Bench is reported in Cro. Eliz. 344, and more fully in Poph. 47; and in the Exchequer Chamber in 2 Anderson 64.
43. See Plowd. 303-7.

XI

PLOWDEN AND THE SUCCESSION

Towards the end of 1566 Plowden turned his mind to the legal issues involved in the question of the succession to the crown. It was a question that exercised the minds of many Englishmen, just as it had plagued the Tudor sovereigns from their beginning on Bosworth Field. With memories of the Wars of the Roses not yet a part of the distant past, the thought of a war of succession was abhorrent to most Englishmen who had vivid memories of the bloodshed that had accompanied the hare-brained attempt of the duke of Northumberland to supplant Mary by Lady Jane Grey. Throughout his reign Henry VIII had been preoccupied with the question, and his tangled matrimonial career, originating with his desire for a son to succeed him, and its attendant succession Acts, served only to complicate the problem; and the question was further bedevilled by the terms of his will by which he attempted to settle the succession in default of heirs of his children, Edward, Mary and Elizabeth.[1]

Henry's younger sister, Mary Tudor, known as 'the French queen',[2] was twice married, her second husband being Charles Brandon, duke of Suffolk, by whom she had two daughters, Frances and Eleanor. Frances married Henry Grey, also created duke of Suffolk, and had three daughters, Jane (who had been executed), Catherine and Mary; Eleanor married Henry Clifford, earl of Cumberland, and had a daughter Margaret who married Henry Stanley, Lord Strange. Henry's will provided that in default of issue of the bodies of Edward VI, Mary and Elizabeth, the crown should 'come to the heirs of the body of the Lady Frances our niece, eldest daughter to our late sister the French queen lawfully begotten; and for default of such issue of the body of the said Lady Frances, we will that the said imperial crown . . . shall wholly remain and come to the heirs of the body of the Lady Eleanor our niece, second daughter to our said late sister the French queen lawfully begotten'.[3] The will thus placed the crown, should Elizabeth die without issue, in the Suffolk line, descended from Henry's younger sister Mary, and excluded the Stuart line, descended from his eldest sister Margaret.

When Elizabeth came to the throne the situation was no better; she was unmarried, with no clearly defined heir, and although she was the focus of Protestant hopes in England, Catholic Europe regarded her as a bastard

---

1. Henry's will (P.R.O., Royal Wills, E.23, iv, pt. 1, pp. 1–17; printed in Rymer, *Foedera*, xv, 110–17) was executed pursuant to the statute 28 Hen. VIII, c. 7 (*Statutes of the Realm*, iii, 655) and 35 Hen. VIII, c. 1 (*Statutes of the Realm*, iii, 955) which empowered the king to declare the descent of the crown either by letters patent or 'by your last will made in writing and signed with your gracious hand'. Copies of the will, with different dates, are in Br. Lib., Harl. MS 293, ff. 107–115; Harl. MS 1877, ff. 41–45, and Harl. MS 5805, no. 18.

2. Because of her marriage to Louis XII of France, Mary Tudor, youngest daughter of Henry VII, was generally known as 'the French queen'.

3. Rymer, *Foedera*, xv, 113.

without any legitimate right to the throne. In the early years of the reign there were, therefore, good grounds for public apprehension at what might happen should the queen die. The obvious solution of the problem was for the queen to marry and have children, and it seems to have been generally assumed that she would do so. That assumption seems to have been behind the request of the commons, made in January 1559, at the very beginning of the queen's first parliament, that she should marry. To that request, however, she replied in effect that she had no immediate intention of marrying and that there was a distinct possibility that she might live and die a virgin.[4]

The first fumbling attempt of the house of commons to deal with the question had met with no success and the problem remained. In the absence of direct heirs the choice of a successor was, at the beginning of her reign, a wide one. The claimant with the best genealogical title to the succession was Mary Queen of Scots who was in the direct line of descent from Henry VII and his wife Elizabeth of York whose elder daughter Margaret had married, as her first husband, James IV of Scotland, the grandfather of Mary Queen of Scots. Mary, however, was a Catholic and as such was obnoxious to the English Protestants; she was, moreover, outside the succession provisions of the will of Henry VIII, and she had been born in Scotland and not in England. Her Scottish birth was a matter of importance and on it was founded the main legal objection to her claim, as it was asserted that no alien could inherit the English crown.

There were two further Stuart candidates for the succession, Margaret, countess of Lennox, and her son Henry Lord Darnley. Their claim to the succession was inferior to that of Mary Queen of Scots because the countess of Lennox was the daughter of Margaret Tudor by her second husband Archibald Douglas, earl of Angus. Although the Scottish queen had a superior right, the countess of Lennox and her son each had the advantage of being born in England but, like Mary, they were outside the provisions of Henry's will.

If the claims of Mary Queen of Scots be ignored, the candidate with the strongest claim to the succession was Lady Catherine Grey, daughter of Henry Grey, duke of Suffolk, and sister of Lady Jane Grey. Catherine Grey's mother, Frances, was the daughter of the younger sister of Henry VIII by her second marriage to Charles Brandon, duke of Suffolk. Her claim was thus genealogically inferior to that of Mary Queen of Scots. Catherine Grey had, however, substantial advantages on her side; she had been born in England of English parents and she could claim that under the provisions of the will of Henry VIII she was the heir to the crown. The Suffolk claim was thus a strong one.

Two further claimants should be mentioned. The first, a Suffolk claimant, was Margaret Clifford who had married Henry Stanley, Lord Strange, the

---

4. *Neale I*, 47–51. The queen's reply included the following sentence: 'And in the end, this shall be for me sufficient, that a marble stone shall declare that a Queen, having reigned such a time, lived and died a virgin.' (*ibid.*, 49).

son of the earl of Derby. Lady Strange's mother was Eleanor Brandon, the younger daughter of Mary Tudor and Charles Brandon, duke of Suffolk, so that her claim under the will of Henry VIII was inferior to that of her cousin, Lady Catherine Grey. The other claimant was Henry Hastings, earl of Hintingdon. He was descended on his mother's side from Lionel duke of Clarence and Edmund duke of York, the third and fifth sons of Edward III; on his father's side he traced his descent from Thomas of Woodstock, duke of Gloucester, the seventh son of Edward III. His title was a Yorkist one and was unlikely to prevail over the Stuart and Suffolk claims, but he was a male, he enjoyed the subsequent support of his brother-in-law, Robert Dudley, and, being an earnest puritan, was acceptable to a vocal section of the nation.[5]

The claim of Mary Queen of Scots to the English throne had been openly asserted at the very beginning of Elizabeth's reign when the Scottish queen was the wife of the dauphin of France. Soon after the death of Mary Tudor the French king, Henry II, had caused his daughter-in-law to be proclaimed as queen of England and at the same time the dauphin and his wife assumed the arms of England in addition to those of France; that claim was maintained when the dauphin succeeded to the French throne as Francis II in the summer of 1559.

On 6 July 1560 English and French commissioners signed the so-called Treaty of Edinburgh by which France and England agreed to a policy of non-interference in Scotland. The treaty included a provision that Mary and her husband, the French king, should abstain from using the arms and title of the kingdom of England, but Mary persistently refused to ratify the treaty, much to the annoyance of Elizabeth who, nevertheless, professed to believe that Mary's claims were instigated by her uncles of the house of Guise and originated from their ambitions.[6]

Soon after the signing of the treaty there occurred a change in the succession situation when, in August 1561, it was discovered that Lady Catherine Grey was pregnant. She claimed that she had been secretly married to the earl of Hertford who was then in France. Edward Seymour, earl of Hertford, was a son of Protector Somerset who had wanted to marry him to Lady Jane Grey. The queen was angry and suspected a conspiracy. Lady Catherine was immediately imprisoned in the Tower where she was joined by Hertford when he returned from France. An investigation into the affair was started at once but it failed to uncover any evidence of a conspiracy. The queen also appointed a commission, under the archbishop of Canterbury, Matthew Parker, to inquire into the validity of the marriage, and after some time it pronounced the marriage to be invalid. While Parker's inquiry was proceeding Lady Catherine gave birth to a son, Edward, who was later known as Lord Beauchamp; and after

---

5. For modern treatments of the succession question, see *Neale I*, 101–13, 129–64, and Levine, *Early Elizabethan Succession Question*.
6. *C.S.P.V.*, vii, 167.

the inquiry was over a second son, Thomas, was born. Both those children were thus bastardized and the Suffolk claim suffered a set-back.[7]

Francis II died in December 1560 and Mary Queen of Scots returned to Scotland on 19 August 1561. In the following month she sent William Maitland of Lethington to London to begin negotiations with Elizabeth on the succession. Elizabeth did not question Mary's right, and even admitted that she preferred her claim to those of her rivals, although she denied that Mary had any right to be queen of England while she herself was alive. In the course of the interviews Elizabeth told Maitland that there would be no other queen of England but herself, so long as she lived, but she added that she would do nothing to prejudice whatever rights Mary Queen of Scots might have. She also dwelt upon the dangers to herself of recognizing her successor during her own lifetime, and emphasized the point by referring to the fickleness of her people and her own experience during the reign of her half-sister: 'I know the inconstancy of the people of England, how they ever mislike the present government and has their eyes fixed upon that person that is next to succeed. . . . I have good experience of myself in my sister's time, how desirous men were that I should be in place and earnest to set me up. And if I would have consented I know what enterprise would have been attempted to bring it to pass, and now perhaps affections of some are altered.'[8] That remained the queen's attitude throughout the remainder of her life.

Despite the queen's dislike of public discussion of her successor, public anxiety on the question was soon given startling expression in the play, *The tragedie of Gorboduc*, written by the puritan Thomas Norton and the courtier Thomas Sackville, both of whom were members of the Inner Temple. Sir John Neale justly described the fifth act of the play as 'nothing less than a tract on the succession, urging immediate parliamentary settlement of the question and the exclusion of Mary Queen of Scots.'[9] The play was first performed in the hall of the Inner Temple on Twelfth Night 1561, and subsequently at court, in the presence of the queen, on 18 January 1562.[10] No record of the queen's reaction to the play has come down to us.

Anxiety over the succession question became acute in October 1562 when the queen fell ill with smallpox, and for a time the court thought she was dying. She had recovered by the end of the year but when parliament assembled in January 1563 the fears engendered by the queen's illness were fresh in each member's mind. Parliament had been called to grant a subsidy, but the commons turned first to the succession. They agreed to petition the queen and persuaded the lords to support their action; each

7. See, generally, Levine, *Early English Succession Question*. 13–29.
8. Maitland's account of his negotiations with Elizabeth in Sept. and Oct. 1561 is printed as an appendix in Pollen, *Letter from Mary Queen of Scots*, 37–45. Maitland's Scottish orthography has been anglicized. *cf.* Read, *Mr. Secretary Cecil*, 229.
9. *Neale I*, 227; *cf.* Neale, *Queen Elizabeth I*, 200.
10. *cf. I.T.R.*, i, pp. lxx, lxxi.

house presented a petition but they got no more than an evasive answer from the queen; parliament was then prorogued.[11]

The queen, no doubt, would have been well content had the question of the succession remained in the unresolved state in which parliament had left it, but it soon raised its head again when manuscript copies of a tract relating to the succession began to circulate. The author of the tract was John Hales who held the lucrative post of clerk of the Hanaper. Hales was an impetuous man who had a long career as an agitator, beginning with the important part that he played in the battle against enclosures under Protector Somerset.[12] In the parliament of 1563 he sat for the borough of Lancaster, and he composed his tract during that session; but although it is cast in the form of a parliamentary speech, it was probably never delivered in the house.[13]

Hale's tract was a defence of the rights of the Suffolk line against those of all other claimants, and he concluded his 'book' by pronouncing Lady Catherine Grey to be the lawful heir to the crown.[14] The first part of the tract is devoted to establishing the validity of the will of Henry VIII.[15] Hales then turned to the claims of Mary Queen of Scots and the countess of Lennox which he dismissed as being excluded by the common law rule that prohibited inheritance by aliens. Lastly he dealt with the Suffolk claim. The validity of the marriage of Charles Brandon, duke of Suffolk, and Mary Tudor had been questioned on the ground that at the time of the marriage Suffolk was married to Margaret Mortimer. Hales therefore developed a long argument to establish the validity of the marriage and the legitimacy of Francis and Eleanor. That enabled him to assert that the daughter of Francis, Lady Catherine Grey, was the rightful and lawful heir to the crown under the terms of the will of Henry VIII.

11. For this session see *Neale I*, 101–13; Levine, *Early Elizabethan Succession Question*, 45–61.

12. In an anonymous pamphlet entitled 'A Lewd Pasquil set Forth by Certain of the Parliament Men', which lampooned 43 members who sat in the session of 1566, he is described as 'Hales the hottest'; Camb. Univ. Lib., MS Ff.v.14, f. 826 (it is partly in Latin and partly in English; there is a copy of the English part in Br. Lib., Stowe MS 354, f. 18).

13. Copies of the tract, with various titles, are in the British Library (Harl. MS 537, art. 4 (ff. 50–55) together with Harl. MS 555, art. 1 (ff. 1–10v); Harl. MS 4666; Sloane MS 827, art. 1 (ff. 1–17v)), the Bodleian Library (Rawl. MS B 7, art. 1 (ff. 1–14); Tanner MS 304, art. 8 (ff. 42–49); Ashmol. MS 829, art. 2, i (ff. 1–11v)), and the Cambridge University Library (MS Gg.iii.34, art. 6 (ff. 145–173)). There are also two copies in P.R.O., S.P. 12/27/33 & 34. The tract was not printed until the 18th cent.; it first appeared in print in [Harbin], *Hereditary Right of the Crown*, App. VII, pp. x–xliii.

14. 'Thus have I declared unto you my Judgement touchinge the right Heyres to the Crowne of England in Remaynder and Reversion; which is, as I take it, praesently the Lady Catherine, Daughter to the Lady Frauncis, both by Kinge H. his will, and also by the Common Lawes of this Realme; and that we be bound both by our Othes and also by our Lawes so to take her.' (see [Harbin], *Hereditary Right of the Crown*, p. xli).

15. The validity of the will was questioned on the ground that it was signed by a blind stamp and not by the king's own hand as required by statute; see, generally, Smith, in *Jo. of Brit. Studies*, ii (1962), 14–27, and Levine, in *Historian*, xxvi (1964), 471–85. When Hales wrote it was widely believed that the will itself was no longer in existence; Hales himself asserted that it had been deliberately destroyed 'to deprive the Heyres of the Lady Frauncis of their Right to the Crowne'; see [Harbin], *Hereditary Right of the Crown*, p. xxvi.

The appearance of Hales's 'book' greatly angered the queen, and within a short time Hales was confined in the Tower. The mere advocacy of Lady Catherine Grey's claim was bad enough but to write specifically against Mary Queen of Scots was worse; as Cecil pointed out, 'The Queen's Majesty continueth her displeasure towards John Hales, for his foolish attempt in writing the book so precisely against the Queen of Scotland's title'.[16] That, however, was not all. Since the archbishop's commission had declared the marriage of Catherine to Edward Seymour to be invalid, her sons were bastards, and it was a weakness of Catherine's claim that she might be unacceptable as a candidate for the throne because her sons were incapable of inheriting the crown after her. To deal with that complication Hales sent Robert Beale, a puritan who later played a conspicuous part in the fight against the *ex officio* oath, to the continent with instructions to obtain the opinions of the leading canonists upon the decision of the archbishop's commission.[17] The queen learned of those activities early in 1564, and her anger against Hales was much increased; the storm that then broke was termed the *Tempestas Halesiana* by Walter Haddon.[18] She was quick to suspect a conspiracy and an investigation was begun.[19] The investigation did not find evidence of a serious conspiracy, but it disclosed the names of several persons involved in the production of Hales's tract, all of whom were acquaintances of Cecil and included the lord keeper, Sir Nicholas Bacon, who was banished from court for a time and forbidden to deal with anything save the Chancery; Cecil, although escaping punishment, was 'not free from suspicion' as he himself put it.[20] Hales had already been sent to the Tower, and he remained there for some time; he was later confined to his house, and as late as February 1568 he was still unable to leave it without the queen's permision.[21] So ended the *Tempestas Halesiana*.

In July 1565 a further change in the succession situation occurred when Mary Queen of Scots married Lord Darnley, the son of the countess of Lennox, thus uniting the two Stuart claims. By marrying a Catholic she incurred the hostility of the Protestant faction in Scotland headed by her half-brother, the earl of Moray, and by marrying a man whose claim to

16. Sir W. Cecil to Sir Thomas Smith, 26 Nov. 1564; printed in Wright, *Queen Elizabeth and her Times*, i, 178, at p. 179.

17. For the opinions of the canonists, see Camb. Univ. Lib., MS Ii.v.3, and MS Dd.iii.84, arts. 5–8; there is a brief summary of their opinions in Bodl. Ashmol. MS 826, art. 4 (ff. 5–6). The documents show that the majority of the canonists consulted by Beale thought that the marriage was valid. See also a Latin tract (19 folio leaves) by Beale in Camb. Univ. Lib., MS Dd.iii.85, art. 18.

18. See Strype, *Sir Thomas Smith*, 122.

19. Incomplete records of the investigation may be found in *Burghley Papers*, vol. 1.

20. Cecil to Sir Thomas Smith, 1 May 1564; printed in Wright, *Queen Elizabeth and her Times*, i, 173, at p. 174. This was alluded to, some thirty years later, in a Catholic book that was probably written partly by Fr. R. Persons, S.J., and partly by Richard Verstegan and others; see Doleman, *Conference about the next Succession*, pt. 2, pp. 1–2. 'R. Doleman' is a pseudonym. See *A. & R.*, no. 271.

21. See John Hales to Cecil, 7 Feb. 1568 (P.R.O., S.P. 12/46/30). His health was still bad at that time.

the English crown was almost as good as her own she increased the fears and hostility of Elizabeth and those in England who were anxious to ensure that she was barred from the English throne. Those were factors that had an important influence on the succession tracts that appeared in the next few years.[22]

Hales's tract was answered by another, put out anonymously, entitled *Allegacions in behalf of . . . the Lady Mary now Queen of Scots against thopinions and bookes set forth in the parte and favour of the Lady Katherin*, which began to circulate early in 1565.[23] That tract is a poorly organized and not very impressive rejection of the arguments set out by Hales; it does not argue the case for Mary Queen of Scots nor even mention her. In December 1565 another anonymous tract appeared, this time a printed book with the title *Allegations against the surmisid title of the Quine of Scotts and the fauorers of the same*.[24] That book, as the title indicates, was concerned to show that Mary Queen of Scots was disqualified from inheriting the crown of England, and it was largely a repetition of one of the principal arguments of John Hales, namely, that the Queen of Scots could not inherit the English crown because of the common law rule against inheritance by aliens.

It was at that point that Plowden entered the pamphlet war. His contribution was much more elaborate than the political squibs with which he was dealing, and was written in two parts, with an interval between the composition of each part.[25] To each of those parts he added a preface in which he described how he came to write it. In the prologue to the first part, which he called a *Treatise*, he said that he was concerned solely to refute the argument that Mary Queen of Scots was disabled from suceeding to the English crown by reason of her foreign birth; he disavowed any intention of dealing with the validity of the will of Henry VIII. He said that there had come into his hands Hales's tract and the printed book, *Allegations against the surmisid title of the Quine of Scotts*, and he expressed the opinion that the legal learning of the two authors was insufficient for the task they had undertaken, and that their tracts were

22. *cf.* Phillips, *Images of a Queen*, 28.
23. Two copies have survived: Br. Lib., Cotton MS Calig. B.ix, art. 112, and Bodl., Ashmol. MS 829, ff. 12–23; it was later printed as an appendix in Atwood, *Fundamental Constitution*, published in 1690. Despite the prefatory note, 'The Printer to the Reader', there is no evidence that the tract was printed before 1690. The prefatory note, which bears the date 20 Mar. 1565 (i.e., 1566 New Style) described the tract as 'certayne allegacions put forth a yere ago, against the heires of the Ladie Marie the French Quene [Mary Tudor]' which indicates that it first appeared some time early in 1565.
24. A copy of this very rare book is in the British Library (shelf-mark C.55.c.3). See *S.T.C.*, no. 17564; the date is 7 Dec. 1565. Manuscript copies exist in the British Library (Cotton MS Calig. B.ix, art. 7; Harl. MS 4627, art. 2), Bodleian Library (Ashmol. MS 829, art. 2, iii), and Cambridge University Library (MS Dd, ix. 14, art. 4a).
25. Contemporary copies exist in the British Library (Harl. MS 849, arts. 1 & 2; and Cotton MS Calig. B.iv, art. 1, which does not contain the second part of the complete work nor the prologue to the first part), and in the Bodleian Library (Rawl. MS A 124, arts. 1 & 2). None of those copies mentions Plowden as the author; there is, however, a later copy in the Bodleian (MS Don. C.43) in which the author is identified as Plowden.

likely to mislead those into whose hands they might come. He considered, therefore, that someone learned in the law should answer them. While he was considering the matter he received the third tract, *Allegacions in behalf of . . . the Ladie Mary now Queen of Scots*, and on reading it 'I conceived that the man that made it was furnished with much good learning in other sciences, howbeit he seemed to me to lack sufficient knowledge in our temporal law.' He therefore thought it necessary, if Hales's tract and the printed book were to be adequately refuted, that the matter should be 'taken in hand by some temporal lawyer, sithence the matter is a point of the law of the realm.'[26]

While he was thus pondering the question he received an 'earnest request' for his opinion from someone that he did not identify but who was probably Thomas Howard, fourth duke of Norfolk and Earl Marshal of England. Feeling that he could not refuse so urgent a request from such a source, and because he himself was interested in the subject, he set to work. 'And therefore, as well for the satisfaction of myself as of you, I have searched the reasons and grounds of the law in the point and have spent a great part of this Christmas 1566 about the same'.[27]

As a result he wrote his *Treatise*, the first part of which is a lengthy exposition of the doctrine of the king's two bodies, in which his treatment is far more elaborate than the account which subsequently appeared in his *Reports*.[28] According to that theory the king had two bodies, the body natural with which he was born and which was subject to all natural infirmities and legal disabilities, and the body politic, an invisible, impassible body that he acquired on his succession to the crown and which was devoid of natural defects and disabilities; the conjunction of the two bodies produced the special and peculiar qualities of the kingship. Plowden argued that, as a result of that conjunction, what the king did in his body politic could not be invalidated nor frustrated by any disability in his natural body. Accordingly, the conjunction of the two bodies modified or excluded a number of common law rules which, but for that conjunction, would have applied to the natural body of the king. Among the results of the conjunction was the removal of such disabilities as nonage (as in the case of Edward VI) and attainder (as in the case of Edward IV and Henry VII) which would have applied to the natural body alone.

In that manner Plowden was able to reach the conclusion that the common law rule which disabled aliens from inheriting land in England had no application to the crown;[29] although the disability was effective

26. Br. Lib., Harl. MS 849, f. 1.
27. Br. Lib., Harl. MS 849, f. 1. For the sequence of subsequent events and for the possible identity of the person who asked Plowden to write his treatise, see Parmiter, in *Innes Review*, xxx (1979), 35–53.
28. See p. 77, *ante*. Kantorowicz, in *King's Two Bodies*, refers to Plowden's treatment of the theory as it appears in his *Reports*, but he does not mention the *Treatise* which was apparently unknown to him.
29. For the development of the common law rule, see *H.E.L.*, ix, 91–4.

where the body natural alone was concerned, once that body was conjoined to the body politic the disability was removed. Plowden emphasized that, in any event, the rule did not relate to every kind of inheritance but only to the inheritance of land; and he pointed out that, strictly speaking, the crown passed by succession and not by inheritance or descent, although the identity of the successor to the crown was, in general, determined by proximity of blood. Accordingly, he asserted that Mary Queen of Scots was not disabled from succeeding to the crown of England by reason of her foreign birth in Edinburgh.

Plowden's argument was applicable to the next in blood to the crown, whether that person were born in France, Spain or any other foreign country 'out of the ligeance of England'. Should any doubt remain, however, he went on to argue, in the second part of his *Treatise*, that neither Scotland nor the Scots were 'out of the ligeance of England', so that the Queen of Scots should not be regarded as an alien and disabled as such from receiving the crown of England. The *Treatise* is a substantial work of some 44,000 words, with a wealth of citation of authorities both legal and historical, and supported by numerous quotations.

As already mentioned, Hales and the anonymous author of the printed pamphlet had also used an argument based on the will of Henry VIII. Plowden had expressly declined to deal with that argument, saying: ' . . . for touching the residue of the matter of the said books it is not mine intent to meddle withall, for if title of the crown in default of heirs of the queen's highness's body be by testament and last will of King Henry the eighth or otherwise given to any, it shall not be by me impugned nor will I enter into the discussion of it'.[30] It seems, however, that after the duke of Norfolk (if he were the person in question) had read Plowden's *Treatise* there was a 'long pause', and then the duke represented to him, with some justification, that it was of little use to show that the foreign birth of the Queen of Scots was no bar to her succession to the crown of England, if that succession had been barred by the terms of Henry's will. Plowden acknowledged the force of that argument and was persuaded to deal with the question of the validity of the will.[31] For that purpose he wrote a further but much shorter tract which he entitled: 'A briffe Declaracion of the invaliditie of the last will of the late kyng of famous memory king Henry the viij^th . . . ',[32] to which he added a prologue setting out his reasons for writing it.

As the nature of the signature on Henry's will is still capable of generating controversy,[33] Plowden's observations on the validity of the will are of contemporary interest. His argument was that, as the law then stood, Henry had no power to dispose of the crown, but parliament empowered him to do so by letters patent under the great seal or by his

30. Br. Lib., Harl. MS 849, f. 1v (prologue to the *Treatise*).
31. Br. Lib., Harl. MS 849, f.31.
32. Br. Lib., Harl. MS 849, f. 31–38.
33. See p. 88, note 15.

'last will made in writing and signed with his most gracious hand'.[34]
Plowden then set out his reasons for thinking that the will had not been
signed with Henry's hand but by stamp, according to a practice which
Henry had adopted towards the end of his reign. The King had then
authorized one of his personal attendants, Sir Anthony Denny, to sign
official documents with his majesty's name. Following doubts about the
legality of the practice, a special pardon was granted to Denny to
relieve him of all criminal liability for all treasons committed by him in
counterfeiting, making, impressing or writing the king's sign manual,
between 20 September 1545 and the date of the pardon, 31 August 1546.
On the same day a commission was issued authorizing Denny, John Gate
and William Clerk to sign all bills, warrants, grants and the like, by stamp
in the name and on behalf of the king. The commission specified that two
of the commissioners should affix the king's signature by means of a blind
stamp, without ink, and that one of them should fill up and blacken with
ink the impression so made. The commissioners were also directed to
prepare schedules of all documents so signed, and the schedules were to be
signed each month by the King.[35] After setting out the evidence which
induced him to believe that the king's will had been signed with the stamp,
Plowden concluded that, as the power conferred by parliament had not
been strictly complied with, the will was not validly executed in so far as it
purported to dispose of the crown.[36]

The composition of the *Treatise* and the *Brief Declaration* was not a
thing to have been undertaken lightly. Any public discussion of the
succession, even in parliament, was calculated greatly to anger the queen,
and the fate of John Hales was sufficient warning of what could befall
anyone minded to undertake the task. An even more recent warning had
occurred in Michaelmas Term 1566, just before Plowden began his *Treatise*:
a moot at Lincoln's Inn, at which the succession had been discussed and the
claims of Mary Queen of Scots rejected, had resulted in the imprisonment of
William Thornton, a bencher of the Inn who had been present.[37] Plowden
himself was well aware of the dangers of what he was doing. In the
prologue to his *Treatise* he wrote: 'For you know right well that in dealing
in titles of kingdoms there is much danger, and specially to the subject.
And in these cases I think the surest way is to be silent, for in silence there
is safety but in speech there is peril, and in writing more.'[38] That a man of

34. 35 Hen. VIII, c.1, s.6 (*Statutes of the Realm*, iii, 956); *cf.* 28 Hen. VIII, c.7, s.9 (*Statutes of the Realm*, iii, 659).
35. For the pardon and commission, see Rymer, *Foedera*, xv, 100, and for the schedule listing the king's will, see *State Papers of the Reign of Henry VIII*, i, 892-8 (and see the note on pp. 628-9).
36. Professor L. B. Smith (*Henry VIII. The Mask of Royalty*, p. 268) was wide of the mark when he wrote, 'Legally the type of signature—holograph or facsimile—made no difference'. There was a rule of law of long standing, clearly set out in *Whitlock's Case* (1608), 8 Co. Rep. at p. 70b, that the authority given by a power must be strictly complied with, if the power were to be validly exercised.
37. *Burghley Papers*, ii, 762; *Neale I*, 133.
38. Br. Lib., Harl. MS 849, f. 1v.

such caution and circumspection as Plowden should have written such a work speaks much for his courage and independence of mind, but it is difficult not to believe that he was relying on the powerful support of the duke of Norfolk who had not then fallen into disgrace. Norfolk, however, appears to have disclosed the existence of the tract to the privy council which caused Plowden some embarrassment.[39] The knowledge that Plowden had written in defence of the right of Mary Queen of Scots may, perhaps, be the reason why his name was included in a list of 'Catholicks in Inglonde 1574' which was probably compiled by a supporter of the Scottish queen.[40]

At much the same time as Plowden wrote his tract John Leslie, the bishop of Ross and a servant of the Scottish queen of long standing, began work on a defence of Mary Queen of Scots which he intended for publication. That work was to be a defence not only against those who slandered her moral character but also against those who denied her right to the English crown.[41] In its published form it was a substantial work divided into three parts or 'books', of which the second was entitled 'The Seconde Booke touchinge the right, title and interest of the foresaide Ladie Marie Quene of Scotlande, to the Succession of the crowne of England.'

At an early stage in the composition of the 'second book' Leslie had, it seems, received some assistance from Sir Anthony Browne. Later, on the advice of Sir Nicholas Throckmorton, who had established friendly relations with the Queen of Scots when she was queen of France and he was English ambassador there, Leslie approached Plowden for help with his book, and sent him a draft by means of Humphrey Sandford. Plowden was at first unwilling to have anything to do with Leslie's book because of the embarrassment which Norfolk had caused him by disclosing his *Treatise* to the Privy Council, but Throckmorton, who knew of Plowden's work and was aware of his views, persuaded him to read the draft. We may imagine that he read it with reluctance, but he made some comments and suggested that the third 'book', concerning government by women, should be omitted, a suggestion that Leslie ignored.[42] Leslie came to England in September 1568 as the special ambassador of Mary Queen of Scots to queen Elizabeth and his book was published in the following year, apparently with the tacit consent of Elizabeth herself, but when a revised edition was printed in 1571 Leslie was in the Tower because of his presumed connection with the Ridolfi plot.

Some twenty years or more after the death of his father, Francis Plowden arranged for the preparation of an elegant manuscript copy of his father's

39. *Burghley Papers*, ii, 29; Parmiter, in *Innes Review*, xxx (1979), 51-2.

40. P.R.O., S.P. 12/99/55, printed in *C.R.S.*, vol. 13, pp. 89-138.

41. It was published in 1569 with the title *A defence of the honour of the right highe, mightye and noble Princesse Marie Quene of Scotlande and dowager of France . . . with a declaration aswell of her right, title & intereste to the succession of the Crowne of Englande, as that the regimente of women ys conformable to the lawe of God and Nature.* The London imprint is false; it was printed in Rheims by Jean Foigny. A second edition, revised, was published in 1571. See *A.&R.*, nos. 452, 453; Southern, *Elizabethan Recusant Prose*, 438-44.

42. See Parmiter, in *Innes Review*, xxx (1979), 52, 53.

work, apparently intended for presentation to king James I, the son of Mary Queen of Scots.[43] What prompted him to contemplate the presentation is unknown. The idea may have arisen out of the parliamentary debates on the proposal of the king for the union of England and Scotland, when arguments similar to those of his father's *Treatise* were aired. On the other hand he may have thought that an expression of his loyalty was needed after he had fallen foul of authority in the summer of 1603, hard on the heels of the 'Bye Plot'. The bailiff of Ludlow had arrested a stranger in whose possession a letter of a compromising nature was found, written to Francis Plowden by his uncle, Ralph Sheldon. Francis Plowden was examined by the chief justice of Chester, Sir Richard Lewkenor, who placed him in custody for a short time and reported the matter to the privy council.[44] Another and perhaps more probable reason was the enactment in 1604 of the first statute of the reign of James I by which parliament acknowledged and declared that the crown of England 'did, by inherent birthright and lawful and undoubted succession, descend and come to [James I] as being lineally, justly and lawfully next and sole heir of the blood royal of this realm'.[45] Whatever the reason, it seems likely that the manuscript was written during the first few years of the reign of James I. In preparing the presentation copy, Francis Plowden combined the *Treatise* and the *Brief Declaration*, and added an address 'To the king's most excellent majesty.' He omitted the whole of the prologue to the *Brief Declaration* and made substantial changes to the prologue to the *Treatise* which then served as a prologue to the whole work.[46] Whether or not the manuscript was presented to the king is a matter of speculation.

43. That copy is now in the Bodleian Library, MS Don. C.43; it identifies the author as Plowden: 'Written by Edmonde Plowden of the Middle Temple an Apprentice in the lawe.' The early history of the MS is obscure. In 1866 it was the property of J. Higginbotham of Pensax Court, Worcs., from whom it passed to the Cawoods of Bewdley. One of the Cawoods was rector of Bewdley and his widow (who died in the early nineteen-thirties) handed the MS, with other papers, to one, M. L. J. Browne. It was bought by the Friends of the Bodleian from T. Thorpe in 1934.

44. See letters and enclosures dated 2 and 6 Aug. 1603, from Sir Richard Lewkenor to the Privy Council (P.R.O., S.P. 14/3/2 & 13). Ludlow is not far from Plowden Hall.

45. 1 Jac. I, c.1.

46. For a fuller discussion of the changes made by Francis Plowden, see Parmiter, in *Innes Review*, xxx (1979), 46-8.

XII

ENGLEFIELD

In the spring of 1567 letters patent had been sealed appointing a new commission of sewers for Buckinghamshire, Oxfordshire and Berkshire in which Plowden was again named a commissioner and as one of the quorum; it is of interest to note that four other Catholic recusants from the Inns of Court were included in the commission: Thomas Fermor and John Yate of the Middle Temple, and James Braybrooke and Francis Yate of the Inner Temple.[1] A year later Plowden was included in a similar commission for Southampton, Berkshire and Wiltshire.[2]

It was in 1568 that Plowden was concerned in the aftermath of some of the litigation that accompanied the sixteenth century mining developments in England. One of the more spectacular features of the Elizabethan commercial scene was the state-supported introduction into England of industrial and mining techniques from abroad. The two pioneering companies, the Company of Mines Royal and the Company of Mineral and Battery Works, were concerned with the winning and working of metals and were the first two companies to be formed in England for the manufacture of articles as distinct from the carrying on of foreign trade. The word 'battery' in the name of the latter company referred to the use of a kind of battering-ram used to force the metal into the desired shapes, and its meaning included hammered brass or copper vessels. The bulk of the finance needed to launch those enterprises, which were founded upon patent monopolies, was provided by English and German merchants, but substantial investments were made by several courtiers, including Cecil, Leicester, Pembroke and Mountjoy. Each company was incorporated by royal charter in 1568.[3]

Before the incorporation of the companies, the patentees had much to do. The patentees of what became the Company of Mines Royal, whose activities were in practice confined to the production of copper in Cumberland, were William Thurland, the Master of the Savoy and a somewhat disreputable clergyman much of whose career was dogged by chronic financial difficulties, and Daniel Hoechstetter, a German expert whom Thurland had brought to England. The patentees of what became the Company of Mineral and Battery Works were William Humfrey, the Assay Master of the Mint who had the ear of Cecil, and Christopher Schütz, a metallurgist from Saxony, who had, however, no German backing.[4]

1. *C.P.R., 1569–1572,* p. 219 (14 May 1567). For the commissions of sewers, see p. 68, *ante.*
2. *C.P.R., 1569–1572,* p. 219 (20 March 1568).
3. For the history of the two companies, see Donald, *Elizabethan Copper,* and Donald, *Elizabethan Monopolies,* respectively.
4. For biographies, see Donald *Elizabethan Copper,* 15–35 (Thurland), and 35–42 (Hoechstetter), and Donald, *Elizabethan Monopolies,* 24–33 (Humfrey), and 33 (Schütz).

In 1564 the queen, by letters patent, had licensed Thurland and Hoechstetter to search for and procure copper ore containing gold or silver in several counties in England and in the principality of Wales.[5] They soon set to work, with workmen brought from Germany, and by October 1566 had extracted a large quantity of ore. The principal place at which they were then working was the waste or mountainous land known as Newlands in Cumberland. At that point the earl of Northumberland objected and put a stop to any further mining. Northumberland claimed that Newlands was part of an area of some 10,000 acres of waste land known as Derwent Fells that had been granted to him by queen Mary in 1557.[6] Since the interruption of the mining operations was likely to prejudice the queen financially the attorney-general laid an information on her behalf against the earl of Northumberland. The earl pleaded his patent and the crown demurred. The demurrer was argued in the Exchequer Chamber before all the judges and the barons of the Exchequer in Michaelmas Term 1567 when the attorney-general, Gilbert Gerard, appeared for the crown, with the solicitor-general, Richard Onslow, and serjeants Christopher Wray and Nicholas Barham; serjeant Thomas Meade, with Robert Bell and another barrister named Shirborne appeared for Northumberland. The case, which was of some importance, was reported at considerable length by Plowden.[7]

The three principal points argued were, first, whether all mines and ores of gold and silver which were in the lands of subjects belonged of right to the sovereign by virtue of the royal prerogative; second, whether mines and ores of copper containing in them gold and silver, which were in the lands of subjects, belonged to the sovereign by prerogative; and third, whether, if so, the grant made by queen Mary to the earl was sufficient to transfer the ores and mines in Derwent Fells to the earl.

Judgment was delivered in Hilary Term 1568. On the first point, the judges were unanimous in deciding that all mines of gold and silver, whether in the lands of the queen or of subjects, belonged as of right to the crown. On the second point, three of the judges, Richard Harpur, John Southcote and Richard Weston, were of opinion that if gold or silver occurred in mines or ores of base metal, in the lands of subjects, the base metal as well as the gold or silver was the property of the subject if the value of the gold or silver did not exceed that of the base metal, but if the value did exceed that of the base metal, the whole went to the crown; they were, however, of the opinion that judgment should be given against the earl because, having admitted that the ore in question contained gold or silver, he had failed to show that the value of the base metal exceeded that of the gold or silver. The remainder of the judges, however, were agreed that if gold or silver occurred in ores of base metal, the crown was entitled to the mine or ore by virtue of the royal prerogative, whether or not the

---

5. *C.P.R., 1563-1566,* 33-4. Gold and silver were royal metals.
6. For the grant, see *C.P.R., 1557-1558,* 179-89, at p. 188 (patent dated 16 Aug. 1557).
7. *The Case of Mines* (1568), Plowd. 310.

value of the gold or silver exceeded that of the base metal; only if the ore or mine in the land of a subject contained no gold or silver was the proprietor of the land entitled to the ore or mine. On the third point they were all agreed that the grant made by queen Mary did not transfer to the earl the ores in question. Judgment was therefore given for the queen, and it was ordered that damages should be assessed by a jury summoned by the sheriff of Cumberland.

Plowden does not seem to have been satisfied by the conclusion of the majority of the judges on the second point, which took an extreme view of the extent of the royal prerogative, and he appended to his report a long note in which he showed a preference for the opinion of the three dissenting judges.[8] The note incidentally shows his wide range of knowledge. 'There seems to me,' he wrote, 'to be a diversity between a mine of copper containing in it gold, and a mine of gold containing in it copper.' He pointed out that the greatest metallurgist of the day, Agricola, in his book *De Re Metallica*,[9] had asserted that some portion of gold or silver occurs naturally in the base metals, so that 'if no regard should be had to the quantity of gold or silver that is found in the base metals (inasmuch as there is naturally some in every base metal), the king would have all the mines of base metals in the realm.' Plowden therefore thought that the conclusion of the majority of the judges was 'grounded upon an ignorance of the nature of base mines'. He concluded his note by suggesting that 'for the better understanding, whether any base mines are void of gold and silver, it is good to know authors and experience, for the truth of this matter ought to direct the judgments of the judges.' It is of interest to note that, fearful of the opposition of landowners, neither Elizabeth nor James I made any attempt to avail themselves of the extended view of the prerogative with regard to mines which the majority of the judges had adopted in that case.[10]

The principal difficulty facing Thurland and Hoechstetter had now been removed, and the Company of Mines Royal was incorporated soon after judgment had been given.[11] The result of the case had consequences that were of interest to others besides the Company of Mines Royal; those concerned in the Company of Mineral and Battery Works were anxious to know how it affected their own patents. On Saturday 25 February 1568 five of the shareholders in that company, Humfrey, Sir William Garrard, Rowland Hayward, Peter Osborne and Henry Codenham,[12] met at

---

8. See Plowd., 338-340.

9. Agricola, *De Re Metallica*, lib. x, cap. 1; English translation by Hoover, p. 439. Georgius Agricola was the latinized name of the German metallurgist, Georg Bauer (1490-1555).

10. *cf.* Stone, *Crisis of the Aristocracy*, 339.

11. For the charter of incorporation, dated 28 May 1568, see *C.P.R., 1566-1569*, pp. 211-2, no. 1195.

12. Sir William Garrard was a haberdasher and Lord Mayor of London, and he and Rowland Hayward (a clothworker, afterwards Lord Mayor of London and knighted) were appointed jointly as the first governors of the company. Peter Osborne was the Lord Treasurer's Remembrancer, and Henry Codenham, an assistant governor of the company, was Auditor of the Mint. For the shareholders generally, see Donald, *Elizabethan Monopolies*, 35-70.

Serjeants' Inn to hear the opinions of Richard Onslow, serjeant Wray, serjeant Roger Manwood and Plowden 'touching the state of the privilege for battery and the use of the calamine stone'.[13]

Thirteen days later Humfrey wrote to Cecil giving him an account of the meeting. He reported that Onslow considered that the queen's 'prohibition [contained in the patents] was by the law effectual because it did not prohibit any man of any thing before known or used within this realm whereby any occupation or liberty of art was infringed.' Wray agreed, and added that 'if privileges were not given by the prince in such cases there would never be brought into the realm any rare arts.' Serjeant Manwood thought that 'though calamine seemed to be an inheritance to the owner as part [of the] soil, yet the prince might prohibit inheritors the use of such things as were before unknown, but of anything known, it could not be done.' Plowden took a different view; his opinion 'was that the prince could not take from [a man] any part of his inheritance, known or unknown, nor forbid him the use of it whatsoever it was, affirming calamine to be his own if it were in his land and so dispose as pleaseth him.' The conference, which lasted nearly three hours, seems to have left Humfrey in a state of some confusion; he told Cecil that at the end of it the lawyers' 'conclusion to my simple understanding was like an endless vice that continually screweth one wheel up and the other down.' The conference left him pessimistic about the future of the company and he asked for Cecil's help.[14]

Shortly afterwards, in Hilary Term 1568, Plowden was concerned in *Mutton's Case*.[15] John Mutton was seized of certain lands in fee on which he levied a fine to the use (declared in certain indentures) of himself and such wife as he should marry. Subsequently he married and later died, and the question then arose whether his widow should 'take any thing by the said indenture and fine, or not, quaere. And by the opinions of Wray and Mead, serjeants, and Plowden, and Onslow, solicitor, she may, and thereto they subscribed their names'; it was held that the wife took a joint tenancy with her husband.

The year 1567 was one in which Plowden assumed new domestic responsibilities. It will be recalled that, after arranging his affairs in England, Sir Francis Englefield went abroad. He left the country with the queen's licence to quit the realm for two years,[16] but when he did not return at the expiration of his licence his vast property was sequestered, virtually the whole of his property in Berkshire and Wiltshire being seized, At the same time Englefield's steward, Humphrey Burdett, was ordered to

13. Calamine stone was zinc carbonate. By a patent granted to Humfrey and Schütz, dated 17 Sept. 1565, they had been granted the right to search for and mine calamine stone in England and the Irish Pale, and to use it for making latten [i.e., a mixed yellow metal similar to brass, an alloy of copper with zinc, tin or other base metal] and all other mixed metals and all kinds of battery wares, etc.; see *C.P.R., 1563–1566,* p. 303, no. 1693.
14. William Humfrey to Cecil, 25 Feb. 1568 (P.R.O., S.P. 12/46/35).
15. *Mutton's Case* (1568), Dyer 274v.
16. See p. 58 *ante.*

receive the income from the seized lands and to pay into the Exchequer from that income the sum of £300 every year and to retain and account for the remainder.[17] Sir Francis Englefield had no children but his brother John had a son, Francis, who had been born on 29 June 1562, about a year before the sequestration of Sir Francis's lands. John Englefield died on 1 April 1567 leaving the young Francis, then under five years of age, as heir and with the reasonable hope of succeeding to what remained of the property of Sir Francis. John Englefield's death involved the Englefields in one of the relics of the feudal system, wardship, which was a considerable burden to many landowners. On the death of his father young Francis became a ward of the queen and his affairs and property fell to be dealt with by the Court of Wards and Liveries which could be expected to make a profitable arrangement for the queen.

Plowden had already undertaken the supervision of the Englefield estates in Shropshire, and when the young Francis became the queen's ward he immediately did what he could to preserve the boy's inheritance from the rapacity of anyone who sought to obtain the wardship. Plowden's nephew, Andrew Blunden, gave a lively account of his initiative on behalf of the Englefields at that time. According to Blunden, Plowden was in London when John Englefield died on the Tuesday after Easter Sunday, and as soon as he learned of his death he took steps to protect the inheritance of the young heir. He went to court early in the morning and sought out the earl of Pembroke with whom, as Blunden said, he was then 'of counsel in law causes'. The earl was a privy councillor and several times previously had urged Plowden 'to espy out some suit to the queen worth five hundred pounds', promising to obtain it for Plowden because he was so much indebted to him. Although the earl was still in bed, Plowden lost no time; he reminded Pembroke of his promise and asked him to obtain for him the wardship of young Francis Englefield. Pembroke replied that he had intended his promise to be for the benefit of Plowden himself and not of some other person, and he said that he was certain that if he obtained the wardship for him, Plowden would not use it for his own benefit but bestow it upon John Englefield's widow or deal with it according to the directions of Sir Francis; 'therefore I pray you, said he, seek out some other thing: this will not be to your profit and I therefore am loth to deal therein'. Plowden, however, was not to be deflected from his purpose and begged Pembroke to leave the whole matter to his discretion, saying that he would accept the wardship at Pembroke's hands 'instead of any good turn as a gift to me by you [sic] honour of £500.'[18]

Seeing that Plowden was not to be moved, Pembroke got out of bed and dressed, and went first to the queen and then to Sir William Cecil, the Master of the Court of Wards. His intervention was entirely successful; he

17. For details of those events, see Parmiter, in *R.H.*, xiii (1975-6), 162-4.

18. *Blunden's MS*, 126. For the earl of Pembroke, see p. 43, *ante*. In 1569, two years after doing his good turn to Plowden, the earl was arrested for supporting the scheme for the marriage of the duke of Norfolk to Mary Queen of Scots, but managed to clear himself. He died in 1570.

'fully obtained [the wardship] for Mr. Plowden, and caused the same to be entered accordingly.' Blunden added that within half an hour of Plowden's departure from the court Lord Hunsdon, the queen's cousin, arrived with the intention of securing the wardship for himself, only to find that he had been forestalled by Plowden.[19] The patent granting the wardship and marriage of young Englefield was sealed on 16 December 1567; the grant was made jointly to Plowden and his old friend Sir Edward Saunders, the chief baron of the Exchequer and a Catholic, and provided for the payment of an annuity of £10 from the death of John Englefield until young Francis should reach the age of fourteen, when the annuity was to be increased to twenty marks.[20]

Having obtained the wardship, Plowden discharged his duties towards his young ward with a notable lack of self-seeking; he did not, as so many other guardians did, make a profit out of his wardship but sought to preserve and improve the property of young Englefield. To quote Blunden again: 'When Mr. Plowden had obtained this [the wardship], how carefully he brought up young Englefield in learning and virtue, what pains, what labour and travail he took in quieting his causes and matters in law, what toils and suits in law he had sundry years together for Tottenhoe [i.e., Tattenhoe in Bucks.], beinge then for the most part litigious in law, how he to his very great charge he quieted the same during the minority of young Mr. Englefield; if they [the Englefields] should deny it, being now fresh in memory, would turn them to great discredit; I dare boldly affirm that in this one matter he did more benefit the young gentleman than he or his uncle [Sir Francis] ever did to Mr. Plowden.[21] Plowden's conduct was all the more remarkable because, as Sir John Carey later observed, 'it is not the use in any place . . . to do good turns gratis.'[22] Plowden, nevertheless, arranged to assist his needy brother-in-law, Richard Sandford; the Sandfords had owned a number of estates but they were dispersed and unproductive, and it appears that by the middle of the sixteenth century the family, who had never been affluent, were in straitened circumstances.[23] Accordingly, Plowden arranged that Richard Sandford should have a 'tenement' in Up Rossall and Udlington and a water-mill at Yetton;[24] that, of course, was property owned by Sir Francis and not by his nephew. Plowden also recommended Richard Sandford's son, Humfrey, to Sir Francis. Humfrey performed numerous confidential services for Sir Francis Englefield and from time to time engaged in the dangerous activity of carrying messages for Englefield to and from England; according to Andrew Blunden, he received twenty marks a year from Plowden.[25]

19. *Blunden's MS,* 125, 126.
20. *C.P.R. 1566–1569,* p. 242, no. 1459.
21. *Blunden's MS,* 128.
22. *Cal. B.P.,* ii, 787 (Sir John Carey to Cecil, 26 May 1602); Carey later became third baron Hunsdon.
23. *cf.* Blakeway, *Isle,* 115–6.
24. Blakeway, *Isle,* 113–4.
25. *Blunden's MS,* 128. For a detailed treatment of the foregoing, see Parmiter, in *R.H.,* xiii (1975–6), 159–77.

Humphrey Burdett continued for some years to act as receiver of the rents and profits of the Englefield lands in Berkshire and Wiltshire, out of which he made the yearly payments of £300 into the Exchequer. On 27 March 1571, however, the queen issued an order to the Treasurer, the Chancellor, the Under-Treasurer and the barons of the Exchequer requiring them to audit the accounts of the sequestration commissioners and of Burdett, and to cause the residue (over and above the yearly sums of £300) 'to be put in respite'; they were also to take into the queen's hands all other goods and lands of Sir Francis that had not already been taken, apart from the lands granted to Lady Englefield for her maintenance, and they were required to pay out of the revenues a yearly sum of £40 to John Englefield's widow, Margaret, as well as the wages and pensions granted by Sir Francis to his servants and to two students at Oxford University. [26] In that way Englefield, although still remaining legal owner of his vast property, was deprived of the entire income derived from it.

By that time, however, other matters more important and more pressing than Englefield's property, were engaging the attention of the government. Anglo-Spanish relations were deteriorating rapidly; in 1567 another religious war had begun in France; the Spanish Netherlands had revolted, bringing down the bloody repression of the duke of Alva and sending refugees to England who brought with them an urgent sense of coming conflict with the Catholic powers; in May 1568 Mary Queen of Scots had fled to England to become the focus of intrigues and plots; there were the activities of the Catholic exiles in Spain and the Low Countries; and in November 1569 came the Northern Rebellion. Finally, in 1570 the pope issued the bull *Regnans in Excelsis* excommunicating and deposing the queen and releasing her subjects from their allegiance. Money was needed to meet the cost of suppressing the rebellion and measures had to be taken to deal with its leaders and also to counter the papal bull. Parliament accordingly assembled on 2 April 1571 and contrived to transact a surprisingly large amount of business in a session that lasted less than two calendar months. [27]

In addition to granting a subsidy, Parliament enacted a new Treason Act, an Act prohibiting the bringing in and putting into execution bulls and other instruments emanating from the papal curia, and an Act confirming the attainder of the northern rebels. [28]

Parliament also passed 'An Acte agaynste Fugytyves over the Sea' which was specifically aimed at the Catholic exiles abroad. [29] The Act recited the traitorous activities of persons that had secretly left England without licence, and asserted that they made secret conveyances of their lands and

26. *C.P.R., 1569-1572,* p. 194, no. 1687.
27. The session ended on 29 May 1571. For the parliamentary history of the session, see *Neale I,* 177-240.
28. 13 Eliz. I, c. 1 (*Statutes of the Realm,* iv, 526; treason); 13 Eliz. I, c. 2 (*Statutes of the Realm,* iv, 528; bulls from Rome); 13 Eliz. I, c. 16 (*Statutes of the Realm,* iv, 549-52; attainders).
29. 13 Eliz. I, c. 3 (*Statutes of the Realm,* iv, 531).

goods in such a way that, although it appeared that their lands were placed at the free disposition of those to whom the conveyance was made, the secret reality was to preserve the property for its owner. The Act therefore enacted that all subjects and denizens who left the realm without the queen's licence and did not return within six months after proclamation for their return, should forfeit the profits of their lands for life, together with all their goods, and similar penalties were provided for persons licensed to leave the realm who did not return after the expiration of their licences. The Act declared that conveyances in trust made by such persons should be void against the crown and provided for the appointment of commissioners to inquire of offenders and of their lands and goods.[30] A commission under the Act was appointed to deal with Englefield's property in Shropshire which sat at Shrewsbury on 29 October 1573.[31]

That legislation, which posed a substantial threat to the Englefield property, must have caused Plowden some anxiety. During that time, however, he was steadily adding to his own property. In March 1569 he bought more land from Sylvester Cowper to add to the property he already owned in Wokefield;[32] his purchase included the manor of Wokefield, and land at Burghfield, Stratford Mortimer and Sulhampstead Bannester.[33] Two years later he made further additions to his Berkshire property; on 25 March 1571 he leased Burghfield Farm for twenty-one years from John Talbot of Grafton, a notable recusant who had been admitted a student in the Middle Temple in 1560.[34] On 15 December 1571 another commission had returned, as part of the Englefield property, particulars of a lease for fifty years of the rectory of Shiplake and its vicarage house and lands, which had been granted on 16 February 1527 to Sir Francis Englefield, and the reversion to which had been granted by Edward VI to the dean and canons of Windsor; on 15 February 1574 Burghley and Sir Walter Mildmay approved the grant to Plowden of the queen's interest in the lease.[35]

---

30. In the following year parliament passed a further Act dealing with fugitives (14 Eliz. I, c. 6 (*Statutes of the Realm*, iv, 598-9), in explanation of the earlier Act, because doubts had been expressed whether the queen might grant leases and other interests out of the lands of fugitives which had been forfeited for their lives.

31. For a detailed account of the foregoing, see Parmiter, in *R.H.*, xiii, (1975-6), at pp. 165-8).

32. For Plowden's purchase of Wokefield Farm, see p. 69, *ante*.

33. Licence for Sylvester Cowper to alienate, 26 March 1569 (*C.P.R., 1566-1569*, p. 407, no. 2404); *V.C.H., Berks.*, iii, 425.

34. See the will of Edmund Plowden (P.C.C. 54 Brudenell; P.R.O., Prob 11/68/429). On 29 Feb. 1572 Plowden granted out of the Farm a yearly rent of £6 13s. 4d. to his son, Francis, to be paid after his death (see Plowden's will). The manor of Burghfield had been owned by the Talbots of Grafton (Worcs.) since 1531 when Henry VIII granted it to Sir Gilbert Talbot. John Talbot, who suffered severely for his Catholicism, died seized of the manor in 1610 and was succeeded by his son, George, who became earl of Shrewsbury on the death of his distant cousin, Edward, 8th earl, who died without heirs (see *V.C.H., Berks.*, iii, 401). For John Talbot, see Sister Callista, in *Worcestershire Recusant,* no. 8 (1966), 15-23. See also *M.T.R.,* i, 129. John Talbot was never called to the Bar.

35. P.R.O., E. 310/22/119, m. 42.

XIII

RELIGIOUS DIFFICULTIES

For the first ten years of Elizabeth's reign the laws relating to the oath and religious conformity had been enforced in the country at large in a haphazard manner, but the events of 1567 and 1568 caused the government to believe that England was facing grave dangers at the hands of the Catholics. Hitherto the Inns of Court had been largely left to their own devices where questions of religious conformity were concerned and it was not until early in 1569 that the first direct governmental move was made against them for matters of religion, and it betrays the council's uncertainty and ignorance of the real state of affairs in the Inns which were suspected of favouring papists. On 24 February 1569 the privy council wrote to John Salven, newly appointed Reader at Lincoln's Inn, to remind him of the obligation to take the oath of supremacy imposed by the statute of 1563,[1] 'which good order, how it hath been observed in that [Lincoln's Inn] and other Houses of Court we do not certainly know'. Salven was ordered to take the oath before taking up his office of Reader and to show the council's letter to 'the Benchers, Ancients and others' of the Inn.[2]

That was followed by an attempt to enforce religious conformity in all the Inns. Twenty-two members of the Inns of Court were summoned before the commissioners for ecclesiastical causes to be examined concerning their attendance at church and reception of communion. Those from the Middle Temple were Richard Palmer, James Gardiner, John Wise and William Tempest, of whom only the first appeared before the commissioners;[3] the notable absence of Plowden's name is, presumably, to be accounted for by his known church-going at that time. The answers of those interrogated were what might be expected of Catholics in the uncertainties of the times, and although none of the answers disclosed a serious case of recusancy the abstract of the examination carries an endorsement in Cecil's hand to the effect that those summoned to appear before the commissioners, including those who did not appear, were to be put out of commons and lodgings in their respective Inns, and were to be forbidden to 'give counsel to any the queen's subjects as common pleaders' or to 'resort to any bar of any court to plead by any manner wise', until they had conformed as evidenced by the testimony of the bishop of London.[4]

---

1. 5 Eliz. I, c. 1 (*Statutes of the Realm,* iv, 402–5); see p. 78, *ante.*
2. *B.B.,* i, 170–1.
3. Richard Palmer, son and heir of John Palmer of Warton, Northants., was admitted to the Inn on 2 July 1552, and James Gardiner, son of Thomas Gardiner of Sawston, Cambs., was admitted on 18 May 1552; both were barristers. John Wise, second son of John Wise of Stanford on Avon, Northants., was admitted on 15 Oct. 1567, and William Tempest, seventh son of Robert Tempest of Holmeside, co. Durham, was admitted on 27 Feb. 1568; both were students. See *M.T.R.,* i, 85, 86, 160, 163.
4. P.R.O., S.P. 12/60/70.

That was followed by letters dated 20 May 1569 from the privy council
to each of the Inns of Court requiring the expulsion of those summoned
before the commissioners. The letters also stated that, in order to avoid
the increase of such contempts and disorders, no person in the Inns, 'being
commonly and notoriously known or vehemently suspected to mislike of
the rites and orders established in this realm for religion, be called or
allowed from henceforth to any degree in that House until the same have
sufficiently purged himself of the said suspicion.'[5] All those concerned
were eventually expelled from their Inns, but none of the Inns made any
strenuous effort to enforce rigidly the instructions of the privy council.[6]

Plowden thus escaped the only real religious 'purge' of the Inns to which
they were subjected, but later in the year he was, for the first time, brought
face to face with one of the problems facing Catholics in Elizabethan
England. The privy council was largely dependent upon the justices of the
peace for local administration and law enforcement, and it expected the
justices to show a good example to those within their jurisdiction. In 1569,
however, the council appears to have become apprehensive that some
justices were not doing all that they should do to enforce the provisions of
the Act of Uniformity and to ensure that the queen's subjects attended
their parish churches on the days prescribed by that statute. In order to
bring about an improvement the council decided that every justice should
be required to subscribe a document acknowledging his duty to observe
the provisions of the Act of Uniformity and promising to repair, with his
family, to his parish church to hear divine service in accordance with the
Book of Common Prayer on the days prescribed by the statute. Accordingly, on 6 November 1569 the council ordered the despatch of letters to
the sheriffs and other authorities requiring them to obtain the subscription
to such a document of the justices within their respective shrievalties.[7]

Plowden was one of the Berkshire justices, and the council's letter was
received by the sheriff of that county, John Fettiplace,[8] on 12 November,
and he immediately arranged for a meeting of justices. On 17 November
the sheriff and six justices, Sir Edward Unton, Robert Keilwey, Edmund

5. cf. B.B., i, 370–2; I.T.R., i, 252–4. The letters to the Middle Temple and Gray's Inn do
not appear to have survived, and the Acts of the Privy Council are missing for the period 4
May 1567 to 24 May 1570. Only the latter part of the letter to the Inner Temple appears in the
manuscript volume of the minutes of the Inner Temple Parliament; in the printed version in
I.T.R. the earlier part has been taken from a copy in the Inner Temple Library, Petyt MS 538/
47, f. 47. There is a corrected draft of the letter in Br. Lib., MS 109, ff. 9–10.
6. For the foregoing, see Parmiter, Elizabethan Popish Recusancy in the Inns of Court,
9–16, and see that essay generally for the reluctance of the benchers of the several Inns to
enforce conformity among their members.
7. cf. P.R.O., S.P. 12/60/47. The responses to the council's circular letter will be found
noted in C.S.P.D., 1547–1580, passim.
8. There were many members of the Fettiplace family in Berkshire and Oxfordshire; John
Fettiplace, of a Berkshire branch, does not appear to have been a recusant although his wife
and two daughters were, and in 1586 he offered a composition of £2 in respect of their recusancy
(P.R.O., S.P. 12/189/54, at f. 139v). Sir Francis Englefield's wife, Catherine, was the daughter
of Sir Thomas Fettiplace of Compton Beauchamp, Berks.; she had ceased to be a Catholic by
1569.

Plowden, Richard Bullock, Roger Young and Griffith Curtis, assembled at
Abingdon where, with the exception of Plowden, they signed the document
required by the council.[9] Hitherto Plowden had gone regularly to the
Anglican services, although he did not communicate,[10] and it seems likely
that he had not given any serious consideration to the implications of doing
so but was content to follow the example of many of his co-religionists.
When, however, he was confronted with the necessity of signing an official
document that rejected important tenets of his faith he hesitated. In their
letter to the council his fellow justices reported that

'Edmund Plowden said that before his coming thither he had not heard
of the said letter and of the contents thereof, but the matter was sudden
to him. And further said that sithens the subscription touched religion
he thought it his part, before he should subscribe, to consider the said
statute, but also most chiefly the said Book [of Common Prayer]
touching the uniformity of common prayer which was very long, and
for the multitude of other matters that he and the rest of the justices
had to deal in there presently, he had no time to consider the said statute
and book, but at our next meeting, which were appointed at Reading
the 25th day of November, he said he would attend upon us and in the
mean time he would consider the said book and statute and then tell us
his full resolution in the points required. And so for that time he did
forbear to subscribe.'[11]

At the same time they wrote to John Yate, a former justice of the county,
asking him to meet them at Wadley on 20 November in order to sign the
document; he did not attend the meeting but sent his excuses. John
Yate, of Buckland was a papist who later suffered financially for his
Catholicism.[12] His younger son, also named John, had been admitted to
the Middle Temple on 8 May 1567, but after being imprisoned by order
of the council 'for attempts touching the state of the kingdom', he was
expelled from the Inn in 1571 and went abroad to become a Jesuit.[13]

At the meeting at Reading on 25 November which Plowden had promised
to attend, there were present the new sheriff, William Forster, Richard
Ward, cofferer of the royal household, John Winchcombe, the grandson
of 'Jack of Newbury', William Dunch and Edmund Docwra, all of whom
subscribed the document. The justices reported that Plowden said

'that he had sithens our assembly at Abendon [Abingdon] fully considered the said statute and book of Uniformity of Common Prayer;
and further said that as touching coming to church and hearing divine
service according to the said book and statute, he had, ever sithens this
service used, come to the church and heard the same service and prayers
according to the same book. And said that, as he thought, no man in
this realm of his profession in the common law and having so much

9. See Justices of Berkshire to the Privy Council, 22 Dec. 1569 (P.R.O., S.P. 12/60/47).
10. See p. 57, *ante.*
11. P.R.O., S.P. 12/60/47.
12. E.g., P.R.O., S.P. 12/117/17 & 17 i (1577); S.P. 12/183/15 (1585).
13. *M.T.R.,* i, 159, 180; Foley, *Records,* vii, 874.

business as he hath had in term time and out of the term had oftener or dulier come to the church and heard divine service according to the said book than he hath done, as they of both the Temples and many others have seen and can testify. And therefore said that touching that point he hitherto hath not been any of those that your honours' [i.e., the privy council's] letters seem to touch. But sithens the subscription required is not only to that point, but is generally to all things in the Act and book, as he saith, and such subscription promiseth allowance, not only presently but in time to come, of all things in the said book; and that there is no book of any part of religion established by the Act which establisheth the said book; and for that upon consideration of the book and Act he conceiveth some scruple in conscience in some things in the said book which he said he would have declared to us if it had been material. And therefore he said he could not with safe conscience subscribe the said letter; for he said he could not subscribe but belief must precede his subscription. And therefore, he said, great impiety should be in him if he should subscribe in full affirmance or belief of those things in which he is scrupulous in belief. And prayed us to certify his sayings unto your honours to the end you might understand that he did not upon stubbornness or wilfulness forebear to subscribe but only upon scrupulosity of conscience. And further said he trusted your lordships, understanding his case, would bear with him in this point. And this is his full resolution, he said to us, refusing for these causes to subscribe, saying that besides the love that of common duty he owed to her highness as a subject, he owed as much more by particular benefit as all that he possesseth is worth; for if of grace she had not foreborne it, she might justly by law have had it from him, and therefore he was the more sorry that he should deny anything that her grace should require, but his conscience, which he cannot remove and which is in God only to alter or change, was the cause he did refuse to subscribe.'

Upon his refusal to sign, his fellow justices, as they were bound to, required him to enter into a bond, in the sum of two hundred marks, which he signed on 20 December; it provided that if, during the space of one year, he were of good behaviour towards the queen and all her subjects, and did personally appear before the council whenever summoned to do so, the bond should be void.[14] The refusal of so eminent a lawyer to comply with the law is striking and is notable not only for the moderation with which it was expressed but for being grounded solely upon a point of conscience. His action rendered him liable to be removed from the commission of the peace and to be deprived of his other offices. It says much for his integrity and prestige as a lawyer that the council were content with the bond, and left him otherwise undisturbed; indeed, they continued

14. See Justices of Berkshire to the Privy Council, 22 Dec. 1569 (P.R.O., S.P. 12/60/47), with the enclosures (47 i, document subscribed by the justices; and 47 ii, the bond signed by Plowden). In the bond Plowden was described as 'of Shiplake' ('Noverint universi per presentes me Edmundum Plowden de Shiplake in Comitatu Oxonie, armigerum . . .').

to entrust him with important duties. It seems, however, that thereafter he did not attend church services.

About a year later a well known papist was elected Treasurer of the Middle Temple. A Parliament held on Monday 27 November 1570 chose Matthew Smith to be Treasurer, and it was agreed that Plowden should remain proctor and promoter of the new hall, both for building and collecting money. Smith had been admitted to the Inn about 1551 and at Christmas 1558 had filled the office of Master of the Revels. From April 1559 he and Plowden's brother-in-law, Ralph Sheldon, were in the chamber of John Mawdeley who had been Treasurer in 1551 and 1552. In June 1563 a Parliament of the Inn ordered that, in consideration of £60 which Smith had lent to the Inn until St. Andrew's Day in the following year, he should be released from his fine of £10 for refusing to be called to the Bar imposed by Gabriel Chambers, the Reader in the previous Lent, and the benchers agreed that he should never be compelled to take up the office of utter-barrister nor any other office. Despite that order he was fined £8 in January 1570 for not reading in the previous Autumn.[15] He remained Treasurer until 1573. On the Saturday following his election Smith appointed another papist, Thomas Pagitt, to be Under Treasurer. Pagitt was almost certainly the same Thomas Pagitt who was appointed Lent Reader in 1583. In that case he was a mere student when he was appointed, since he was admitted to the Inn in 1563 but was not called to the Bar until early in 1575; he was chosen Treasurer of the Inn in 1599 and died in 1614.[16]

Following the alarm caused by the Northern Rebellion and the bull *Regnans in Excelsis,* the archbishop of Canterbury, Matthew Parker, became concerned at what he believed to be the bad state of religion in the Inns of Court. On 17 June 1571 he wrote to Lord Burghley recalling that about two years earlier the action of the council had reduced the Inns of Court to better order about religion, but he complained that the Inns 'do now of late grow again very disordered in over bold speeches and doings touching religion', and that that had occurred as he thought 'for want of due execution and observation of your lordships' said decrees and ordinance'.[17] He therefore asked Burghley to obtain from the council a letter, of which he enclosed a draft, by virtue of which he hoped that 'there will be some better order and reformation therein to the furtherance of religion'.[18]

The archbishop's complaint had a sympathetic reception and, although the council did not adopt Parker's draft, it addressed a letter to the 'Bishop of London [Edwin Sandys] and others the Ecclesiastical Commissioners' which began by setting out the letters and instructions sent to the Inns of Court by the Council in May 1569 'for the reformation of a sort of

15. *M.T.R.,* i, 118, 141-2, 170.
16. Williamson, *Middle Temple Bench Book,* 83, 316.
17. I.e., those of 20 May 1569; see p. 105, *ante.*
18. Archbishop Parker to Lord Burghley, 17 June 1571; printed in Bruce and Perowne, *Correspondence of Matthew Parker,* 384-5; *cf.* Strype, *Life of Matthew Parker,* 73-5.

persons, about that time detected to be in the same Houses, of disordered demeanour and perverse disposition, especially against the laws and orders ecclesiastical of the church'. The council went on to inform the commissioners that they were credibly informed that the former disorders had revived, 'or rather increased', and that was due, it was said, partly to the failure of the benchers to enforce the council's orders and partly to the remissness of the ecclesiastical commissioners themselves. The commissioners were, therefore, required speedily, before the end of term, to send 'for some of the ancients and benchers of the discreetest and dutifullyest of every House or Inn of Court", and also of the Inns of Chancery, to inquire of the disorders concerning the observance 'of the laws ecclesiastical and the rites of the church', and, if they found that such disorders were likely to increase, they were to suggest the means 'to reform or otherwise to correct the parties offending, and to limit some good orders for the due service of God in those Houses, and to stay and reform the rest from the entry into like offences'.[19]

There is in existence a set of interrogatories to be put to five members of the Middle Temple which may have been drafted by Parker in connection with this investigation of the religious state of the Inns.[20] Four of those to whom the interrogatories were to be put are referred to only by their initials, but they can easily be identified as George Horde, Thomas Pagitt, John Stone and Edmund Plowden; the fifth, referred to by name, was Matthew Shaftowe. They were to be asked whether they went to the Temple Church at service time and received communion there, and whether they had in their possession 'a certain lewd libel intituled A knack to know a knave'.[21] Pagitt was to be asked, among other things, whether he had been preferred to his office as Under Treasurer 'chiefly by Mr. Plowden and Mr. Smythe the chief Treasurer of the House', whether he had taken the oath on being admitted to office, and whether he had 'purposely disappointed any being of good religion from having of chambers in the House'. In two further interrogatories to be put to Plowden, he was to be asked whether 'there were some that you suspected to have preferred [i.e., informed against] you, and that you would mischief them', and whether he had any popish or seditious books in his possession. Whether those

19. Br. Lib., Lansd. MS 15, ff. 158r-v (printed in *B.B.,* i, 454-5). Strype printed a version, with small verbal differences from the letter in the Landsdowne MSS, but he dated the letter 1581 instead of 1571 (see Strype, *Annals,* III, i, 44-6).

20. See Inner Temple Lib., Petyt MS 538/47, ff. 342r-v. The MS is endorsed in a later hand 'The Councells letters with interrogatories, and the Archb for removing Papists owt of the Inner Temple'; the endorsement is confusing, since two sets of interrogatories have been placed together. The first set is apparently to be dated 1571, whereas the second set, which closely agrees with the interrogatories described by Strype (*Life of Grindal,* 224) should be dated early in 1570. The council's letter, referred to in the endorsement, is now missing.

21. It has not been possible to identify the 'lewd libel' here referred to. Save for its title it had, presumably, nothing to do with an anonymous play (perhaps by Robert Greene) entitled *A most pleasant comedie, intituled A knacke to knowe a knave* (*S.T.C.,* no. 15027) which was printed in 1594; it was entered at Stationers' Hall on 7 Jan. 1594 (Arber, *Transcript of the Register,* ii, 304). The 'lewd libel' must have been in MS form.

interrogatories were ever put to the five members of the Inn is unknown; there is no record of their answers and the report which the council required the commissioners to make does not now appear to be in existence.

One result of the commissioners' report appears to have been the issue by the privy council, in the queen's name, of orders addressed to each of the Inns of Court; those orders were signed on 31 May 1574 and were entitled 'Orders necessary for the government of the Inns of Court established by commandment of the Queen's Majesty, with the advice of her Privy Council and the Justices of her Bench and the Common Place in Westminster.'[22] Among other things, the orders prohibited the admission to an Inn of Court of more in number than the chambers of the Inn could accommodate and forbade the building of new chambers and the admission of more than two persons to an existing chamber. The purpose of such requirements was, doubtless, partly to assist the government's campaign to restrict building in London (a campaign that was largely fruitless), partly to control the increasing numbers entering the Inns, and partly to make easier the supervision of the Inns and the detection of those whom the government regarded as dangerous or undesirable. The orders also provided that no one should have any chamber or be in commons if he 'upon public admonition once given by any Reader, Bencher or utter-barrister, doth not come and remain at the usual common prayers at the church and chapels of the same House'; and that no one should be admitted to plead in any court unless, in addition to his professional qualifications, he should, upon admonition as before, be at common prayer.

At the same time a survey was made of the Inns of Court which set out the number of chambers in each Inn, and the number of benchers, utter-barristers and 'other gentlemen' accommodated therein.[23] It is not clear what degree of accuracy may be attributed to it, but on the assumption that the errors are small, it shows that the total number of those in the Inns of Court in 1574 was 761 who, with the exception of 132 who had no accommodation in the Inns, were distributed among 408 chambers. In the Middle Temple there were eleven benchers, forty utter-barristers and 139 'other gentlemen', making a total of 190, of whom 130 were accommodated in ninety-two chambers and sixty had no accommodation in the Inn.

22. *A.P.C.*, viii, 246–8. The orders also appear in the records of the Inner Temple, the Middle Temple and Lincoln's Inn: see *I.T.R.*, i, 276–8; *M.T.R.*, i, 200–2; *B.B.*, i, 391–2. The orders do not appear in the records of Gray's Inn under any date in 1574, but a version appears on their re-issue in 1584 under the date 8 Feb. 1584 (see *G.I.P.B.*, i, 60–2). The orders are also printed in *D.O.J.*, 312. On 13 May 1580 three members of the Middle Temple, John Marston (father of the playwright), William Spatchurst and William Simmes were put out of commons 'for their practice contrary to' the orders (*M.T.R.*, i, 233).

23. 'A survey of the chambers and societies of all the Innes of Courte togethr with certayne devyses for the government of the worthie and necessarie sorte and for the exclusion of the unworthie and unnecessarie number and sorte thereof. Maie 1574'; P.R.O., S.P. 12/95/91 (printed in *I.T.R.*, i, 468–70).

XIV

PLOWDEN'S COMMENTARIES

In the year 1571 Plowden published his *Commentaries* or *Reports* of cases decided in the superior courts during the reigns of Edward VI, Mary and Elizabeth I, and that was an event of great importance for the legal profession and for the law itself. For centuries lawyers had used, for their professional purposes, the series of notes of cases and arguments known as the Year Books. The Year Books, produced by lawyers for lawyers, stretch in an almost continuous series from the reign of Edward I to the reign of Richard III, but in the reigns of Henry VII and Henry VIII they became intermittent, and the last printed Year Book is for Trinity Term, 27 Henry VIII, that is, 1535.[1]

The precise nature of the Year Books, and how and why they came into existence, are still matters of controversy among legal historians, but one may be allowed to conjecture that with the growing organization of the legal profession, there grew up in the Middle Ages some sort of system of reporting which enabled lawyers to know what was happening in the royal courts. The Year Books were of immense importance in the development of medieval law so that when, in 1535, they finally ceased to appear, a serious gap was left.

Lawyers, however, did not rely entirely on what was provided by others; they kept manuscript notebooks in which they entered notes of arguments and judgments, and of other matters that were useful to them in their professional work. There are hundreds of such manuscripts still in existence and most of them consist almost entirely of notes, either long or short, of decided cases. Those who were fortunate enough to possess a good collection of cases were often asked by their fellow practitioners for the loan of the book, and while such books were on loan they were often copied, not always accurately. Practitioners and students were not the only borrowers of such collections; publishers, too, were anxious to get hold of them, and they were not always very scrupulous in the methods they used.

So numerous were the defective and inaccurate collections of reports circulating in manuscript that when, in 1600, Sir Edward Coke published the first part of his *Reports*, he castigated the undesirable results that such collections sometimes produced; he wrote:

'I have often observed, that for want of a true and certain report, the case that hath been adjudged, standing upon the rack of many running reports (especially of such as understood not the state of the question) hath been so diversely drawn out, as many times the true parts of the case have been disordered and disjointed, and most commonly the right reason and rule of the judges utterly mistaken. Hereout have sprung many absurd and strange opinions, which, being carried about in a

---

1. For the Year Books, see e.g., Holdsworth, in *L.Q.R.*, xxii (1906), 360–82; Bolland, *The Years Books*; Simpson, in *L.Q.R.*, lxxxvii (1971), 94–118; *H.E.L.*, ii, 525–56.

common charm, and fathered on grave and reverend judges, many times with the multitude, and sometimes with the learned, receive such allowance as either beguile or bedazzle their conceits and judgments.'[2]

Like many of his fellow practitioners, Plowden assembled his own collection of cases; from an early period in his career he assiduously attended the courts and moots to take notes of what he heard. His own description of his method of working at that time has already been quoted,[3] and he went on to say:

'And finding that I reaped much profit and instruction by this practice, I became at last disposed to report the arguments and judgments made and given in the King's Courts upon demurrers in law, as abounding more copiously with matter of improvement, and being more capable of perfecting the judgment, than arguments on other occasions.[4] Upon this I undertook first one case and then another, by which means I at last collected a good volume. And this work I originally entered upon with a view to my own private instruction only, without the least thought or intention of letting it appear in print.'[5]

The existence of Plowden's private collection of reports became, in time, well known and they were so highly regarded by his fellow lawyers that he was, as he said, asked by 'some of the judges and other grave and learned men' to publish them. He was unwilling to do so, but he was forced to change his mind when he heard that a publisher was preparing to print an unauthorized version of them.

'I thought it my duty to decline making public my own disjudication of the arguments of men more learned than myself, and to keep the work for my own private advantage, and thereby to avoid the censure of affecting a more acute and discerning judgment than I really had. But by and by an accident happened, which inclined me, and (as I may say) forcibly compelled me to make this work public. For having lent my said book to a very few of my intimate friends, at their especial instance and request, and but for a short time, their clerks and others knowing thereof got the book into their hands, and made such expedition, by writing day and night, that in a short time they had transcribed a great number of the cases, and especially of the first, contrary to my own knowledge and intent, or of those to whom I had lent the book; which copies at last came to the hands of some of the printers, who intended (as I was informed) to make a profit of them by publishing them. But the cases being transcribed by clerks and other ignorant persons who did not perfectly understand the matter, the copies were

---

2. 1 Co. Rep., pp. xxvi–xxvii (preface).
3. See p. 13, *ante*.
4. A demurrer [from the French *demorrer*, to wait or stay] was a pleading which admitted the facts stated in the opponent's pleading, and asserted that those facts did not constitute a sufficient case in law to entitle that party to the relief claimed; upon demurrer, the issue of law arising thereon was determined by the court which decided whether or not the party demurring was bound to answer his opponent's pleading, and until such judgment the party 'waited'.
5. Plowd., p. iii (preface).

very corrupt, for in some places a whole line was omitted, and in others one word was put for another, which entirely changed the sense, and again in other places spaces were left where the writers did not understand the words, and divers other errors and defects there were, which, if the copies so taken had been printed, would have greatly defaced the work, and have been a discredit to me. And besides this, they had omitted to transcribe the pleadings according to the records, and had only transcribed the cases and arguments upon them, so that the benefit, which the reader would have reaped from the records of the pleadings in this book, (which is also a Book of Entries[6] of all others most sifted and tried) would have been totally lost. Wherefore, in order to prevent and avoid these defects, I considered with myself whether it was not better for me to put this work in print. During which consideration letters were sent to me by all the justices of both benches, and by the barons of the Exchequer, requesting and encouraging me to make it public. And at last, upon these and other motives, and hoping that it might be of some benefit to the students of the law, I resolved (as you see I have done) to put it in print.'[7]

The book was published by Richard Tottel in October 1571; his own copy with his marginal notes is preserved at Plowden Hall. It was reprinted in 1578 with a second series of reports together with a table of notable matters compiled by William Fleetwood, the recorder of London. There were several later folio editions of the two parts, and all of them were in Law French; an English translation was first published as a folio volume in 1779, and again in two octavo volumes in 1816.[8] The title *Commentaries or Reports* is, perhaps, misleading to a modern reader who expects something in the nature of Blackstone's *Commentaries* and finds that the book is confined to reports of cases. Plowden explained the title as follows: 'I have given a name to the whole work, and have called it my Commentaries or Reports, which word (Commentary) in one sense signifies a register or memorial of acts or sayings. And so, seeing this book contains the acts and sayings of others touching the matters therein treated of, I think the word (Commentary) is a proper name for it.'[9] On the title page Plowden described himself as 'Edmund Plowden of the Middle Temple, Esq., an apprentice of the common law'.[10]

6. Books of Entries were, in essence, books of precedents in pleading. The earliest was that of Pynson in 1510, which was followed by 'the old Book of Entries' in 1546, while a third was published by William Rastell in 1566; see *H.E.L.*, v, 383-6.
7. Plowd., pp. v-vi (preface).
8. All quotations from Plowden's Reports, in English, have been taken from the edition of 1816.
9. Plowd., p. viii (preface).
10. In the Law French editions, 'Edmund Plowden un Apprentice de le Common Ley'. In the heading of the preface he addressed his fellow lawyers: 'Edmund Plowden, to the students of the common law of England, and especially to his companions of the Middle Temple, wisheth increase of learning' (Edmund Plowden a les Estudents de les common Leyes de Engleterre, & principallment a ses Compaignions de le melieu Temple souhayte encrease de scavoir).

Plowden's *Reports* were startlingly new. He himself had no doubt that they far surpassed any of the reports that had hitherto been available: 'And (in my humble apprehension) these Reports excel any former books of reports in point of credit and authority, for other reports generally consist of the sudden sayings of the judges upon motions by the serjeants and counsellors at the Bar, whereas all the cases here reported are upon points of law tried and debated upon demurrers or special verdicts, copies whereof were delivered to the judges who studied and considered them, and for the most part argued in them, and after great and mature deliberation gave judgment thereupon, so that (in my opinion) these reports carry with them the greatest credit and assurance.'[11] His reports made a radical departure from the practice of earlier reporters who usually gave little more than short summaries of special points in the argument and frequently omitted to mention the judgment; such reports originated in the days when advocacy was chiefly concerned with framing the issues of law in the case, while the decision was of secondary importance to the reporters. The progressive supersession of oral by written pleadings brought about a change in the emphasis of argument in court; the questions then argued were concerned with the effect of the written pleadings, rather than with the nature of the issues and the form they should take. That in turn had its effect on the style of the law reports. The entries in the Year Books and similar reports were frequently no more than an account of a dialogue between judges and counsel that led to the formulation of an issue, but with written pleadings the issue was already defined and what then concerned the reporter was the argument upon that issue and the law laid down by the court as a result. That meant that the written pleadings became a necessary part of the report, and as the decision of the court became of increasing concern to the reporter, the arguments of counsel diminished in importance. That change made a substantial contribution to the development of the modern conception of the binding power of decided cases.

Plowden confined his reports to those cases in which a point of law fell to be decided; as he himself wrote, 'in this book there is no record entered but such upon which there was either a demurrer in law, or a special verdict given, concerning a point of law, in both which cases the matter was thoroughly sifted and debated at the Bar and at the Bench also, and in the end either approved or disapproved, for the causes shewn in this book, by the judgment of the court.'[12] Plowden's reports in which, unlike the Year Books, he gave each case a name, are therefore in striking contrast to what had gone before. He began at the beginning with a full and lucid heading for each case, which included the names of the parties, the date of the argument, the court concerned and the term in which the

11. Plowd., p. vi (preface). For demurrer, see p. 112, *ante*, note. A special verdict is where the jury finds the facts of a case and leaves to the court the application of the law to the facts so found.
12. Plowd., p. vi (preface).

proceedings were instituted. In the body of his report he set out a copy of the official record and of the pleadings, a full note of the arguments of counsel and judges, and the substance of the final judgments. Thus the practitioner had in one reliable report all that he needed. In that way Plowden set a new standard of law reporting which has influenced all subsequent law reporters, and his *Reports* not only satisfied a need for accurate reports of recent cases, but created a continuing demand for them which is still being met by his successors.

Plowden took great care to make his reports as accurate as possible, and he often sought the assistance of the judges and counsel who had taken part in the cases he reported. In the preface to his *Reports* he said that in almost all the cases which he undertook to report, he obtained copies of the 'record' of the cases and studied the points of law arising thereon before the case was argued. Then, 'after I had drawn out my report at large, and before I had entered it into my book, I shewed such cases and arguments, as seemed to me to be the most difficult and to require the greatest memory, to some of the judges or serjeants who had argued in them, in order to have their opinion of the sincerity and truth of the reports, which being perused and approved by them I then entered into my book.'[13] In that respect he appears to be the originator of a practice that has continued to the present day. In one case in which Plowden appeared for the defendants, the court said merely that judgment should be given against the plaintiffs; whereupon 'the apprentice [Plowden] said, may it please your lordships to shew us, for our learning, the causes of your judgment', and Catlin, the chief justice, having done so, Plowden was able to include a short note of it in his report.[14] And when, for any reason, he was unable to be present during some part of the argument in a case that he was reporting, he was careful to obtain a reliable report from those who could supply it, and to record the fact in his report.[15] In a case in the King's Bench in which William Fleetwood and Plowden appeared for the plaintiff, the question arose whether the action were maintainable; after the argument all four judges assembled at Serjeants' Inn in Fleet Street, in the chambers of the chief justice, Robert Catlin, to consider the matter and were unanimous that the action was maintainable, and afterwards Plowden was able to obtain from Catlin the principal reasons for the judges' decision.[16]

A reporter has, of necessity, to summarize the arguments he reports and so must possess the ability to distinguish the relevant from the irrelevant. Plowden described his own practice in that respect:

'I have for the most part reported cases in a summary way, collecting together the substance (as it appeared to me) of all that was said on the

13. Plowd., pp. vi–vii (preface).
14. *Sharington* v. *Strotton* (1566), Plowd., 298, at pp. 308–9.
15. See e.g., *Wimbish* v. *Tailbois* (1550), Plowd. 38, at p. 46; *Assize of Fresh Force* (1553), Plowd. 89, at p. 93; *Hill* v. *Grange* (1556), Plowd. 164, at p. 170; *Hales* v. *Petit* (1562), Plowd. 253, at p. 261; *Cole's Case* (1571), Plowd. 401; *Newis* v. *Lark* (1572), Plowd. 403, at p. 410; *Nichols* v. *Nichols* (1574), Plowd. 477, at p. 482; *Eare* v. *Snow* (1576), Plowd. 504, at p. 514.
16. *Chapman* v. *Dalton* (1564), Plowd. 284, at p. 292.

one side, and on the other, and oftentimes of all that was said by the judges themselves, without reciting their arguments *verbatim*. In which case I have purposely omitted much that was said both at the Bar and at the Bench, for I thought that there were few arguments so pure as not to have some refuse in them, and therefore I thought it best to extract the pure only, and to leave the refuse, then and yet holding that to be the best method of reporting.'

He went on to say that

'although I have omitted many things which were said, as being deemed by me less material than that which is here reported, yet I have not thereby (as far as I am capable of judging) given just cause of offence to any. For neither in them nor in others have I suppressed any sentence which I remembered and thought to be very material, but I have expressed the matter intended truly, and for the most part in the words of the party who spoke it, sometimes indeed in other words added by myself, shewing the matter more fully, but never (to the best of my knowledge) departing from the sense or intent of the party touching the matter'.[17]

Nevertheless, from time to time he inserted notes of his own, but he always made it clear that his observations were not part of the argument or judgment. Some were no more than asides, such as his engaging observation that 'Sir Humphry Brown, who was then one of the justices, did not argue at all, because he was so old that his senses were decayed, and his voice could not be heard.'[18] In *Stowel* v. *Lord Zouch* Plowden stated bluntly that he had omitted from his report 'divers cases' cited by serjeant Bendlowes because he considered that the statute, in respect of which they had been cited, did not extend to the matter argued.[19] Others were what would, perhaps, nowadays be termed practice notes, such as how a petition should be brought in the court of Exchequer by a person who had a rent issuing out of land in the king's hands;[20] or a note on the current method of proceeding to obtain a writ of consultation by way of bill of attachment upon a prohibition, which Plowden considered greatly inferior to the older method upon a writ of *fieri facias*;[21] or the note that where a person was convicted in the Exchequer of an intrusion into crown lands, upon a bill of intrusion brought in that court, the proper procedure was to put him out of possession by a special writ of *amoveri facias*.[22]

Occasionally Plowden's notes were lengthy and amounted to essays on particular legal topics. An example is provided by the long note which appears at the end of the report of the case of *Eyston* v. *Studd*,[23] in which

17. Plowd., pp. iv, vii.
18. *Wrotesley* v. *Adams* (1559), Plowd. 187, at p. 190. Sir Humphrey Browne was one of the judges of the Common Pleas and uncle of Anthony Browne who had been degraded from the position of chief justice to a puisne at the beginning of Elizabeth's reign.
19. Plowd. 353, at p. 375.
20. *Sir Henry Nevil's Case* (1570), Plowd. 376, at p. 383.
21. *Soby* v. *Molins* (1574), Plowd. 468, at p. 471.
22. *Walsingham's Case* (1579), Plowd. 547, at p. 561.
23. Plowd. 459, at pp. 465–8.

he expounded the concept of what he called Equity as applied to the interpretation of statutes. Plowden was alive to the growing importance of statutes in English law and he was concerned to build a consistent and reasonable system of statutory interpretation based on his conception of Equity.[24] Plowden's attempt may not have been entirely successful, yet he made a significant contribution to the doctrine of statutory construction.

The success of Plowden's *Reports* was immediate and lasting, and their influence has long been recognized. William Fleetwood, once the recorder of London, considered Plowden's reports to be the best means of learning the common law.[25] That students found it so is demonstrated by the survival of a substantial number of students' commonplace books which contain summaries of and extracts from Plowden's *Reports*.[26] For example, young Thomas Egerton, later Lord Ellesmere and lord chancellor, when he was a student, copied extracts from Plowden into his commonplace book, and when he composed the treatise on the interpretation of statutes known as the *Discourse* he added extracts from the first part of Plowden's *Reports*.[27] Another treatise on the same subject, by Sir Christopher Hatton, is heavily indebted to Plowden.[28] Students continued to use Plowden's *Reports* until well into the eighteenth century.

Further testimony to the success and great practical utility of Plowden's *Reports* is provided by the frequency with which they were printed, and by the fact that that great maker of abridgements, Thomas Ashe, found it worthwhile to publish an abridgement of Plowden's *Reports* in 1607, which later was translated into English by Fabian Hickes and published in 1650.[29] Plowden's influence is clearly visible in the work of that later and greater reporter, Sir Edward Coke, who regarded Plowden's Reports as 'exquisite and elaborate'.[30] Coke defined a report as 'a public relation, or a bringing again to memory cases judicially argued, debated, resolved, or adjudged in any of the king's courts of justice, together with such causes and reasons as were delivered by the judges of the same';[31] and elsewhere he observed that 'in the reports and arguments of matters in law, the point adjudged is principally to be observed, and not matters of discourse which do not tend to the point adjudged.'[32] Those statements might well be a description of Plowden's work, and they indicate that the new conception of a law report, initiated by Plowden, was gaining ground.

Plowden was the first to publish his own reports under his own name in his own lifetime. It is true that his friends Sir James Dyer, chief justice of

24. *cf. Reniger* v. *Fossa* (1550), Plowd. 1; *Hill* v. *Grange* (1556), Plowd. 164; *Stradling* v. *Morgan* (1560), Plowd. 199. See p. 161, *post.*
25. Fleetwood, *Annalium*, Epistola.
26. See Abbott, *Law Reporting*, 218.
27. See Egerton. *A Discourse upon . . . Statutes*, ed. S. E. Thorne, pp. 94–7; Plucknet, in *L.Q.R.*, lx (1944)., 242–9; *cf.* Radin, in *Illinois Law Review*, xxxviii (1943), 16–40, where the authorship of Egerton is questioned.
28. See Hatton, *A Treatise concerning Statutes.*
29. See Beale, *Bibliography*, 110 (R 491).
30. 2 Co. Rep., p. viii (preface).
31. Co. Litt. 293a.
32. *Case of Alton Woods* (1594–1600), 1 Co. Rep. 40b, at p. 52a.

the Common Pleas, and serjeant William Bendlowes were also reporters, but their reports were not published until after their deaths, and years after the publication of Plowden's *Reports*.[33]

It is probable that the aim of both Dyer and Plowden was to bring greater certainty into the process of decision-making; there were, nevertheless, substantial differences between their individual approaches. Dyer, whose reports retained much of the older note-book characteristics of the Year Books, was chiefly concerned to preserve what he regarded as a coherent body of law based on immemorial custom. By contrast, Plowden's interest was the provision of effective remedies for persons whose rights had been infringed, and if that meant that the law must be altered to meet the needs of justice, he was content that it should be so; indeed, one of his favourite aphorisms was 'Blessed be the amending hand'.[34] Dyer was a great lawyer, but he was typical of his age in regarding law as existing in a rarefied atmosphere, largely independent of human needs and aspirations as they were felt at the time. Plowden, on the other hand, never lost sight of the close connection between law and the contemporary activities of men. For example, when he appeared with Thomas Bromley in 1565 in a case in the King's Bench, he cited Aristotle's *Politics* in which, he said, Aristotle had devised for the instruction of the world 'a public-weal with laws and governments, perceiving that it would be in vain to make laws but to a people, and that people are necessary before laws'.[35]

Plowden's *Reports* are concerned only with points of law and have little interest for anyone who is not a lawyer. There is, however, one exception to that general statement, the famous case of *Hales* v. *Petit*[36] which was argued early in Elizabeth's reign and raised a question of forfeiture. As reported by Plowden it was a claim by the widow of Sir James Hales for damages for trespass to certain land known as Graveney Marsh in Kent which she and her husband had held jointly under a lease for a term of years. After the death of Sir James Hales, one of the judges of the Common Pleas, a coroner's inquest found that he had drowned himself in a stream near Canterbury and a verdict of *felo de se* was recorded.[37] Thereupon the lease was seized by the crown as being forfeited for felony, and was then granted by letters patent to Cyriac Petit, a Catholic, and John Webb, the latter of whom subsequently died. Petit then entered upon the land, which was the trespass complained of. The question arose: since

33. Dyer died in 1582 and his reports were first published in 1585 from his own manuscript bequeathed to his nephews; Bendlowes died in 1584 and his reports were published in 1661.

34. See p. 164, *post*.

35. *Sharington* v. *Strotton* (1565), Plowd. 298, at p. 303.

36. Plowd. 253. For an account of earlier proceedings, see Parmiter, in *Kent Recusant History*, no. 3 (1980), 74–6.

37. During Mary's reign Hales was imprisoned for several months during which he was induced to renounce his Protestantism, but his recantation so preyed upon his mind that he attemped to commit suicide; he was released in April 1554, a few months before his death. Despite that and the jury's verdict there are, according to Edward Foss, grounds for thinking that the judge, who was then aged 85, fell accidentally into the stream as he was crossing it by an unfenced bridge; see Foss, *Judges of England*, v, 373.

Hales and his wife were joint tenants under the lease and Hales alone had become *felo de se*, was the lease forfeited during the lifetime of Hales, thus depriving the widow (who had committed no felony) of her interest? If the forfeiture occurred after Hales's death, his widow would be entitled to the lease by survivorship. The court decided that the lease was forfeited.

Leaving aside, however, the legal questions involved, Plowden's report of the case has two points of general interest. During the course of the argument the nature of suicide was minutely discussed, and Chief Justice Dyer in his judgment devoted some space to the inherent wrongfulness of suicide, a part of his judgment that was derived directly from the *Summa* of St. Thomas Aquinas.[38] The ultra-metaphysical arguments of the judges and counsel on the nature of suicide became known to William Shakespeare (probably from Plowden's *Reports*) and he made fun of them in the grave-diggers' scene in *Hamlet*.[39]

38. *cf.* Aquinas, *Summa Theologica*, IIa IIae, Q. 26, A. 5, and IIa IIae, Q. 64, A. 5.
39. Act v, scene 1.

XV

MIDDLE TEMPLE AND THE BAR

Plowden's father-in-law, William Sheldon, died on 23 December 1570. Some years earlier Sheldon had moved to Lower Skilts in Warwickshire, leaving his heir, Ralph, in possession of his estate at Beoley which had been the centre of his manifold activities for about a quarter of a century. Sheldon had bought the substantial estate of Lower Skilts from James Duffyld early in Elizabeth's reign, and had built there a house of brick on the site of a former Grange of the suppressed priory of Augustinian canons at Studley. It was there that he died. Some three weeks later he was buried with considerable funeral pomp in the chapel in Beoley church where his son later erected an imposing monument to his memory. Robert Cooke, Clarenceux king of arms, and other officers of arms travelled from London for his burial and among the mourners was Edmund Plowden.[1]

Plowden's long period in charge of the building of the new hall in the Middle Temple had now come to an end. There is no record of the completion of the building, but it seems likely that it was in use by the end of 1570 or soon thereafter. The hall, on which Plowden had lavished so much care, was a notable addition to the buildings of the Inn. Built of brick with stone dressings, it was 100 feet in length, including the passage behind the screen at the east end, and 40 feet wide save at the west end where bays on either side gave additional width. The principal feature of the hall was, and is, a splendid hammer beam roof, the graceful timbers of which impart to the room a unique and dignified charm. The screen was not erected until a few years later, the date usually given being 1574. The hall was provided with a fireplace, situated near the centre of the room, from which the smoke emerged into the open air through the lantern in the roof above; that fireplace no longer exists, having been removed as a result of an order of the benchers on 12 February 1830.

When the hall was first built the entrance was not surmounted by the present tower (which was added in 1832), but by two chambers. The space underneath the hall, now used for storage, cellarage and kitchens, was used for chambers, and there was another at the east end. On the dais at the west end of the hall stands the bench table which is over twenty-nine feet in length and made of polished oak; the oak is said to have come from trees in Windsor forest and to have been the gift of queen Elizabeth, and tradition has it that she also gave to the Inn the Cupboard or table which stands below the bench table. In the stained glass in the window of the south bay at the west end of the hall the central space is occupied by Plowden's name and arms, with the date 1573, together with a Latin inscription: 'Hoc perfecit opus legum cultoribus hujus maxima cura viri;

---

1. See Barnard, *The Sheldons*, 16, 17. Sheldon's will (P.C.C. 8 Horley), which is very long, was executed on 3 June 1570, and a codicil was added on 28 Sept. 1570; it was proved on 10 Feb. 1571.

sit honos his omne per aevum' (the very great care of this man brought this work to completion for those who cultivate the laws; to them be honour through all time). The date 1573 probably indicates the year in which the work of building and fitting out the hall was finished, but it must have been in use earlier, since the date 1570 was a prominent feature of the window behind the gallery over the screen.[2] At a Parliament held on 26 November 1571 Plowden submitted his accounts for the building of the hall, and Thomas Farmer, Gabriel Chambers, Matthew Dale and Fabian Phillips were appointed auditors.[3] Presumably the completion of the hall was marked by some sort of festivity, but the records of the Inn contain no mention of anything of the kind; the minutes of Parliament, however, consistently ignore all festivities unless they resulted in disciplinary measures against a member of the Inn.

The old hall was soon put to a new use in order to relieve the serious overcrowding of the Inn. None of the Inns was able at that time to accommodate all its members, and the survey made in 1574 shows that of the 190 members of the Middle Temple 60 had no chambers in the Inn.[4] The orders of 31 May 1574, by which the privy council had prohibited the building of more chambers in the Inns of Court, contained an exception in favour of the Inn which provided 'that in the Middle Temple they may convert their old hall into chambers, not exceeding the number of ten chambers.'[5] The Inn immediately took advantage of that permission. On 28 November 1574 Thomas Meade was admitted to a chamber 'to be newly built in the old hall', and in the following February the upper part of the old hall was assigned to Edward Fenner, John Agmondesham and John Boyes, to build chambers to be held for life; in November 1577 two chambers which had been built over the walls of the old hall by James and John Brett, Alexander Hamond and George Franklin, were assigned respectively to the two Bretts and to Hamond and Franklin for life, and in the following year eight chambers built by Alan Bellingham at the upper end of the old hall were granted to him for life.[6] The benchers evidently paid little heed to the limit imposed on the number of new chambers they could build.

At about the same time Bishop's Castle, the nearest town to Plowden's Shropshire home, received its first charter of incorporation; although in the past the town had received a number of privileges from the bishop of Hereford, whose property it was and from whom it derived its name, it had never achieved corporate status as a borough. On 16 July 1573 letters

2. *W.H.T.*, 229-33. Dugdale (*D.O.J.*, 188) gives 1572 as the date of completion of the hall.
3. *M.T.R.*, i, 183. Unfortunately, those accounts have disappeared.
4. See p. 110, *ante*.
5. *A.P.C.*, viii, 246; *M.T.R.*, i, 200; *I.T.R.*, i, 276; *B.B.*, i, 391; *D.O.J.*, 312.
6. *M.T.R.*, i, 203, 209, 218, 219. In Feb. 1584 William Nelson of the Inner Temple was admitted 'to the north part of the old hall where Mr. Forde kept his office', at a rent of 26s. 8d. p.a.; *M.T.R.*, i, 266. Edward Fenner was a bencher in 1576 and a serjeant in 1577 when he was knighted; he was appointed a judge of the King's Bench in 1590. John Boyes was a bencher in 1580 and Treasurer in 1598; he was knighted in 1603.

patent were sealed granting the town the status of a free borough and incorporating its inhabitants as the bailiff and burgesses of the borough of Bishop's Castle. The governing body was to consist of the bailiff and fifteen chief burgesses who were empowered to elect the bailiff from among their number and to co-opt new members. The letters patent named Robert Mason as the first bailiff, and among the chief burgesses were Plowden and his nephew, Andrew Blunden.[7]

Early in 1575 Plowden increased his property in Shropshire by the purchase of a lease of the rectory of Lydbury North which, like the manor which he had bought earlier, had been owned by the Augustinian Abbey of Wigmore until its suppression. Before Plowden's purchase, a lease of the rectory for twenty-one years, together with the tithes of corn and a yearly pension from the manor of Plowden (in lieu of tithes), had been granted to William Doddington by letters patent dated 11 July 1571; the grant was stated to have been made because Doddington first informed the queen that the rectory had been concealed at the time of the surrender of the monastery.[8] It seems that Plowden bought the lease and then procured the grant of a new lease to himself. Letters patent dated 9 February 1575 granted a lease of the rectory, together with the tithes and the pension, to Plowden for life with remainder as to one moiety to his eldest son Edmund, and as to the other moiety to his second son Francis, for life; the grant required the surrender of the patent granted to Doddington and it was stated, oddly enough, to have been made to Plowden because he was instrumental in recovering for the crown the premises which had been concealed at the surrender of the monastery.[9]

Meanwhile his professional life was as busy as ever, and only a few examples can be given. In 1570 he argued an important case in the Exchequer on behalf of Sir Henry Neville.[10] In 1530 the archbishop of Canterbury, William Warham, had granted to Sir Henry Neville and his father Sir Edward, for their joint lives and the life of the survivor, the office of keeper of the park and deer of the episcopal manor of Aldington, near Canterbury, together with an annual rentcharge issuing out of the manor. In 1538, however, Edward Neville was attainted of treason and executed for his part in the supposed conspiracy of the Poles and Henry Courtenay, marquis of Exeter. With the attainder of Edward Neville the crown claimed that the office and rentcharge had been forfeited, and since the death of queen Mary the rentcharge had not been paid. Eventually Sir Henry Neville, as survivor of the two grantees, petitioned the barons of the Exchequer for payment of the rentcharge, including all the arrears. The case was argued on demurrer in Easter Term 1570 and the court gave

7. *C.P.R., 1572-1575*, 14, 15; Weinbaum, *British Borough Charters, 1307-1660*, 95. *cf.* Dukes, *Antiquities of Shropshire*, 97-8; Eyton, *Antiquities of Shropshire*, xi, 203.

8. *C.P.R., 1569-1572*, 291. Doddington was auditor of the Exchequer, of first fruits and tenths, and of the Mint.

9. *C.P.R., 1572-1575*, 491. *cf.* Dukes, *Antiquities of Shropshire*, 270, 271. In 1591 the lease was renewed for three lives in favour of Francis, whose brother had died in 1587.

10. *Sir Henry Neville's Case* (1570), Plowd. 377.

judgment in Neville's favour; a writ then issued to the Treasurer and chamberlains of the Exchequer ordering them to pay all the arrears and to continue to pay the rentcharge every year.

Some three years later Plowden appeared for Sir Thomas Wroth in a similar case.[11] In October 1546, when Wroth was gentleman usher of the privy chamber to prince Edward (afterwards king Edward VI), Henry VIII by letters patent granted to him for life an annuity of £20. A few months later Henry VIII died and the annuity was never paid. Like Neville, Wroth eventually petitioned the barons for payment of the annuity. The case was argued on demurrer in the Exchequer in Trinity Term 1573 when Plowden appeared for Wroth. The court decided that Wroth was entitled to his annuity for life and, accordingly, a writ issued to the Treasuer and chamberlains of the Exchequer ordering them to pay all the arrears due up to the date of judgment and thereafter to pay the annuity to Wroth during the remainder of his life.

Those two cases are of importance because they were much discussed in *The Bankers' Case*[12] at the end of the seventeenth century, which had a considerable influence on the development of the petition of right as a remedy against the crown, and they formed the basis of the opinion of Holt, C. J., in that case, that money could be paid out of the Exchequer on the authority of an order of the court of Exchequer.

During the fifteen-seventies Plowden's name figured frequently in the reports. For example, in Easter Term 1572 he appeared for Lord Paget in a case concerning real property,[13] and in the following term he was concerned in a case relating to contingent remainders.[14] In Michaelmas Term of the same year he appeared in a case relating to the right to emblements. A man conveyed some of his land on trust, to the use of himself and his wife for their lives, but he died soon after sowing the land. The court held that the man's widow, and not his executors, were entitled to the crop, but subsequently, by the award of Dyer, C. J., and Plowden, the executors were awarded a fourth part of the threshed grain as recompense for the seed that produced the crop.[15]

Plowden's assistance was also sought by Edward Seymour, earl of Hertford, in his long drawn out struggle to re-establish his fortunes, and early in 1580 he drafted a number of petitions for submission by the earl to the queen. And in the complicated litigation against the earl by Lord Wentworth, Henry Knyvett and Henry Middlemore, which extended over many years and was not settled until 1580, Plowden was one of several distinguished lawyers who represented the earl, the others being John

11. *Sir Thomas Wroth's Case* (1573), Plowd. 452. Plowden's report of this case was read and revised by Saunders, C.B., who also supplied Plowden with the reasons of the judges, which were not stated in open court; see pp. 455, 459.

12. (1690–1700), 14 St. Tr. 1. *cf. H.E.L.*, ix, 32–9.

13. *Lord Paget's Case* (1572), Dyer 308, pl. 74.

14. Anon. (1572), Dyer 314, pl. 96.

15. Anon. (1572), Dyer 316, pl. 2. Emblements are growing crops of those vegetable productions of the soil which are annually produced by the labour of the cultivator.

Jeffrey and Roger Manwood, William Fleetwood, John Popham, Christopher Yelverton and Edward Baber.[16] In Easter Term 1574 he appeared with the solicitor-general, Thomas Bromley, and William Lovelace in an action relating to the title to some land which raised a technical point concerning discontinuance of possession; he was unsuccessful.[17]

In 1575 Plowden appeared in a case in the King's Bench where his argument touched upon England's early claims to sovereignty of the sea. The subject of fisheries in the North Sea and the waters surrounding the British Isles was of great importance in the Tudor period, but since the time of Edward III considerable liberty of action had been allowed to all foreign fishermen. The middle years of the sixteenth century, however, saw a rapid decay of the English sea fisheries, and the revival of the industry became an important political objective. The first published scheme for revitalizing the fishing industry was put forward by Dr. John Dee, that remarkable man who was philosopher, mathematician, antiquarian, political thinker and reputed magician. In 1577 Dee published his *Perfect Art of Navigation* in which he dealt with the fisheries and the boundaries of the British seas, and proposed that a tribute be exacted from foreign fishermen to be used for the maintenance of a naval force, which he called 'The Petty Navy Royal', for keeping the seas and supervising the fisheries.[18]

Two years before Dee's book appeared his political proposals had been given a legal foundation in Plowden's argument in *Sir John Constable's Case*.[19] The nature of the case seemed far removed from the topics dealt with by John Dee, as it arose on a *quo warranto* brought by the crown against Constable (for whom Plowden appeared) to inquire into his right to wreck of the sea taken on the foreshore adjoining his manor of Holderness on the coast of the East Riding of Yorkshire.[20] Constable pleaded that he took the wreck between the low water mark and firm land ('entre le low water mark et le firme terre adjoyant a le Manor du Holderness'); that the duke of Buckingham had been seized of the manor and that wreck of the sea had always been appurtenant to the manor; that

16. *H.M.C., Bath*, 178, 187-9.

17. Dyer 333b, pl. 30.

18. Dee, *General and Rare Memorials pertayning to the Perfect Arte of Navigation*. The book is only part of a much larger work, the remainder of which was never published; it is often known by its running title, *The Brytish Monarchie*. For a summary of Dee's views and proposals, see Fulton, *Sovereignty of the Sea*, 99-105.

19. The record of the case on the Coram Rege Roll is in P.R.O., K.B. 27/1254, Rex, rot, 2, mm. 1-3v; the argument for the crown is reported in 1 And. 86, and Plowden's argument is in Br. Lib., Harg. MS 15, ff. 95v-96v (a translation of which is printed in Moore, *History of the Foreshore*, 225-32). The case was followed in 1599 in *Sir Henry Constable's Case*, Br. Lib., Lansd. MS 1088, f. 69.

20. *Quo warranto* was a writ issuing out of the King's Bench against a person who claimed or usurped any office, franchise or liberty, to inquire by what authority he supported his claim, in order to determine the right. Wreck comprised such goods (including the ship or cargo or any part thereof) which, after a shipwreck, are afloat or cast upon the land by the sea. Wreck belonged to the crown, but a right to wreck was often granted to lords of manors.

Buckingham was attainted and the manor forfeited to the crown; that Philip and Mary granted it to the earl of Westmorland with wreck of the sea appertaining to the manor; and that the earl conveyed it to Constable who took the wreck in virtue of the right conveyed to him.

The attorney-general, Gilbert Gerard, appeared for the crown, and his argument was, in effect, that if wreck were appurtenant to the manor, it passed to the crown on the attainder of Buckingham and merged, and the general words of the patent granting the manor to Westmorland were insufficient to pass the right to wreck of the sea. It was also argued that, even if such a right were appurtenant to the manor, the foreshore, where the wreck was taken, could not be parcel of the manor nor of the county in which the manor was situated. It was in relation to the second limb of the crown's case that Plowden developed the wider aspects of his argument. As to that, he said, 'we ought to consider to what place the bounds of England extend, and then to whom the property of the sea and of the land under the sea belongs, and to whom belongs the property of the land between the greensward and the low-water mark, and within what county and parish the said soil is.' Plowden argued that 'the bounds of England' extended to 'the middle of the sea adjoining which surrounds the realm; but the queen has all the jurisdiction of the sea between France and this realm by reason of her title to France, and so it is of Ireland; but in other places, as towards Spain, she has only the moiety'.[21] It was the same, he said, with the sea as with great rivers.

Turning to the question of ownership, he said that 'although the queen has jurisdiction in the sea adjoining the realm, still she has not property in it, nor in the land under the sea, for it is common to all men, and she cannot prohibit any one from fishing there, and the water and the land under it are things of no value and the fish are always removable from one place to another.' Turning to the precise place where the wreck had been taken, he said that 'as to the property of the place between the greensward and the low-water mark, this belongs, as it seems to me, to him who has the greensward adjoining, and it is admitted by the queen, even in her quo warranto, that it is in the county adjoining, for she demands by what warrant we took the wreck in such a place within the county of York.'[22] After many adjournments the attorney-general entered a *nolle prosequi* in Easter Term 1579 and the action ceased.[23]

The 'bounds of England' as set out by Plowden in his argument were the same as those adopted by John Dee in his book published in 1577, but Dee asserted that the fisheries within those bounds should be appropriated

---

21. Br. Lib., Harg. MS 15, f. 95v; translation in Moore, *History of the Foreshore*, 227–8.

22. Br. Lib., Harg. MS 15, f. 96; translation in Moore, *History of the Foreshore*, 229–30.

23. P.R.O., K.B. 27/1254, Rex, rot. 2, m. 3v. The Coram Rege Roll recorded that 'predictus Gilbertus Gerrard, armiger . . . viso placito predicti Johannis Constable, militis, per ipsum in forma predicta superius placitato, maturaque deliberacione inde habita diligentaque [sic] per ipsum unacum litteris patentibus predictis ac Actu parliamenti et Indenturis predictis et plene intellectis, dicit quod ipse ulterius versus prefatum Johannem Constable, militem, in hac parte pro dicta domina Regina prosequi non vult. Ideo cessatur processus versus eum omnino.'

to England and a levy imposed on those who fished in them.[24] Plowden's argument owed something, no doubt, to the opinions of the Italian jurists such as Bartolus of Saxo-Ferrato and Baldus Ubaldus whose authority was then very high, but it was influential in a later period; in Stuart times it was developed, on somewhat different lines, by John Selden in his *Mare Clausum* and by Hugo Grotius in his *Mare Liberum*. In a sense, therefore, Plowden may be taken to have initiated the long continuing argument as to the bounds of England and the sovereignty of the seas.

In the following year Plowden was engaged in another *quo warranto* case, concerned with property near his own home of Plowden Hall.[25] In 1547 Edward VI had granted to Sir William Paget[26] the manor of Earnwood in Shropshire, together with three woods, all of which had formed part of the possessions of the earldom of March which had passed to the crown.[27] Three months after the grant had been made to him Paget conveyed the manor and woods to Thomas Seymour, the brother of Protector Somerset and recently created baron Seymour of Sudeley, but on Seymour's attainder for treason in 1549 his property was forfeited to the crown. In 1563 queen Elizabeth granted to Robert Dudley, later earl of Leicester, the manor, park and borough of Cleobury Mortimer together with 'all and every lands, woods, &c. belonging to the said manor of Cleobury Mortimer, or heretofore deemed part or parcel of the same manor.'[28] The three woods which Paget had conveyed to Seymour with the manor of Earnwood had been from time immemorial part of the manor of Cleobury Mortimer, and Leicester began to exercise rights of ownership in them. In 1576 the crown challenged his right to do so and proceedings by way of *quo warranto* were begun against two Cleobury yeomen, Richard Bishop and Thomas Thornton, who had entered upon the woods.

It was the contention of the crown that the three woods had been severed from the manor of Cleobury Mortimer and had remained in the hands of the queen when the grant was made to Leicester. The defence of the two yeomen was that they were merely acting as the servants and under the orders of Leicester who was the real defendant in the proceedings. Some ten years earlier Leicester had given Plowden a yearly retainer,[29] and Plowden appeared for the earl in the proceedings. The attorney-general, Gilbert Gerard, who appered for the queen argued that that part of the grant, already quoted, relating to the woods, was void for uncertainty,[30]

24. In 1579 Dee gave a fuller descripton of the limits of the British seas, in a tract which he wrote at the request of Sir Edward Dyer; see Br. Lib., Harl. MS 249, art. 13, and Royal MS 7. C. xvi, art. 35.
25. See Blakeway, in *T.S.A.S.*, 3rd ser., viii, (1908), 92–5.
26. Paget was created baron Paget of Beaudesert in 1549; he was one of the exectuors of the will of Henry VIII and a supporter of Protector Somerset.
27. When Edmund Mortimer, earl of March, died in 1424 without issue, his property went to his sister Anne, countess of Cambridge, whence it descended to her grandson, Edward IV.
28. Blakeway (op. cit., p. 94) gave the date of the grant as 7 June 1563; the Patent Rolls, however, date the grant as 9 June 1563 (*C.P.R., 1560-1563*, 543).
29. See p. 82, *ante*.
30. Blakeway (op. cit., 95) stated that the argument was that the grant was void for 'infinity'; that is clearly a slip and presumably 'uncertainty' was intended.

and he asserted that the woods had been severed from the manor of Cleobury Mortimer some sixteen or seventeen years before the grant to Leicester, that is, when Paget conveyed them to Seymour. Plowden had little difficulty in disposing of the argument that the grant of the woods was void, and he answered the remainder of his opponent's argument by pointing to the record where it was stated that at the time of the grant of Edward VI the woods were parcel of the manor of Cleobury Mortimer. The court accepted Plowden's argument and gave judgment for Leicester.

In Michaelmas Term 1577 he was concerned, in *Calverley's Case*, with contingent remainders, a topic that was then undergoing development at the hands of the lawyers. The case is one of several instances which show the high regard in which Plowden's exposition of a point of law was held by his fellow practitioners, for copies of his argument (and of that of his opponent, John Popham, who later became chief justice of the King's Bench) began to circulate among lawyers, and at least five of them are still in existence.[31] His argument in another case on contingent remainders, perhaps argued in Trinity Term 1581, was also widely circulated.[32]

31. Br. Lib., Harl. MS 6707, ff. 85-87; Camb. Univ. Lib., MS Ii.v. 20, ff. 7v-11; Bodl., Rawl, MS C.85, ff. 152v-164v; Longleat Ho., MS 240, ff. 116v-120; Harvard Law Sch., MS 2079, ff. 57-63. Dyer, in his report of the case which is confined to the wardship aspect, said (Dyer 354b) 'And therefore it seems to me that the opinion of Plowden is reasonable' (Et ideo il semble a moy, que l'opnion de Plowden est reasonable).

32. Br. Lib., Harl. MS 6707, ff. 87v-89 (headed 'Le opinion de Ed Plowden de midle temple en un case touchante le toller per lacte del tenant de terr, le futur vse appoint de surder'); Lansd. MS 1078, ff. 104-106; Harg. MS 15, ff. 6-9v; Harg. MS 373, ff. 88-97; Lincoln's Inn Lib., Mayn. MS 29, ff. 252-257, and Misc. MS 361, f. 152v. All the reports have a similar heading.

XVI

MORE RELIGIOUS DIFFICULTIES

For Plowden the year 1577 was not only busy but vexatious. On 14 March 1577 the privy council ordered that a letter be sent to Plowden informing him that, as 'certain rogues naming themselves Egyptians' had been apprehended in Berkshire after the Assizes were over, a special commission of oyer and terminer had been sent to the Berkshire justices specially for the trial of the gypsies; Plowden was appointed a commissioner 'for the better assistance of the justices there', and as some of the gypsies were charged with high treason he was 'required to make his repair forthwith into the said county' and there assist the justices with his counsel and advice. The sheriff and justices of Berkshire were informed of those arrangements and, since other gypsies of the same troop had been arrested in Oxfordshire, the sheriff of Oxfordshire was instructed to send them to Berkshire for trial with the others.[1]

At about that time Plowden was concerned with a west country quarrel between the two Dorset towns of Weymouth and Melcombe Regis. For many years the two towns had disputed the ownership and profits of the harbour that divided them until parliament in 1571 hoped to put an end to the wrangling by passing 'An Acte for thincorporacion and unitinge of Weymouthe and Melcombe Regis in Dorsett Shiere.' The Act did not have the desired effect, and eventually the privy council decided to intervene because, since the passing of the Act, 'between the inhabitants of either town sundry jars have risen concerning certain petty customs challenged to be proper to either town'. Accordingly, the council committed the matter to the solicitor-general (Sir Thomas Bromley), Plowden, Edmund Anderson and George Fettiplace for the purpose of bringing the quarrels to an end. They were not successful and the council noted that 'there hath not been such end made therein as were convenient'. The council was forced to take further action and in June 1577 they wrote to the judges of Assize instructing them to examine two persons from each town who had been sent to them by the council, and ordering the judges 'to make some final end therein according to justice, that they may be thoroughly quieted and their lordships not further troubled therewith.' Their lordships were disappointed; the judges were no more successful than Plowden and his colleagues had been, and the 'jars' continued for years to come.[2]

In 1577 the government and leading churchmen were becoming concerned at the increase in the number of papists in the country, whose attitude towards attendance at church had become stiffer since the first seminary priests had arrived in England in 1574. In the summer of 1577 the

1. *A.P.C.*, ix, 311–2.
2. *A.P.C.*, ix, 368. For an account of the long dispute between the two towns, see Weinstock, *More Dorset Studies*, 5–17. The Act of Parliament was not printed in *Statutes of the Realm*, but see the table of p. xxxi of vol. 4.

newly appointed bishop of London, John Aylmer, wrote to Sir Francis
Walsingham about the matter: he said that he and the archbishop of
Canterbury had 'received from divers of our brethren, bishops of this
realm, that the papists do marvellously increase, both in number and in
obstinate withdrawing of themselves from the church and service of God'.
Aylmer considered that the penalties hitherto inflicted on papists had been
largely ineffective and he urged Walsingham to persuade the queen that in
future heavy fines should be imposed and their payment exacted in every
case.[3] Although the government did not adopt the policy of inflicting heavy
financial penalties on Catholics until 1581, the necessary first step was
taken in October 1577 when the privy council ordered the bishops to make
returns of all the recusants in their dioceses, setting out their names and
the value of their lands and goods.[4]

A month later, however, the council realized that there had been 'omitted
the Inns of Court, which last two [sic][5] places [are] greatly infected with
popery'. The council therefore directed, on 17 November 1577, that a
letter be sent to the lord keeper, Sir Nicholas Bacon, because they 'do
think it meet (the said Inns being privileged places and under his lordship's
jurisdiction) to desire him forthwith to appoint in every such Inn some
persons well affected in religion to take the charge to inquire of the
recusants, and to deliver unto his lordship a perfect certificate of their
names and values as near as they may.' The lord chief justice was directed
to take the like course with the Inns of Chancery.[6] The certificates
demanded by the council were returned by the end of the month, and the
short time taken to make the neccessary inquiries is reflected in the frequent
omission of christian names and places of origin, while the 'values' of
those appearing in the certificates are given in only a few cases.[7]

The investigation of the Middle Temple was undertaken by two benchers,
William Fleetwood and John Popham, at a time when Fleetwood was very
active hunting papists in and around London.[8] The first three names in the

3. John Aylmer, bishop of London to Secretary Walisngham, 21 June 1577 (P.R.O., S.P.
12/114/22; printed in *C.R.S.*, vol. 22, pp. 1–2.

4. The letters of the privy council were dated 15 Oct. 1577; they are not registered in *A.P.C.*
but the date is frequently mentioned in the letters from the bishops enclosing their returns. An
amended draft of the letter is in P.R.O., S.P. 12/116/15. The bishops' returns (but not the
covering letters, save that from the archbishop of York) are printed in *C.R.S.*, vol. 22,
pp. 1–101, 108–14. For a discussion of them, see Trimble, *Catholic Laity in Elizabethan
England*, 81–8; and for a criticism of Professor Trimble's methods, see Manning, *Religion and
Society in Elizabethan Sussex*, 255–8.

5. The Innter Temple and Middle Temple were (and are) extra-parochial, and so not subject
to episcopal jurisdiction; see *W.H.T.*, 395, 480.

6. *A.P.C.*, x, 94, 95.

7. The certificates, each dated Nov. 1577, are as follows: P.R.O., S.P. 12/118/68 (Middle
Temple): S.P. 12/118/69 (Inner Temple);S.P. 12/118/70 (Lincoln's Inn); S.P. 12/118/71
(Gray's Inn). They are printed in *C.R.S.*, vol. 22, pp. 101–7, and the certificate for the Inner
Temple is also printed in *I.T.R.*, i, pp. liv–lvi. The certificate for the Inns of Chancery is in
P.R.O., S.P. 12/118/38 i and is printed in *C.R.S.*, vol. 22, pp. 107–8. The certificates appear
to be confined to papists and do not include any puritans.

8. See Harris, in *R.H.*, vii (1963–4), 106–22.

certificate, under the heading 'These forbear to come to church here at the Temple', were those of Edmund Plowden, Walter Curson and William Cowper, with the note, 'what they do in the country or what livelihood they be of we know not.' Altogether the certificate named twenty-six recusants which was approximately fourteen per cent of the total mebership of the Inn enumerated in the survey of of 1574.[9] The certificate, however, included the names of some who had been expelled earlier for religious reasons, or had fled abroad or been reconciled; if those names are deducted from the total number recorded in the certificate, there were only six recusants in the Middle Temple, or about three per cent. Nevertheless there are substantial reasons for thinking that all the certificates, and especially that relating to the Middle Temple, seriously underestimated the number of papists in the Inns of Court.[10] A noteworthy omission from the Middle Temple certificate was the name of Matthew Smith, a papist who had been elected Treasurer on 8 December 1570 and had then appointed another papist, Thomas Pagitt, as Under Treasurer.[11]

Soon after the Middle Temple certificate had been returned some Protestant members of the Inn complained to the privy council about Plowden's papist activities, and among other matters of complaint was his conduct in relation to the compilation of the certificate. It was said that 'he opposed himself openly against such benchers as furthered that certificate', so that not all the papists in the Inn were included in it; thus, when the names of twenty-four members 'known or suspected for papists were by good search of such as were appointed to the purpose presented to the benchers, whereof some have forsaken the realm as it is affirmed by such as seem to know it, none at all were certified', and it was asserted that Plowden arranged for his own means to be omitted from the certificate contrary to the requirements of the council. It was said, quite correctly, that ever since 'the Bull came in that Felton was executed for [*Regnans in Excelsis*]' Plowden had not come to church or received the sacrament, and it was also said that when he was admonished, by order of the queen and the privy council, to conform himself, he refused to do so and arranged for the person who had admonished him to be put out of commons. A rather frivolous complaint asserted that, when Henry VIII had been commended 'for rooting out the pope and his power', Plowden had openly called him a 'great slouch' who was like 'a bull in a common and that Justice Mountegue [Sir Edward Montague] was his butcher to execute whom he would.' Further complaints asserted that Plowden tried to ensure 'that none should be called to the bench but such as will bear with these abuses', and that 'by his practice and [the] friendship that he procureth, and the severity and sincerity of other houses, the Middle Temple is

9. See p. 110, *ante*.
10. For an analysis of the certificates and a discussion of their shortcomings, see Parmiter, *Elizabethan Popish recusancy in the Inns of Court*, 21-9.
11. See p. 108, *ante*. Pagitt's name appears in the certificate of 1577 under the heading, 'These have been removed from the fellowship for a time and after reconciled and so contynue as we thinke'.

pestered with papists and not to be amended without your honours' especial aid'; despite those assertions, the draftsman went on to say that 'the most of that Society [Middle Temple] and all the best affected in religion except some two or three of his [Plowden's] dearest and most familiar friends' were anxious that Plowden's activities should be stopped. In asking the council to provide a remedy it was said that Plowden 'applieth all his forces and friendship to suppress religion and the professors thereof, and to prefer papists and their superstition'.[12] The author of that ill drafted document is unknown, but it seems fairly clear that his statements could have represented the opinions of only a handful of the members of the Inn; the council seems to have taken a realistic view of it, and the complaint went unheeded.

While he was still embroiled in the difficulties surrounding the return of papists for the privy council, an event took place in the recently completed hall of the Middle Temple which must have given Plowden much pleasure. He had devoted much time and effort to the building and beautifying of the hall, and in Michaelmas Term 1577 it was used for the Serjeants' Feast which is the earliest recorded entertainment given in the new hall. By the end of 1576 death and promotions to the bench had reduced the number of serjeants to three: Nicholas Powtrell, a serjeant since 1558, Thomas Meade of the Middle Temple who had received the coif in 1567, and old William Bendlowes who had been a serjeant for more than twenty years. To make up their number the queen called seven new serjeants of whom only one, Edward Fenner, was a member of the Middle Temple; the others were William Ayloff, Edward Baber and Francis Wyndham, all of Lincoln's Inn, Francis Gawdy and Edmund Anderson of the Inner Temple, and Robert Shute of Gray's Inn. The visit of the new serjeants to the courts at Westminster in order to be sworn, had had to be postponed to November on account of the plague;[13] that ceremony was followed by the Serjeants' Feast customarily given by the new serjeants to a large and distinguished company. In the course of the ceremonies at Westminster the new serjeants were required to listen to several lengthy exhortations, including one from the chief justice of the Common Pleas, Sir James Dyer, who, among other things, 'did counsel them not to use delays, nor to give deceitful counsel to take away any man's right by untrue vouchers, . . . not to be captious one upon another, nor to mock one another, but to be discreet, to ride with six horses and their sumpter in long journeys'.

For the feast in the hall of the Middle Temple, the new serjeants and their guests were accommodated at four tables: privy councillors and

12. P.R.O., S.P. 12/144/45; there is a copy in S.P. 12/144/46. The document is unsigned and undated; it is endorsed '2 Decembre 1580'. The complaincte against Mr. Plowden', but since opposition to the certificate is stated to have occurred 'in conference this terme about the execucion thereof', the true date of the document appears to be Dec. 1577.

13. Robert Ball, of the Middle Temple, had been called to the degree of serjeant-at-law in Jan. 1577, and was immediately thereafter raised to the position of chief baron of the Exchequer; he died of the plague in July of the same year and was one of the many victims of the notorious 'Black Assizes' at Oxford.

noblemen sat at the upper table; the Lord Mayor of London and the aldermen sat at a table on the south side of the hall, while on the north side was a table for the new serjeants; a long table in the centre of the hall accommodated the judges, the barons of the Exchequer, the Master of the Rolls, the old serjeants and the law officers; and the whole company was served by the officers of the feast and the young gentlemen of the Middle Temple. The new serjeants, waring their robes and coifs, were separated from each other by a space of two yards, and each was attended by his carver, cup-bearer and sewer who came from the new serjeant's old Inn; 'and so', observed Dugdale, 'they dine with sober countenances and little communication.'[14] If the new serjeants did not derive much enjoyment from the feast, it seems that their guests did.

14. *D.O.J.*, 119-27.

XVII

PROFESSIONAL LIFE

In 1578 Plowden and the solicitor-general, Thomas Bromley, together advised Sir Nicholas Lestrange who had been chamberlain of the duke of Norfolk's household until the duke's downfall in 1571, for which they received thirty shillings. In the following year Bromley was appointed lord chancellor and knighted, and in Trinity Term 1580 he went out of his way, when on the bench, to state the good opinion he had of 'the great discretion, circumspection and honesty of Mr. Plowden'.[1]

It was about that time that Plowden gave assistance to a fellow Catholic, Francis Tregian of Golden, not far from Truro in Cornwall, who had been arrested on serious charges. Tregian was a well known recusant who had two notable enemies, each for his own reasons bent on Tregian's ruin: Richard Grenville, then sheriff of the county, with whom Tregian had earlier fallen out, and Sir George Carey, the Knight Marshal and a cousin of the queen, who was anxious to gain possession of Tregian's estate. One of the first of the seminary priests to come to England, Father Cuthbert Mayne, had lived at Golden disguised as Tregian's steward since his arrival in the west country in the spring of 1576. In the summer of 1577 Tregian's house was raided by the sheriff and his assistants, and Mayne, Tregian and a number of others were arrested. When the house was searched there were found among Mayne's possessions an *Agnus Dei* and a copy of the papal bull proclaiming the Jubilee Year of 1575 and the indulgences that could be obtained in that year. Those were dangerous possessions as a statute of 1571[2] made it treason to obtain from Rome any bull containing anything whatsoever, and also made it a *praemunire* to aid or maintain a person obtaining such a bull; the same Act made it a *praemunire* to bring into the realm or receive any *Agnus Dei*.

Father Mayne, Tregian and several others were sent to Launceston gaol and interrogated. As a resul of those interrogations and of the interrogations ordered by the privy council, seven indictments were preferred against Mayne, Tregian and the others, and their trial was to take place at the Winter Assizes which were due to open at Launceston on 16 September 1577. Meanwhile, however, Tregian had been summoned to London by the privy council and he appeared there on 12 September; on the last day of that month he was committed close prisoner in the Marshalsea in the custody of the Knight Marshal, Sir George Carey.

In the absence of the assize records and because of the confusing nature of contemporary and later accounts, it is not easy to determine the course of the complicated legal proceedings that followed. It seems, however, that despite Tregian's enforced absence in the London prison, the trials

1. Gurney, in *Archaeologia*, xxv (1834), at p. 565. Bromley's observation is quoted from Cooper, *Athenae Cantabrigienses*, i, 502. For Nicholas Lestrange, see *D.N.B.* and Neale, *Elizabethan House of Commons*, 195.
2. 13 Eliz. I, c. 2 (see p. 102, *ante*).

of those charged on the indictments, including Tregian, proceeded at Launceston on 16 September before the two assize judges, Roger Manwood, then a judge of the Common Pleas, and John Jeffrey, then a judge of the King's Bench. The most serious of all the charges were that Father Mayne had obtained a bull of absolution from Rome and that Tregian had aided and maintained him, and also that Father Mayne brought an *Agnus Dei* into the realm and that Tregian had received it. On the first of those charges, Father Mayne said that the bull found in his possession was, in fact, a copy of the bull proclaiming the Jubilee of 1575, which had been printed in Douai where he had bought it. He argued that as the bull had expired on the last day of 1575 it was no longer an effective bull and that, being a copy printed in Douai, it was not a bull obtained from Rome. According to the account written by Tregian's son, the sheriff, Grenville, rose from his place in court and urged one of the witnesses in a menacing manner to make a statement damaging to Tregian, and the judges apparently allowed him to do so. The jury did not take long to reach a verdict, but when they returned to court Grenville again left his place, in the sight of the judges, and spoke to the jury very vehemently. The jury found all the prisoners guilty on all the charges.

At the *allocutus*, when the prisoners were asked whether they had anything to say why sentence should not be passed upon them, Father Mayne again put forward his argument that the bull was no longer effective and had not been obtained from Rome. That argument seems to have made an impression on Jeffrey, but Manwood took the view that the date of expiry was irrelevant; a whispered discussion between the judges then took place which Manwood cut short, saying that he would give judgment. Father Mayne, as a convicted traitor, was sentenced to be hanged, drawn and quartered, and Tregian, although he was not present and had not pleaded to the indictment, was sentenced to the penalties of *Praemunire*.

The validity of Tregian's conviction and sentence was open to question and the matter was referred to the privy council, probably by Jeffrey. Tregian was summoned to appear before the council once more. Grenville, however, was determined that the sentence should stand, and he immediately went to London and persuaded the privy council to issue a warrant for the execution of Father Mayne who was put to death at Launceston on 30 September 1577.

Meanwhile, on 12 October, Tregian wrote a letter from his 'close cabin in the Marshalsea' to the earl of Leicester, a connection of his wife, in which he complained of the envy and malice of his enemies who wished to despoil him of his property. He asked for Leicester's help in order that 'my indictments may be removed by the common process of *certiorari* into her Majesty's Bench, that there I may receive ordinary trial, by the law, of mine innocency'.[3] Leicester does not appear to have given him any

---

3. Br. Lib., Cotton MS Titus B. vii, f. 46; in the version of the letter printed in Boyan and Lamb, *Francis Tergian* (at p. 53) there is an omission of a whole phrase from the relevant passage.

assistance, but his friends succeeded in obtaining a writ of *certiorari* to remove his indictments into the King's Bench.[4] The indictments now being in the King's Bench, Tregian was permitted the assistance of counsel to argue those points of law that arose, and on 9 June 1578 the privy council instructed the Knight Marshal to allow Tregian to consult, in Carey's presence, serjeant Thomas Gawdy and Plowden. The argument put forward by Gawdy and Plowden seems to have been a strong one, so that the Knight Marshal, fearing that Tregian might succeed, as many lawyers seemed to think he would, contrived to have judgment stayed until the end of Trinity Term brought about an automatic adjournment of the case; meanwhile Carey persuaded the privy council to order Tregians's return to Launceston to stand his trial there at the next assizes. That was done and Tregian was convicted and sentenced to the penalties of *Praemunire*. As a result he was stripped of all his property which was later given to Carey; Tregian himself remained in prison until 1601 when he was released on parole, and two years later he went abroad and died in Lisbon in 1608.[5]

Even the greatest of lawyers occasionally makes a mistake and Plowden was no exception, but Plowden's contemporaries seem to have thought that even his mistakes were worthy of being recorded. William Leonard, the reporter, noted a case heard in 1578 in which Plowden had given bad advice to a sheriff with regard to a writ of extent. The judge, Roger Manwood, observed that the sheriff's return to the writ was insufficient and tactfully remarked that 'perhaps Master Plowden did not know' of an entry on the roll which indicated that execution had not taken place.[6] Another and more serious mistake was recounted by William Hudson in his treatise on the Star Chamber. In the sixteenth century a theory had grown up that the court of Star Chamber owed its origin to the statute 3 Hen. VII, c. 1, of 1487, and that the jurisdiction of the court was limited by its provisions, whereas the statute, like earlier Acts, had merely defined some branches of the council's jurisdiction which the circumstances of the time had rendered especially important. The theory was not in accord with historical fact and was condemned by the leading lawyers of the day. Nevertheless, on one occasion Plowden inadvertently subscribed to the theory, which provided Lord Chancellor Egerton with an anecdote he liked to tell and which illustrates the esteem in which Plowden was held by his colleagues. Hudson wrote:

'I well remember that the Lord chancellor Egerton would often tell, that in his time, when he was a student, Mr. Serjeant Lovelace put his

4. According to the account written by Tregian's son in 1593 (Oscott MS 545, printed in Morris, *Troubles*, 1st ser., 63-140; see p. 100), his friends obtained 'a writ of *capias*', but in view of Tregian's own letter to Leicester, and because none of the various writs of *capias* was appropriate in the circumstances, it has been assumed that the writ in question was *certiorari*.

5. For the proceedings against Tregian see Oscott MS 545 (printed in Morris, *Troubles*, 1st ser., 63-140); Inspeximus dated 5 June 1581 preserved in the church of the Englsih Martyrs, Launceston; *A.P.C.*, x, 6, 7, 29, 41, 85, 249, 259, 276-7, 279, and xi, 231-2, 237, 241, 380, *H.M.C.*, *Rutland*, i, 113; Rowse, *Tudor Cornwall*, 346-54; Boyan and Lamb, *Francis Tregian*, 45-83.

6. *Colshil and Hastings' Case* (1578), 2 Leon. 12, at p. 13.

hand to a demurrer in this court, for that the matter of the bill contained other matters than were mentioned in the statute of 3 Hen. VII, and Mr. Plowden, that great lawyer, put his hand thereto first, whereupon Mr. Lovelace easily followed. But the cause being moved in court, Mr. Lovelace, being a young man, was called to answer the error of his ancient, Mr. Plowden, who very discreetly made his excuse at the bar, that Mr. Plowden's hand was first unto it, and that he supposed that he might in anything follow St. Augustine.'[7]

Just as St. Augustine of Hippo was the oracle of the schools of theology, so in his time was Plowden the oracle of the law.

In 1579 Plowden was engaged in the last stages of an important case that had begun ten years earlier. The case arose on a bill of intrusion, exhibited in Hilary Term 1569, and was concerned with the title of the crown to extensive landed property in Kent forfeited on the attainder of Sir Thomas Wyatt after his unsuccessful rising in the reign of queen Mary.[8] The case was argued on demurrer in the Exchequer in Michaelmas Term 1571 when serjeant Nicholas Barham and Plowden appeared for the queen, and serjeant Roger Manwood and John Bullock for the plaintiffs Thomas Walsingham and John Gillibrand. After a long argument judgment was eventually given for the queen. However, it so happened that the Common Pleas, in a case raising precisely the same legal issue, had given judgment the other way, a circumstance that encouraged Walsingham and Gillibrand to bring their case into the Exchequer Chamber on a writ of error. It was first argued there in Trinity Term 1578 when Henry Beaumont appeared for the plaintiffs in error and Edward Flowerdew for the queen. The full argument took place in Hilary Term of the following year when serjeant Thomas Gawdy appeared for the plaintiffs in error and Plowden appeared alone for the queen as serjeant Barham had been one of those who died during the notorious 'Black Assize' held at Oxford in the summer of 1577. The argument took place before the lord keeper, Sir Nicholas Bacon, the lord treasurer, Sir William Cecil, and all the judges of the King's Bench. The argument was a long one and towards its close Plowden raised a point on the pleadings; he asserted that the defect was such that it 'would prevent the reversal of the judgment, let the matter in law turn out how it might'. After the close of the argument the case was adjourned to the second Saturday in Easter Term, but in the intervening vacation, on 19 February 1579, Bacon died and the writ of error abated. Thomas Bromley was

7. Hudson, *Treatise concerning the Court of Star Chamber*, written apparently in the reign of James I, and printed, not altogether accurately, in Hargrave, *Collectanea Juridica*, ii, 1-240; see p. 51, and *cf.* Hawarde, *Les Reportes del Cases in Camera Stellata*, 301-2. There is a substantial number of manuscript copies of Hudson's treatise still extant (e.g., Br. Lib., Lansd. MS 622, Harl. MSS 736, 1226, 1689, 4274, 6235, 6256, Harg. MSS 251, 290, 291, Stowe MS 419, Add. MSS 11681, 26647; Huntington Lib. MS E1 7921; Bodl., Douce MS 66) of which the most reliable is generally agreed to be Harl. MS 1226. William Lovelace, of Gray's Inn, was advanced to the degree of serjeant-at-law in 1567; he had appeared with Plowden in several cases, for instance, on behalf of Bonner in 1564 (see p. 78, *ante*), and in an action heard in 1574 (see p. 124, *ante*).

8. *Walsingham's Case*. Plowd. 547; and see p. 38, *ante*.

appointed lord chancellor on 26 April and a new writ of error was then obtained. Eventually the lord chancellor announced that the court were all agreed that the judgment below should be affirmed, and he ordered the Queen's Remembrancer to enter judgment accordingly. Thereupon Plowden asked the lord chancellor what was the ground of the judgment; was it the matter in law or was it the point of pleading? The lord treasurer replied 'that they themselved knew the causes thereof well enough, but that it was not necessary for them to show it openly.' That answer did not satisfy Plowden and in a note at the end of his report of the case he recorded that he made private but unsuccessful efforts to discover the reasons for the judgment.

It has often been asserted that queen Elizabeth I offered Plowden the office of lord chancellor if he would change his religion and that Plowden refused.[9] There is now in existence no written evidence to support the assertion, although in the Plowden family and in the legal profession (especially in Plowden's own Inn, the Middle Temple) there is a tradition that he did receive an invitation from the queen to accept the office of lord chancellor. Support for that tradition has been found in two documents said to have been in the possession of the Plowden family which are no longer in existence. The first was the offer itself. Serjeant Woolrych, whose work was published in 1869, stated categorically, 'A letter has been preserved at Plowden Hall, the ancestral mansion, written by Queen Elizabeth to the Serjeant [i.e., Plowden] containing an offer to make him Lord chancellor, if he would consent to change his religion'.[10] The text of the letter has not survived. Serjeant Woolrych, followed by Miss Barbara Plowden, stated that it had been lost in rather curious circumstances. He said that Mr. Edmund Plowden, who died in 1838, told the resident chaplain at Plowden Hall that he had found among the family papers a letter from queen Elizabeth to Plowden offering him the office of lord chancellor if he would change his religion. The chaplain believed that Mr. Edmund Plowden lent the letter to a lawyer of his acquaintance who died soon afterwards without returning the letter.

The second document is the letter in which Plowden is said to have refused the queen's invitation; the text, as printed by Serjeant Woolrych for the first time, is as follows:

'Hold me, dread sovereign, excused. Your Majesty well knows I find no reason to swerve from the Catholic faith, in which you and I were

9. E.g., Woolrych, *Lives of Eminent Serjeants*, i, 114–6; *B.M.P.*, 17–8; Strickland, *Lives of the Queens of England*, iii, 544; Foley, *Records*, iv, 538–9; *H.E.L.*, v, 372 (Holdsworth qualifies the statement with the phrase 'it is said'); O'Sullivan, *Edmund Plowden*, 20 (O'Sullivan qualifies the statement with the phrase 'it seems likely'). An earlier account of the traditional story was printed in 1805 in Plowden, *Historical letter from Francis Plowden*, at pp. 30, 31; the relevant passage in this rare pamphlet contains several factual errors (I am indebted for this reference to Mr. Clifford Llewis 3rd of Media, Penn., U.S.A.). Francis Plowden died in 1829.

10. Woolrych, *Lives of Eminent Serjeants*, i, 114. No such letter now exists at Plowden Hall. It is a tribute to Plowden's reputation that serjeant Woolrych claimed him among his eminent serjeants, describing him as 'an ornament to our history', although Plowden was never a serjeant.

brought up. I can never contenance the persecution of its professors. I should not have in charge your Majesty's conscience one week before I should incur your displeasure, if it be your Majesty's royal intent to continue the sytem of persecuting the retainers of the Catholic faith.'[11] That document also is no longer in existence. Serjeant Woolrych said that it was taken from a copy, adding in a footnote that it was 'copied from Miss Eliza Plowden's papers'.[12] The nature of the copy is not indicated; we have no knowledge of when or why the copy was made, nor of the date when the original disappeared, and there is no recorded statement by anyone who saw the original document. It is, moreover, questionable whether a cautious lawyer of the sixteenth century would have employed the language attributed to him by serjeant Woolrych.

If such an offer had been made to Plowden, the most probable time of the incident was during the interval of some eight weeks between the death of Bacon and the appointment of Bromley, when Plowden was appearing for the queen in *Walsingham's Case*. There are, however, several reasons for doubting the truth of the traditional story. Indeed, the story of the queen's offer to Plowden does not stand alone; it is one of a series of similar stories which describe the offer by the queen of a position of importance to well known Catholics in return for their change of religion. Thus, it has been said that John Feckenham, the last abbot of Westminster who stoutly maintained his religious faith, and Father Edmund Campion, S.J., who died a martyr, where each offered the see of Canterbury; Francis Tregian was said to have been offered a viscounty; and it has also been said that the woolsack was offered to Sir Anthony Browne, the Catholic judge, when Bacon was in temporary disgrace on suspicion of having assisted John Hales in the preparation of his succession tract.[13] It is not improbable that the account of the offer to Plowden is one of those cases where a stock story has been successively attached to the names of well known persons.

During the closing years of the fifteen-seventies Plowden was engaged in a good many heavy cases. For instance, in 1579 he was one of the lawyers who composed the differences between the archbishops of Canterbury and York which arose over a lease of some property in Battersea in Surrey. The origin of the dispute went back some years. The dean and chapter of York owned a house in Battersea, together with about eighty acres of land, which was used for the convenience of the archbishops when they came to London for sessions of parliament or attendance at court. The property had been let on a long lease, one of the terms of which

11. Woolrych, *Lives of Eminent Serjeants*, i, 115; it is also printed, from Woolrych, in *B.M.P.*, 18, and Hamilton, *Chronicle of the English Augustinian Canonesses*, i, 222.
12. Woolrych, op. cit., i, 115; Miss Eliza Plowden was the daughter of Francis Plowden who died in Paris in 1829.
13. For a discussion of the traditional story and for a consideration of some reasons for doubting its truth, see Parmiter, in *Downside Review*, xc (1972), 251-9; for the example of Brown (not mentioned in that article) see Doleman, *Conference about the next succession* (1594), pt. 2, pp. 1-2, *cf.* Titler, in *Downside Review*, xcii (1974), 62-7.

required the tenant to vacate the property whenever the archbishop wished to reside there. That lease came into the hands of one, Hill, who disliked the condition of the lease which required him to vacate the premises from time to time; he ploughed up the land and kept it in tillage, while he made the house so incommodious that it could not be used as a lodging for the archbishop. Things became so bad that Thomas Young, who was archbishop of York from 1561 to 1568, tried to evict Hill and recover the property at Battersea; the case was mishandled, however, and judgment was given against Young who was also ordered to pay Hill £60 damages.

That success emboldened Hill to make matters even more awkward for the archbishop, and he began felling timber and suing the archbishop's workmen for trespass. When Edmund Grindal succeeded Young as archbishop of York in 1570 he began looking for means to rid himself of his troublesome tenant. Eventually he consulted Thomas Bromley, then solicitor-general, William Ayloff, who in 1577 was appointed a judge of the King's Bench, Plowden and 'Mr. Wilbraham'.[14] The lawyers advised the archbishop that the lease to Hill was void and that a new lease should be granted to the archbishop. Accordingly, the dean and chapter granted a lease of the Battersea property to the archbishop for his life; and subsequently, with a view to getting rid of Hill, the archbishop granted a sub-lease for twenty-one years to Richard Ratcliff and Richard Frampton, two of his servants. When, however, Grindal was translated to Canterbury in 1576 and Edwin Sandys was enthroned as archbishop of York in 1577, the latter took exception to Grindal's retention of the lease, and a dispute developed between the two archbishops. Sandys complained that Grindal, by failing to surrender the lease when he was translated to Canterbury, had acted to the prejudice of the archbishop of York; Grindal, on the other hand, said that he had retained the lease in order to protect his sub-lessees whose tenancies the new archbishop of York had called in question. Plowden and his fellow lawyers appear to have been able to bring about a settlement without recourse to litigation.[15]

The year 1579 also saw the culmination of some lengthy legal proceedings in which Plowden was successful in protecting the interests of several Cheshire gentlemen in some property claimed by the dean and chapter of Chester.[16] The dispute originated in the reign of Edward VI when Sir Richard Cotton, the comptroller of the king's household, was instrumental in securing the imprisonment in the Fleet of William Clyffe, the dean of Chester, and two of the prebendaries. While they were confined Cotton coerced them into conveying to himself almost all the estate, chiefly confiscated monastic lands, that had been granted by Henry VIII to the newly established diocese of Chester. Clyffe's two successors made

14. Strype, *Life of Grindal*, 366; there were two members of the Bar named Wilbraham whose initials were R. and T. respectively, but it is not known which of them is here referred to.

15. See Strype, *Life of Grindal*, 259-60, 364-7.

16. Copies of, or extracts from, many of the documents relating to the proceedings are contained in Br. Lib., Harl. MS 2060, art. 35; see also Harl. MS 2071.

strenuous efforts to set aside the conveyance to Cotton, and in the course of those efforts the chapter discovered that Henry's original grant was void because of the accidental omission of the word *Cestrie* in the decription of the grantees, thus failing to identify the particular ecclesiastical corporation to which the grant hade been made. That meant that the lands in question were still vested in the crown and that dean Clyffe and the prebendaries had no title to convey to Cotton. Accordingly, they petitioned queen Elizabeth to carry out her father's intention by making a fresh grant of the lands to the dean and chapter. Meanwhile, however, Cotton had realized that his own title was open to question and he made what he could out of the transaction by contriving quick sales of portions of the land to a number of Cheshire gentlemen who were glad to increase their landholdings at very modest prices.

As a result of the petition by the dean and chapter the matter was twice argued in the Exchequer, first by serjeant John Popham on behalf of the crown and by Thomas Egerton for the Cheshire gentlemen, and second by serjeant Thomas Gawdy for the crown and Plowden for the Cheshire men. Before judgment was given, however, Plowden's clients became aware, probably as a result of his advice, that they were likely to lose their case. Accordingly, they sought the help of the earl of Leicester and promised him six years' rent of the lands in dispute. What followed is a vivid illustration of one feature of the administration of the law in the sixteenth century. Leicester saw to it that the proceedings were stayed and a commission was issued for hearing the matter before the privy council, of which Leicester was himself a member. Eventually a compromise was reached, the sensible nature of which seems to reflect the influence of Plowden. All the parties to the dispute surrendered whatever interests they had to the queen, and in 1579 she granted the estates in question to the various gentlemen who claimed them, subject to certain rentcharges payable out of the respective estates; those rentcharges the queen then granted to the dean and chapter, and for many years they formed the principal part of the endowment of the diocese.[17]

Plowden appears to have had a retainer from the dean and chapter of Christ Church, Oxford, to advise them from time to time; on 8 November, 1580, he signed a receipt for £10 'for my whole year's fee due unto to me at the feast of St. Michael the archangel last past.'[18] He also had a retainer from the earl of Rutland who does not seem to have been so prompt to pay his fee as the dean and chapter; at any rate, in February 1584 the earl's agent, Thomas Screven, reminded him that he owed Plowden twenty marks for his annuity.[19]

In 1581 the corporation of Abingdon sought Plowden's advice in the curious comedy that arose out of the refusal of Thomas Tesdale to be mayor of Abingdon when he was elected to that office in 1581. Tesdale had been a clothier to the army but later, as a malster, he settled at

---

17. Br. Lib., Harl. MS 2060, art. 35; Harl. MS 2071; Lysons, *Magna Britannia*, ii, 573n.
18. Bodl., Tanner MS 283, f. 189v.
19. *H.M.C.*, *Rutland*, i, 160–1.

Abingdon where he took a considerable part in local affairs and, as might be expected of a man of considerable business ability, he progressed from one local office to another. In 1577 be became a governor of Christ's Hospital in Abingdon, of which he was master in 1580; and in 1580 he was elected principal burgess of Abingdon. About that time, however, he moved to Glympton in Oxfordhsire where he amassed a considerable fortune, part of which went, after his death, towards the endowment of Pembroke College in Oxford which was erected out of the existing foundation of Broadgates Hall. When, however, the corporation of Abingdon elected Tesdale mayor in 1581 he declined the office on the ground that he no longer lived in Abingdon; presumably his new and prospering busisness in Glympton left him little time in which to attend to the municipal affairs of Abingdon. On his refusal to be mayor the corporation committed him to prison, but he was excused on payment of a fine of forty shillings. Before ordering the imprisonment of Tesdale the corporation appears to have consulted Plowden, for the chamber accounts of the borough for the year 1580-1 show that the town clerk, John Hallywell, received the sum of twenty shillings which he had 'paid to Mr. Plowden for counsel about the election of Mr. Tesdall'.[20]

Towards the end of 1581 the trial and execution of the Jesuit, Father Edmund Campion, and others took place, events that made a considerable impact on several lawyers, especially those of Gray's Inn.[21] The trial took place in November in the King's Bench before the chief justice, Sir Christopher Wray, and two of his puisnes, William Ayloff and Thomas Gawdy. The prosecution was conducted by the Queen's Serjeant, Edmund Anderson, later chief justice of the Common Pleas, the attorney-general, John Popham, and the solicitor-general, Thomas Egerton. Wray, though careful to maintain in public an attitude of indifference in religious matters, was very probably of Catholic inclination; Gawdy, on the other hand, was sympathetic to puritanism, while Anderson had a hatred of every kind of non-conformity and it was, no doubt, his personal hostility and the violence of his language that did most to secure the conviction of Campion and his fellow prisoners. The trial attracted a good deal of attention, especially among the lawyers, and Plowden was among those who visited the court. It may be supposed that Wray had little relish for the task on which he was engaged, and when he saw Plowden among the crowd he sent a message asking him to withdraw; whereupon Plowden left the court.[22]

Plowden was still active in his own Inn. In the summer of 1580 a Parliament of the Middle Temple decided that all petitions for the erection of new buildings in the Inn should be referred to three benchers, Plowden, Matthew Dale and Myles Sandys.[23] It was about that time that the benchers

20. See Preston, *Church of St. Nicholas, Abingdon*, 429. For Thomas Tesdale, see *D.N.B.*, s.v. 'Tesdale, Teasdale or Tisdale, Thomas'.
21. *cf.* Parmiter, *Elizabethan Popish Recusancy in the Inns of Court*, 44–5.
22. Simpson, *Edmund Campion*, 307.
23. *M.T.R.*, i, 234 (20 June 1580). Dale became a bencher in 1575 and Sandys in 1578 (Williamson, *Middle Temple Bench Book*, 79, 81).

made orders relating to religious conformity but Plowden does not seem to have been troubled thereby. On 25 November 1580 a Parliament ordered that all members of the Inn should receive communion three times a year and that those thereafter admitted to the Inn should enter into a bond so to do. It was also ordered that on every Sunday and holiday one of the butlers should take a note of those who were absent from church and certify the names of the absentees to the masters of the bench, or, in their absence, to the senior utter-barristers, 'by whose direction those who refuse to come to church shall be amerced.'[24]

The Inner Temple had also made orders relating to conformity,[25] but so little was done by either house to make their orders effective that early in 1582 the Master of the Temple, the puritan Richard Alvey, approached the benchers of both Inns about the matter. On 9 February of that year a Parliament of the Middle Temple considered a request from Alvey

> 'that, in accordance with letters from the Privy Council, they would appoint overseers and collectors for this House and Fellowship, to take the view of all resident and in commons who do not resort to church, or being there, do not demean themselves according to the laws; as also for doing other services for the church. As the cause concerns also the Inner Temple they [the benchers of the Middle Temple] have desired Her Majesty's Attorney General [John Popham] and Mr. Morryce to confer with the Inner Temple and report.'[26]

The conference appears to have taken some time. It was not until 2 July that the benchers of the Middle Temple agreed to the appointment of overseers, but the Inner Temple did not do so until 27 January 1583. Then both Inns agreed to the appointment of two gentlemen from each house to act as overseers who should report to Alvey those that did not go to church; if his private admonition did not produce reform, the names of the offenders were to be disclosed to the benchers of the Inn to which they belonged, and the benchers would then take such measures as they thought fit. That arrangement does not seem to have been made with much enthusiasm by the bench of either Inn, nor with much expectation that it would be easy to persuade any member to spy upon the religious observances of his fellows, for the benchers left the implementation of the arrangement very largely to the Master of the Temple when they specified that the overseers were to be 'such as he [Alvey] can persuade to take upon them that office and charge, and therewithal such as the benchers of the same Houses shall well like and allow of.' On 4 November 1583 the Middle Temple appointed Henry Sumaster and Robert Moyle to 'certify to the bench what gentlemen have not come to the church and have not received communion'.[27]

24. *M.T.R.*, i, 239.
25. *cf*. I.T.R., i, 304 (15 May 1580).
26. *M.T.R.*, i, 248. Popham became a bencher in 1568 and James Morris (or Morryce) in 1578 (Williamson, *Middle Temple Bench Book*, 76, 81).
27. *M.T.R.*, i, 252, 263, *I.T.R.*, i, 320, 321.

Presumably in an attempt to quieten Alvey's importunities the benchers of both the Inner Temple and the Middle Temple at that time made orders relating to church services; it was ordered that communion should be administered four times a year 'in such order as the laws and Her Majesty's injunctions prescribe', and it was provided that the ordinary service in the Temple church should not begin before seven in the morning out of term nor before half-past six in term time.[28] And when in November 1581 it became necessary to confer with the Inner Temple about the right of Richard Alvey to a house near the Temple Church, the Middle Temple appointed John Agmondesham and Plowden as their representatives, despite the latter's well known Catholicism.[29]

Plowden remained a subject of interest to those who informed the government of the activities of recusants. Sometime between 1572 and 1578 an informer compiled a list of certain papists in London with notes of the places at which some of them heard Mass.[30] The list contains an entry consisting of three bracketed names, Sir Thomas Offley, Dr. Edward Atslowe and Plowden, who were said to go 'to Baron Browne's house at old Fish Street Hill to hear Mass.' That appears to indicate the place where Plowden was accustomed to hear Mass in the fifteen-seventies, but the matter is far from clear. The first two entries in the list are, 'Baron Browne of the Exchequer' and 'Baron Lord of the Exchequer of Redcross Street.' Robert Browne had been appointed a baron of the Exchequer in 1550 and it is tempting to assume that the place where Plowden heard Mass was his house. Browne, however, died early in 1559 and Robert Lord, who was appointed to the court in 1566, died sometime before 20 January 1576 when he was succeeded by Thomas Greek.[31] It is not easy to understand why an informer who compiled his list in the fifteen-seventies should include a man who had been dead for many years. Unfortunately little is known of either Robert Browne or James Lord, but if it be assumed that Browne, a Catholic, had lived in a house in Fish Street Hill, which ran northwards from old London Bridge to Eastcheap (the Monument now stands on its former route), a solution to the puzzle may be provided by

28. *M.T.R.*, i, 253 (2 July 1582); *I.T.R.*, i, 321 (27 Jan. 1583). The hours prescribed were not unduly early in a period when early rising was common; parliamentary committees frequently met at 5, 6, or 7 a.m. (e.g., *Commons Journals*, i, 96, 97, 99, 102, 111, 115, etc.), and Sir Edward Coke is reputed to have habitually risen at 3 a.m. (Woolrych, *Life of Sir Edward Coke*, 195). According to Lord Campbell, James Dyer (afterwards chief justice of the Common Pleas and the author of the reports which bear his name), when a young man, attended the courts every morning from 7 a.m. to 11 a.m. to make notes of cases (J. Campbell, *Lives of the Chief Justices of England*, i, 180).

29. *M.T.R.*, i, 248.

30. P.R.O., S.P. 12/25/118. The document is headed 'Davie Jones' and was probably compiled by Walsingham's spy of that name. It lists 'Dr. Burkotte', that is, Burchardt Kranich who died in Oct. 1578, and 'Lady Paulet Widow, wyfe to Sir Hughe' whose husbandd (formerly commander and governor of Jersey) died in 1572; the document must, therefore, have been compiled between 1572 and Oct. 1578. The lists presents several problems.

31. Foss, *Judges of England*, v, 470, 515; *M.T.R.*, i, 122. Browne's will (P.C.C. 2 Chaynay) was proved in 1559 and confirmed by sentence dated 5 July 1566 (P.C.C. 19 Crymes).

the further assumption that the house continued to be occupied by his family and to be known as 'Baron Browne's'.[32]

Plowdens's Catholicism, however, did not deter him from giving assistance to a parish of the established church. The Plowdens' house in Shrewsbury was in the parish of St. Mary's and when, on the night of 28 October 1579, a violent storm caused serious damage to the beautiful parish church, destroying two windows, bringing down stone, iron and glass, and lifting the lead from the roof, Plowden was among those who contributed money to repair the damage.[33]

On 14 December 1581 Plowden's eldest daughter Anne was married, a few months before her twenty-first birthday.[34] Her husband was Francis Perkins of Ufton Court in Berkshire, some fifteen miles from Plowden's house at Shiplake, and only a short distance from his property at Wokefield and Burghfield.[35] The Ufton estate and other property had been owned by Richard Perkins, uncle of Francis, who had married Elizabeth, daughter of Sir John Mompesson. Since he had no children Richard Perkins settled his property on his nephew, but reserved a life interest for himself and his wife. Richard Perkins died in 1562 but his widow, who subsequently married Sir John Marvyn, lived on at Ufton until her death in the summer of 1581. On Lady Marvyn's death, Francis Perkins inherited the Ufton and other estates which his uncle had settled, and by her will Lady Marvyn bequeathed to her nephew all her landed property in Wiltshire. She appointed Edmund Plowden to be one of the overseers of her will and bequeathed him 'in token of good will' the sum of £3 6s. 8d.[36]

Anne spent most of the rest of her life at Ufton Court and as she and her husband were staunch recusants who suffered much for their religion, the house became something of a recusant centre and was equipped with several priest-holes. The house was raided and searched in September 1586 and again in 1599; in 1600 Perkins was convicted of recusancy at the Old Bailey (as a resident in the parish of St. Dunstan-in-the-West) and in November of that year began to pay the monthly fine of £20 under the statute of 23 Eliz. I, c. 1. Francis Perkins died in 1615, but Anne survived him for twenty years, dying in 1635; their tomb is in Ufton parish church. One of their descendants, Arabella Perkins, acquired an unusual fame; she was the 'Belinda' of Pope's *Rape of the Lock*.[37]

32. 'Dr. Burkotte' (see note 30) and Dr. Good of Chancery Lane are also listed as going to Mass at 'Baron Brownes'.

33. Owen and Blakeway, *History of Shrewsbury*, ii, 355–7.

34. The date of Anne's marriage is stated in the will of Edmund Plowden, P.C.C. 54 Brudenell (P.R.O., Prob 11/68/429).

35. Ufton lies partly in three parishes, Burghfield, Mortimer and Sulhampstead.

36. Will of Elizabeth Lady Marvyn (P.C.C., 37 Darcy; P.R.O., Prob 11/63/256), made 28 July 1581 and proved 27 Sept. 1581. See also Sharp, *History of Ufton Court*, 83 et seq.; *V.C.H., Berks.*, iii, 244–5, 439, 443; Rylands, *Visitations of Berkshire*, i, 119.

37. See Hodgetts, in *R.H.*, xii (1973–4), 100–13; Sharp, *History of Ufton Court*, 91–3. In her will (P.C.C. 76 Pile) Anne Perkins declared that 'I hold the Catholic auntient and apostolique Roman faith'. For Perkins's recusancy fines, see *C.R.S.*, vol. 53, p. 154, and vol. 57, pp. xxxiv–xxxv, 2–3.

Plowden's younger daughter Mary did not, apparently, marry until after her father's death; at any rate, she was under twenty and unmarried on 2 January 1582 when Plowden made his will. Her husband was Richard White of Halton in Essex. Their second son Thomas, born in 1593, was ordained priest and for a time was president of the English College in Lisbon; better known under his alias Blacklo, he became one of the most controversial figures in seventeenth century English Catholicism.[38]

Lady Marvyn was not the only person to appoint Plowden as the overseer of a will. Some, like her, may have been influenced by family and religious ties, such as his brother-in-law, Anthony Daston, who besides appointing him overseer left him forty shillings and a gold ring.[39] In some cases there may have been an attempt to avoid forfeiture for recusancy by creating secret trusts which was perhaps the case in the will of Lady Petre, the widow of Sir William Petre. She died in 1582 and by her will she appointed four trustees to administer part of her land under the supervision of Plowden.[40] Religion may also have played a part in the case of Sir Thomas White who died in 1567. White was a Catholic who had amassed an enormous fortune in trade. As master of the Merchant Taylors' Company he had participated in the foundation of the Merchant Taylors' School, and he was instrumental in opening up trade with eastern Europe and Russia by means of the Muscovy Company of which he was one of the promoters. Out of his great wealth he founded in 1555 St. John's College in Oxford in order 'to strengthen the orthodox faith, in so far as it is weakened by the damage of time and the malice of men'. In his will he made generous provision for his college and among other bequests was the gift of a black gown to Edmund Campion, then a fellow of the college but who later became a Catholic and was executed as a Jesuit priest; it was Campion who spoke White's funeral oration. White named as his executors his widow and brother-in-law together with Sir William Cordell, the Master of the Rolls, and he appointed Plowden one of the overseers of his will and left him forty shillings and a black gown for his pains.[41]

Old friendship as well as religion may have been the motive of other testators such as Sir Edward Saunders who died at the end of 1576. Saunders was a Catholic who had been appointed chief justice of the King's Bench by queen Mary but on the accession of queen Elizabeth was degraded to the position of chief baron of the Exchequer. He was somewhat

38. For Blacklo, see *D.N.B.*, s.v. 'White, Thomas'; Anstruther, *Seminary Priests*, ii, 349; *C.R.S.*, vol. 69, pp. 185-6; Shanahan, in *Essex Recusant*, vii (1965), 78-85, and viii (1966), 33-7; Bradley, 'Blacklo and the Counter Reformation' in Carter, ed., *From the Renaissance to the Counter Reformation*.

39. P.C.C. 31 Dyer (1572). Anthony Daston married Anne Sheldon, sister of Plowden's wife, as her second husband. See Whitfield, in *N. & Q.*,ccxi (1966), 122-5; see also Whitfield, in *N. & Q.*, ccvi (1961), 364-72.

40. Foley, in *Essex Recusant*, ii (1960), at p. 51.

41. P.C.C. 36 Stonard (P.R.O., Prob 11/49/264). White's will was made on 8 Dec. 1566 and proved on 21 Dec. 1567. The quotation is from the college statutes, quoted in *V.C.H.*, *Oxon.*, iii, 251. For White, see *D.N.B.*; Loftie, *History of London*, i, 325-6; Dickens, *Englsih Reformation*, 314.

older than Plowden, having been admitted to the Middle Temple in 1524, but they had much in common. On 30 October 1576 Saunders transferred to five trustees, one of whom was Plowden, all his 'goods and chattels real and personal moveable and unmoveable' to be held on certain trusts declared in the deed and on such other trusts as he should declare in his will. When he came to make his will ten days later he appointed the same persons to be his executors and gave to each of them 'a piece of plate of the value of five pounds or five pounds in ready money.' He also gave ten pounds to his friend Robert Atkinson, a Catholic barrister of the Inner Temple who had been expelled from his Inn in 1570 for religious reasons.[42] Plowden was also chosen as a overseer by a friend and neighbour, Griffith (or Griffin) Barton of South Stoke in Oxfordshire, who owned land at Burghfield. Barton named his sons-in-law as executors and appointed Plowden as one of overseers of his will and gave him five marks.[43]

42. P.C.C. 41 Carewe (P.R.O., Prob 11/58/299). The will was made on 10 Nov. 1576 ('being at this presente sicke in body') and proved on 13 Dec. 1576. The trustees and executors were Sir Walter Mildmay (chancellor of the Exchequer), Edmund Plowden, William Saunders (cousin), and two 'trustie and welbeloved servantes', Humphrey Dyke and Lawrence Eyton.
43. P.C.C. 10 Arundell (P.R.O., Prob 11/62/75). The will was made on 4 March 1578 and proved on 21 March 1580.

XVIII

ENGLEFIELD AGAIN

Meanwhile the troubles of Sir Francis Englefield had continued to engage Plowden's attention. He had recognized the danger to Englefield's property posed by the legislation of 1571 relating to fugitives overseas, and had been worried by the political activities of Sir Francis in the Low Countries.[1] Englefield shared the enthusiasm of many of the exiles there for a vague plan for the invasion of England to restore the Catholic religion and to liberate Mary Queen of Scots. In order to further that plan, the 'enterprise', Englefield, accompanied by Dr. William Allen who had recently founded his seminary at Douai, went to Rome where they arrived on 14 February 1576 for a discussion with the cardinal of Como, Ptolomeo Galli, and the Spanish ambassador, Don Juan de Zuñiga. As a result the cardinal, who was then the papal secretary of state, advised Allen and Englefield to return to the Low Countries and await the outcome of events after Don John of Austria had taken over his new responsibilities as governor of the Spanish Netherlands later in the year. Englefield left Rome in May 1576, in a spirit of optimism, and reported to a friend that 'the enterprise would probably begin within twelve months'.[2]

Before he left Rome, Englefield dealt with his estates in England. According to Andrew Blunden, Plowden 'aforeseeing [Sir Francis Englefield] might commit folly and be attainted', had for some time been urging Englefield to settle his estates so as to preserve them, as far as possible, should he incur the queen's displeasure. For that purpose Plowden had enlisted the help of serveral of those associated with Englefield, and in particular Humphrey Sandford. Englefield was reluctant to part with the actual possession of his estates and put off a decision for a considerable time. At length, however, he gave way to Plowden's persuasions and 'willed Mr. Plowden to put it in order and form of law'.[3] When, years later, Humphrey Sandford was examined about the matter before Sir Roger Manwood, the chief baron of the Exchequer, he said that Sir Francis had made an assurance of his lands to the use of his nephew, Francis, and that the deed had been drafted by Plowden who sent it to Englefield enclosed in a letter. The letter went by way of Thomas Wotton, a London merchant who was then in Antwerp, and was delivered into the hands of Englefield by Humphrey Sandford himself. Sandford said that the draft deed had been written on paper by one of Plowden's clerks, Thomas

1. See p. 103, *ante*.
2. See Loomie, *Spanish Elizabethans*, 21–3; Cleary, in *R.H.*, viii (1965–6), 300–22, especially pp. 310–12; Memorial of Allen and Englefield for the Invasion of England [Feb. 1576], printed in *C.R.S.*, vol. 58, pp. 284–92.
3. *Blunden's MS*, 134. By that time Englefield was seriously troubled by defective eyesight; see Englefield to Roger Baynes, Madrid, 10 May 1596 (extract printed in Knox, *Letters and Memorials of William Cardinal Allen*, 137 n. 1): 'Being nowe more then 24 yeares synce myselfe could write or reade, and having in that tyme treated with so many greate personages of matters important by the eies and pennes of such servantes as I trusted'.

Harrington, and in Rome it was engrossed on parchment by Englefield's secretary, Edmund Dyer. So far as Sandford could recall, Englefield executed the deed about the end of February or in March 1576 in the English Hospital, in the presence of a number of Catholic exiles, including Allen. When the deed had been executed, it was handed to Humphrey Sandford to take back to England.[4]

The document signed by Englefield on that occasion was of some importance and proved to be a substantial obstacle in the way of the final seizure of his lands by the queen. By that deed Englefield settled all his manors, lands and hereditaments on himself for life and after his death on his nephew, Francis, and the heirs male of his body lawfully begotten, with remainders over. Those provisions were, however, subject to two provisos: the first was that, should Sir Francis have lawful male issue, all the uses and limitations of the deed should be void; and the second was that if Sir Francis should, by himself or any other person, at any time during his life deliver or offer to his nephew, or his heirs, executors or assigns, a ring of gold to the intent to make void the uses and limitations expressed in the deed, then thenceforth all the estates, uses and limitatons so expressed should be void and of no effect, and thereupon all the lands comprised in the deed should be 'in such sort, estate and degree' as they were before the deed had been made.[5] The unusual provision relating to the tender of a ring, by which Englefield might resume full ownership of his estates at any time, ultimately proved to be a serious weakness of the deed; it is probable that Plowden was compelled to include that provision in order to overcome Englefield's reluctance to part with possession of his estates and induce him to sign the deed. The words introducing the proviso stated that the reason for the condition was that Sir Francis did not think it convenient to settle the inheritance upon his nephew absolutely, so long as Sir Francis himself were alive, without a bridle to restrain his nephew who might later be found to be prodigal or given to intolerable vices. It seems likely that that phrase, drafted by Plowden, was a contributory cause of the extreme animosity which young Francis Englefield later displayed towards the Plowdens and Sandfords.[6] By executing the deed Sir Francis divested himself of the fee simple ownership of his estates and acquired instead merely a life interest; in other words, the purpose of the deed was to reduce Englefield's interest in his estates so that in the event of his incurring a forfeiture all that would be lost would have been his life interest while the remainders were preserved for his heirs.

At the time that Sir Francis executed the deed in Rome his nephew was

4. *Blunden's MS*, 156, 157 (additional matter printed at the end of the MS). The date of Sandford's examination was 19 Feb. 1590.

5. For the terms of the deed, see *Sir Francis Englefield's Case* (1591), Poph. 18; *Englefield's Case* (1591), 7 Co. Rep. 11b; and the preamble to the statute 35 Eliz. I, c. 5 (1592), 'An Acte confyrming the Quenes Title to the Lands of Sir Frauncis Englefeild' (*Statutes of the Realm*, iv, 849).

6. For an account of the conduct of young Francis Englefield after Plowden's death, see Parmiter, in *R.H.*, xiv, (1977–8), 9–25.

almost fourteen years old. Since his father's death in 1567 he had been brought up largely in Edmund Plowden's house where, apparently, he lived a quiet and studious life, and when he was nearly twenty he was admitted a member of his guardian's Inn, the Middle Temple, on 3 February 1582; he was admitted 'specially' on payment of a fine of £5 and was bound with John Hedworth and Francis Moore.[7] The circumstances that he was admitted specially meant that he was not required to attend the exercises of learning during the vacations.

During virtually the whole of young Englefield's minority Plowden had his wardship from which he could have derived a handsome profit had he been so minded. Andrew Blunden, who took a practical view of such a situation, stated that he 'did sundry and oftentimes deal with Mr. Plowden to that end [and] prayed him to have consideration of his own estate if there were not some secret trust betwixt Sir Francis and him therein that either he should enforce him [i.e., the young Francis] to marry one of his daughters or to pay for the marriage'.[8] Plowden, however, was more concerned for the well-being of his ward than for his own pecuniary advantage; young Englefield's twenty-first birthday was on 29 June 1583 and about five months before that date Plowden made him a present of his wardship.

In January 1583 young Englefield was staying at Plowden's house at Shiplake in Oxfordshire, together with his mother and his maternal uncle, Francis Fitton. After dinner on 20 January Plowden went into his 'new parlour' and called them to him, and there seems to have gathered there a number of others including his son-in-law, Francis Perkins, and his nephews Humphrey Sandford and Andrew Blunden. Blunden later recounted that, when the family party had assembled, Plowden told his ward that he had obtained his wardship, not with the assistance of the Englefields, but with the help of Lord Pembroke as the requital of a good turn which Plowden had done him. He went on to say that he was in no way beholden or bound to Sir Francis Englefield or to any of his friends, so that he did not feel called upon to bestow so great a benefit as the wardship upon any of them. He said that young Englefield's expectations were great and that he himself might find the wardship and marriage a profitable commodity; indeed Lord Montague had already offered him £2,000 for it. Since there was no secret arrangement between Sir Francis and himself, he was free to make what he could of the wardship. With that rather ominous preamble, he asked those present what they had to say. Andrew Blunden, who must have watched the scene with keen interest, observed that 'These words thus uttered with a stern countenance somewhat amazed and appalled them all: for they knew not what he [Plowden] would do, and knew right well that they had much abused him and that he was privy thereunto'.

7. *M.T.R.*, i, 247. Francis Moore was the son of Edward Moore of East Ilsley, Berks. (Ilsley was an Englefield manor) and became an associate bencher of the Middle Temple in 1603, a serjeant-at-law in 1614, and was knighted in 1616; he was the author of Moore's Reports (see Williamson, *Middle Temple Bench Book*, 92).

8. *Blunden's MS*, 126.

Young Englefield, his mother and his uncle all answered, in effect, that they trusted in his goodness as at all times, and they could not ask anything of right but only of gentleness. What then was said was described by Andrew Blunden as follows:

'Well then, said Mr. Plowden, my good will towards the house of Englefield hath always been firm, is and shall be on my part; I do freely and frankly give it to you. . . . And take it for a gift of £2,000. And in recompence of it I crave no benefit for myself or any of my own children; but here I have in my house my cousin Humfrey Sandford, my sister's son, and his wife and son of their children; he hath served your uncle Sir Francis in the parts beyond the seas many years at my charges, for I gave him every year twenty marks standing to serve Sir Francis besides many other wants I supplied him; and his father also gave him somewhat, all which he spent in your uncle's service, and did to him most acceptable service as Sir Francis himself hath by his letters to me often confessed, and promised to do for him, and will if time would serve. In consideration of this service done to your uncle, and for this my liberality towards you, when such things as be in his father's hands shall come to your disposition,[9] that you will make a lease thereof to him, his wife and son for their three lives at the old rent. And this is a matter of no great importance; I do not account it worth £200 betwixt strangers . . . and yet this may ease them, their father my brother-in-law having almost utterly consumed himself. This gladded Mr. Englefield himself, his mother and uncle Fitton; they thanked Mr. Plowden most lovingly, confessed his infinite goodness to them, that they would perform this request to the uttermost, yes and what else they would not do. Then said Mr. Plowden, Nay Mr. Englefield, look that you perform this indeed, for it is likely, and I expect, that I shall be dead before it shall come to your hands to perform, but my soul will look and require that you perform it, and from this day forward take him for one of your own, and here I remit him to you.'[10]

The hopes and expectations kindled on that occasion at Shiplake did not last for long. In May 1582 a messenger whom the Spanish ambassador, Bernardino Mendoza, had sent to Scotland disguised as a dentist was captured and, although he managed to escape by bribing his guards, he left behind him a mirror in the back of which were found some letters. Those letters disclosed the existence of the 'enterprise' against England which the Catholic exiles abroad were planning. Walsingham immediately set his well trained and efficient spy system to work, and by May 1583 his spies were keeping a close watch on a young man, Francis Throckmorton, who, Walsingham learned, had visited the French embassy by night and was an agent of Mary Queen of Scots. Throckmorton was arrested in his house in November and his papers were seized. He was severely racked and the statements which he made under torture, together with his papers,

9. Richard Sandford had, apparently, only a limited interest in the estate on which he lived.
10. *Blunden's MS,* 126–9; the quotation is on pp. 128, 129. For the date of young Englefield's promise, see ibid., 148.

disclosed to Walsingham the details of what came to be known as the Throckmorton Plot. Among other things, Throckmorton disclosed that Sir Francis Englefield had advised the king of Spain to invade England, and that a short while before his arrest Throckmorton himself had been in correspondence with Englefield about the Spanish forces needed to support a rising in England. Throckmorton and Englefield were attainted of treason, and Throckmorton was executed in June 1584. With the attainder of Sir Francis, the future of the Englefield estates was put at very serious risk.

By the time the threat to the Englefield property materialized Plowden was no longer alive to assist the family. In the end almost the whole of the vast estates of Sir Francis Englefield were seized by the crown, but an act of parliament was needed to secure the queen's title.[11] In the course of those catastrophic events an extremely acrimonious dispute developed between the Sandfords and Andrew Blunden on the one hand and young Francis Englefield, his mother and uncle on the other, during which the Englefields did not hesitate to make serious but unfounded accusations about what they considered to be the discreditable conduct of Edmund Plowden in his handling of the Englefield affairs. Young Francis disregarded his promise to Plowden and did his utmost to eject the Sandfords from their home. He went so far as to tell Richard Sandford, then an old and sick man, that he must be out of his house in a month; Richard Sandford was extremely distressed by that ultimatum and asked to be taken to Plowden Hall where he died within a few weeks of his arrival there.[12]

11. 35 Eliz. I, c. 5 (1592, 'An Acte confyrming the Quenes Title to the Lands of Sir Frauncis Englefeild'; *Statutes of the Realm,* iv, 849).
12. For a full description of the events after Plowden's death, see Parmiter, in *R.H.,* xiv, (1977-8), 9-25.

XIX

THE LAST YEARS

By the end of 1581 Plowden was about sixty-three years of age, and on 2 January of the following year he made his will, in which he described himself as 'Edmund Plowden of Burfeilde in the countie of Bark esquire otherwise called Edmund Plowden of Shiplacke in the countie of Oxforde Esquire sonne and heire of Humfrey Plowden of Plowden in the countie of Salopp Esquier deceased'. He appointed his eldest son Edmund as his sole executor and his nephew Andrew Blunden as overseer of his will.[1]

His executor was authorized to determine his place of burial, but he expressed the wish that, if he should die in London, his body might 'be buried in the Temple Church where the body of my late loving wife Katherine Plowden lieth' and that his body should 'lie between her body and the wall on the north side of the chapel there where she is buried'; on the other hand, should he die 'in or about' Burghfield, he wished to be buried there. His executor was to arrange the order of his burial 'and the charge thereof, which I would not have great'.

He left money to be given to twelve poor householders in each of the parishes of Burghfield and Shiplake, and he gave to 'the parson of Burghfield ten shillings, and to the vicar of Shiplake thirteen shillings [and] four pence for all tythes by me negligently forgotten and not paid to them.' He provided that his house at Shiplake should be maintained at the expense of his estate for three months after his death, during which time his servants should receive their usual wages and their meat and drink; and gifts were made to each of the servants at Shiplake. He then provided that all the professional fees outstanding at his death should be recovered and divided equally between his two clerks, Humphrey Purcell and Thomas Harrington; but he stipulated that, 'because the arrearages of Sir John Littleton and Sir John Perrott are great, and they have put me to little or no pain sithence the first part were due', the fees owing by them should be considered by his executor and reduced by such amount as his executor thought right. All his books of receipt and similar documents were to be delivered to his clerks to enable them to get in the outstanding fees.[2] Humphrey Purcell was also to have all Plowden's wearing apparel in London.

Various interests in landed property were given to his son Francis. He left to his daughter Mary an annuity of £10 to be paid to her until 26 March 1592 so long as she remained unmarried, and an annuity of four marks to Humphrey Purcell for a similar period. In addition Mary was to receive on her twentieth birthday or on marriage 600 marks 'as her marriage money' and forty marks to buy her wedding apparel. He also provided for the payment of the remainder of the marriage portion promised to Anne on her marriage to Francis Perkins, should any part of it remain unpaid at

1. P.C.C. 54 Brudenell (P.R.O., Prob 11/68/420).
2. That is, presumably, the reason why those papers are no longer in existence.

his death. He added a provision that Francis Perkins, Thomas Vachell, Andrew Blunden and William Wollascot might increase or decrease the sum payable to Mary as they thought fit; he went on to say, 'I heartily beseech my loving friends Mrs. Englefield [the mother of young Francis Englefield] and my sister Pollard[3] being widows and my daughter Anne Perkins to oversee my said daughter Mary and to have care of her, to whose order and direction I leave the said Mary charging her to be obedient to them as to me'.

The will made further provision for servants by way of annuity and legacy, and required his son Edmund, his heir, to grant without fine a lease for sixty years of his land at Acton in Shropshire to Thomas Harrington, his clerk, 'in consideration of his long service to me'. Plowden was also concerned for the future well-being of one of his former servants, Margaret Holmes, who had left his service when she married Paul Wilkinson, a papist who was imprisoned in Oxford gaol 'for matter of recusancy'.[4] In his will he recorded that 'Margaret Holmes hath long served me and my wife deceased and is now married unto Paul Wilkinson, and I know not what she will do or where she will abide after my decease, and therefore cannot now resolve what to do for her or how to reward her although she has well deserved at my hands'; he therefore left it to his son Edmund to provide for her and charged him 'to be good and friendly to her and not to suffer her to lack'. The will, which he stated had been written 'wholly with the hand of John Meysie[5] and myself', was witnessed by eleven persons, including his son-in-law Francis Perkins and his nephew William Wollascott.

A year after he had made his will there occurred an event which must have given Plowden much pleasure. On 2 February 1583 his son and heir, Edmund, was admitted to the Middle Temple; he was admitted 'specially' and no fine was taken 'because his father was of the bench.' On the following day his second son, Francis, was similarly admitted.[6] On 10 February Francis was admitted to the chamber of John Scawen and Richard Daston (who was related to Plowden's brother-in-law Anthony Daston and later was Treasurer of the Inn) on the surrender of the latter; again no fine was taken 'because his father has been very kind to the House and is one of the Masters of the Bench.'[7] Later in the year, on 16 November, Plowden's nephew William Wollascott was admitted to the Inn, the fine on admission being only forty shillings 'at Mr. Plowden's request'; his sureties were Andrew Blunden and young Edmund Plowden.[8] Young Edmund died in 1587, but Francis remained in the Inn until October

3. Philippa Sheldon was the sister of Plowden's wife, Catherine Sheldon; she was the widow of Anthony Pollard whose brother, Sir John Pollard, was succeeded in 1557 by Plowden as deputy chief steward, south parts, of the duchy of Lancaster; see p. 50, *ante,* note 31.
4. P.R.O., S.P. 12/255/46. See also S.P. 12/189/54, and Br. Lib., Lansd. MS 55, f. 166 (printed in *C.R.S.,* vol. 22, p. 124).
5. Plowden's brother-in-law; Plowden's sister Joyce married Leonard Meysie.
6. *R.A.M.T.,* i, 50; *M.T.R.,* i, 255.
7. *M.T.R.,* i, 256.
8. *M.T.R.,* i, 263.

1594, but he was never called to the Bar.[9]

Despite the fact that by contemporary standards Plowden was now an old man, he remained in practice. What was probably his last important case was heard in Easter Term 1583 when he appeared in the Exchequer on behalf of his fellow Catholic, Sir Thomas Tresham of Rushton in Northamptonshire. Tresham, who was then about forty years of age and the owner of extensive estates in Northamptonshire and elsewhere, was being steadily impoverished by the accumulation of fines for recusancy, an extravagant style of living, and his financial support of the impecunious recusant Lord Vaux.[10] He had been admitted to the Middle Temple in November 1560 and was knighted in 1575.[11] During the fifteen-seventies Tresham's attempts to improve the rents payable by the tenants on all his manors led him into litigation that began in 1571 and which involved hearings in the Star Chamber, the King's Bench, the Chancery, and Assizes.[12] Among others he sued one George Robins for possession of the manor of Great Houghton in Northamptonshire. John Tresham, the grandfather of Sir Thomas, had settled the manor in tail for the benefit of himself and his heirs, subjet to a condition that if he or one of his heirs alienated the manor or suffered any feigned recovery, or should discontinue, it should revert to its original owner or his personal representatives.[13] In 1526, after the death of John Tresham, his son, also called Thomas, conveyed the land by means of a recovery to Thomas Godden and John Robins and it eventually came into the possession of George Robins, the son of John, who in 1572 had levied a fine by which he conveyed the land to William Belcher without a licence to alienate.[14]

By the reign of Elizabeth the device of a recovery to bar an entail had achieved the status of a common assurance and it was accepted that 'everyone may suffer a common recovery, and so make the most of his land, and bar their issues'.[15] Sir Thomas Tresham's claim to the land had two main branches, the recovery suffered in 1526 which, it was argued, was in breach of the condition of the original entail, and the fine of 1572 which had been levied without licence to alienate. Plowden's argument in the Exchequer before all the barons was a long one, and its quality is indicated by the number of surviving manuscript notes of it, some of

9. *M.T.R.*, i, 345: ' 11 Oct. [1594] . . . Mr. Henry Blomer to the chamber of Messrs. Plowden and Miller in place of the former.' Thereafter Francis Plowden disappears from the records of the Inn.

10. For Tresham and his financial difficulties, see Finch, *Wealth of Five Northamptonshire Families,* 66–69, 179–84; *C.R.S.,* vol. 57, pp. 116–7.

11. *R.A.M.T.,* i, 25; Finch, op. cit., 72.

12. For those early proceedings, see P.R.O., C. 3/175/11; Sta. Cha. 5/T3/38, 5/T8/23, 5/T10/3, 5/T24/20.

13. 'ou permittent auscun recovery par fraude ou covin'; a 'feigned recovery' was a device invented to evade the statute *De Donis Conditionalibus* (13 Edw. I, c. 1), whereby a tenant in tail enlarged his estate tail into a fee simple and so barred the entail; see *H.E.L.,* iii, 111–20, 246.

14. A 'fine' was an action that was compromised in court, on terms approved by the court, by which land was conveyed from one person to another; see *H.E.L.,* iii, 236–45.

15. *Willion* v. *Berkley* (1562), Plowd. 223, at p. 244, *per* Weston, J.

which are very long.[16] In the event he won his case and judgement was entered for Tresham. Some sixteen years later Tresham referred to the litigation in a long letter written in the Summer of 1599 when he was confined in the Fleet prison as a recusant; the letter was mainly devoted to his grievances against those he considered to be his enemies, and especially one whom he referred to as 'Fulcis', that is, George Fulshurst who married Muriel, daughter of Lord Vaux by his second wife. In the course of the letter Tresham wrote: 'I have lived forty years owner of my lands in Northamptonshire and never there had in all that time but one suit, and that for above a hundred pound of inheritance, detained wrongfully from my ancestors and me almost eighty years. I recovered it by many years suit, albeit the then Marquis of Northampton (my near kinsman and one of [my] mightiest adversaries) and the judges of that circuit, also all the puritans and preachers combined therein against me. Had not my right been good and my means to recover it well managed, I could not possibly have prevailed.'[17]

Old habits die hard. Mention has already been made of the lawyers' habit of 'putting cases',[18] and Plowden seems to have indulged in it almost to the end of his life. Many of the cases so put were recorded in lawyers' notebooks and in reports, but frequently it is not clear whether the point of law was a hypothetical one or had arisen in an actual case, for it was common for counsel to seek the opinion of the judges on points of law which did not arise in cases pending before them.[19] In a collection of notes and short reports of cases once owned by Nicholas Jordan of the Inner Temple, there is a note that in Hilary Term 1583 Plowden put to the Lord Treasurer, Lord Burghley, a question concerning certain rights in two acres of land and a dovecote; Burghley appears to have sidestepped a legal discussion by saying that it would be necessary to look at the relevant records.[20] In the same notebook there is recorded another 'putting of cases' in Plowden's chamber in the Middle Temple during Michaelmas Term 1584.[21]

16. See Bodl., Rawl. MS. C. 85, ff. 55v-64 (the foliation is confusing). The report (which is confined to a preliminary statement of facts and Plowden's argument) begins with the words, 'John Tresham . . . fut seisie en fee del manor de Houghton in com. Northumberland . . .', presumably a *lapsus calami* of the scribe. Other reports are: Br. Lib., Lansd. MS 1072, f. 95, Add. MS 35951, f. 26v; Lincoln's Inn, Mayn. MS 82, ff. 57v-75; Camb. Univ. Lib., MS Ff.v.4, ff. 344-61v.
17. *H.M.C., Var. Coll.,* iii, 98. Tresham's assertion that he was involved in 'but one suit' is wide of the truth.
18. See p. 16, *ante.*
19. E.g., Cro. Eliz., 174; Cro. Eliz., 753; Br. Lib., Harg. MS 388, f. 239. A short report by Dyer (Dyer 314, pl. 95) appears at first sight to be a note of a hypothetical point, as it begins, 'Fuit move pur question per Bendlowes . . .', but it was in fact the gist of the important case of *Clere* v. *Brook,* Plowd. 442, in which serjeants Gawdy and Bendlowes appeared for the plaintiff and serjeants Lovelace and Barham for the defendants.
20. Br. Lib., Harg. MS 373, f. 212. In the 17th cent. the MS (mainly reports of cases) was given the title 'Jordan's Collectanea' by Edward Umfreville to whom it once belonged. It seems unlikely that Nicholas Jordan was the compiler as he was not admitted to the Inner Temple until 1588; he was called to the Bar in 1597 and became a bencher in 1613.
21. Br. Lib., Harg. MS 373, ff. 223-4.

XX

DEATH

Plowden died on 6 February 1585.[1] Since he is buried in the Temple Church, according to his wish should he die in London, it seems likely that he died there, most probably in his chamber in the Middle Temple. Four days later his nephew, Andrew Blunden, was called to the Bar.[2]

For the protection of any rights the sovereign might have as the result of the death of a subject who was thought to hold land as tenant in chief of the crown (according to the old feudal tenures), it was customary for the county escheator to hold an inquisition post mortem, either in obedience to a writ of *diem clausit extremum* or by virtue of his office. The escheator summoned a jury to inquire, upon oath, of what lands the tenant was seized at the time of his death, by what rents or service they were held, and the name and age of his heir, in order that the sovereign might be informed of his right of escheat or wardship or other advantages accruing to him. If the heir were an adult, livery of seisin was granted to him on his appearance in court and performance of homage, and on payment of a fine or relief; if, however, he were a minor, he and his estates remained in wardship until he reached full age. Inquisitions post mortem continued to be held until 1660 when feudal tenures were abolished.

The inquisition post mortem that followed the death of Edmund Plowden was held at Reading on 13 March 1585 by Reade Stafford, the escheator for Berkshire.[3] It shows that at the time of his death Plowden was a considerable landowner, but he held only one estate, that of the manor of Wokefield, as tenant in chief of the crown. The return of the jury stated that in Berkshire he owned two messuages (or dwelling-houses with outbuildings and land) in Burghfield, together with three messuages in Wokefield as well as the manor; a substantial part of that land was said to be in the occupation of Andrew Blunden at the time of Plowden's death. The bulk of his property, however, was in Shropshire. In addition to the family estate, together with a messuage and water mill,[4] there was land and other property in Choulton and Eyton, Lydbury North, Lee and Oakley, and Bishop's Castle, as well as at Totterhill, Longton, Myndtown, Longfield and Acton. All that property was inherited by his heir, Edmund, who proved his will disposing of the remainder of his property on 23 November 1585.

A notable ommission from the inquisition was Plowden's property at Shiplake where he had spent much of his time when he was not in London.

1. The date of death is stated in the inq. p. m. (P.R.O., C. 142/206/13; Ward 7/21/108). See also the inscription on his tomb in the Temple Church, and *Athen, Oxon.,* i, 504-5.
2. *M.T.R.,* i, 274.
3. P.R.O., C. 142/206/13. For the transcript delivered to the Court of Wards and Liveries, see P.R.O., Ward 7/21/108.
4. Plowden was stated to hold the manor of Plowden and its associated lands of the queen, as of her manor of Bishop's Castle, by service unknown; he was seized of the property in tail male.

That appears to be due to the circumstances in which Plowden came into possession of Shiplake. It will be remembered that the queen granted to Plowden her interest in the lease of Shiplake which has been forfeited by Sir Francis Englefield.[5] That lease expired in 1577, but as he continued to live there and made provision in his will for its maintenance at the expense of his estate for three months after his death, his tenure of the property must have been extended by another lease that has not yet been discovered. A lease was a chattel (or chattel real) and, as chattels were outside the purview of an inquisition post mortem, the lease was excluded from the inquisition. Soon after Plowden's death, however, the queen, by letters patent dated 10 December 1585, granted a lease of the land formerly held by Plowden at Shiplake, and some land in Berkshire, to Andrew Blunden and Plowden's two sons, Edmund and Francis, for their joint lives and the life of the survivor.[6] According to Cooper, 'it is to be presumed that this grant was a recognition by her majesty of the merits of the greatest and most honest lawyer of his age.'[7] The young Edmund did not live to enjoy his inheritance for long; he died unmarried in August 1587 and was succeeded in the family estates by his younger brother, Francis, who lived sometimes at Plowden Hall but chiefly, it seems, at Shiplake.[8]

Nearly ten years after his father's death Francis Plowden scored a victory in the court of Exchequer which would probably have pleased Edmund Plowden. In 1587 parliament had passed a statute which sharply increased the penalties for recusancy and provided a new procedure for their recovery.[9] Under the new Act the justices of the peace were no longer able to proceed to conviction upon indictments for recusancy, and all such indictments were thenceforth to be tried in the King's Bench, at Assizes or at general sessions of gaol delivery. The Act also provided that a recusant, once convicted, should pay not a single fine calculated at the rate of £20 per month under the Act of 1581,[10] but should be liable, without further conviction, to pay into the Exchequer twice yearly a sum calculated at the rate of £20 per month from the date of his conviction until he conformed. If the recusant failed to pay the cumulative penalty the queen was empowered, by process out of the Exchequer, to seize all the recusant's goods and two-thirds of his landed property. Among the procedural changes the Act provided

'that upon the indictment of such offenders a proclamation shall be made at the same Assizes or Gaol Delivery in which the indictment shall be taken, if the same be taken at any Assizes or Gaol Delivery, by which it shall be commanded that the body of such offender shall be rendered to the sheriff of the same county before the said next Assizes or Gaol

5. See p. 103, *ante*.
6. P.R.O., C. 66/1267, m. 39.
7. Cooper, *Athenae Cantabrigienses*, i, 502. If there is any truth in that suggestion it seems more likely that it refers to the original grant of 1574, rather than that of 1585.
8. See Inq. p. m. taken at Theale, Berks., on 3 April 1588 following the death of Edmund Plowden, jr. (P.R.O., C. 142/221/123).
9. 29 Eliz. I, c. 6 (*Statutes of the Realm*, iv, 771–2).
10. 23 Eliz. I, c. 1 (*Statutes of the Realm*, iv, 766–7).

158

EDMUND PLOWDEN

Delivery to be holden in the same county. And if at the said next Assizes or Gaol Delivery the same offender, so proclaimed, shall not make appearance of record, that then, upon such default recorded, the same shall be as sufficient a conviction in law of the said offender whereof the party so standeth indicted as is aforesaid, as if upon the same indictment a trial by verdict thereupon had proceeded and been recorded . . .'[11]

It will be observed that the Act enabled the crown to obtain a conviction for recusancy in the absence of the recusant, since a default of appearance was to be taken as sufficient for a conviction. Indeed, it then became possible for a recusant to be convicted while wholly unaware of the proceedings against him, and those circumstances were most likely to arise where the indictment of a provincial recusant such as Francis Plowden was preferred in London by reason of his possession of a house in the capital.

Francis Plowden was a victim of the new procedure. At the time in question he had a chamber in the Middle Temple and on that basis proceedings against him were instituted in London. On 28 June 1591 a true bill was found against him at the sessions of the peace held at Guildhall. Three days later he was proclaimed in the Justice Hall adjoining Newgate prison where the commission for the delivery of that gaol was executed. Upon his non-appearane to the proclamation he was convicted, and parts of his lands in Berkshire and Shropshire, including Plowden Hall, were seized in April 1592.

Presumably the first intimation that he had of the proceedings against him was the arrival of the sheriff to demand the forfeiture of his property. As a result of the seizure he instituted proceedings in the Exchequer claiming that his conviction was illegal, and his appeal was heard by the barons of the Exchequer in Michaelmas Term 1594.[12] The argument for Francis Plowden was that, according to the statute, the proclamation should have been made at the same sessions as those in which the indictment had been taken, whereas in his case the indictment had been taken at the Guildhall sessions and the proclamation made in the Newgate Gaol Delivery. The attorney-general, Edward Coke, who appeared for the crown did not dissent from that argument and the barons of the Exchequer held that Francis Plowden's conviction was unlawful and he was discharged. The entry on the Recusant Rolls of the seizure of his property was vacated and thereafter the name of Francis Plowden disappeared from the rolls.[13]

11. 29 Eliz. I, c. 6, s. 5 (*Statutes of the Realm,* iv, 772).
12. For the record of the proceedings, see P.R.O., E. 368/477, m. 133. He is there referred to as 'Franciscus Plowden de London', generosus, alias dictus Franciscus Plowden de Shiplake in Comitatu oxonie, generosus'.
13. For a valuable analysis of the Act of 1587, see Dom Hugh Bowler's illuminating introduction to the second Recusant Roll, *C.R.S.,* vol. 57, pp. xxii–xliii. In 1614 Coke referred to the case of Francis Plowden, and said that the indictment should have been removed into the King's Bench for further process; see *Foster's Case,* 11 Co. Rep. 56b, at p. 63b (where he wrongly referred to 'Edw. Plowden'). It seems that at the time of Plowden's conviction the opinion was prevalent that justices of the peace had no power to proclaim recusants, an opinion which was not shared by either the barons of the Exchequer in 1594 or Coke in 1614.

Francis died on 11 November 1652 at the age of ninety and was buried at Shiplake.[14] One of his sons, named Edmund after his grandfather, held several official positions in Ireland and was knighted in Dublin in 1630. In 1634 Charles I, as king of Ireland, granted him a charter erecting the province of New Albion in America as a county palatine and creating him its governor. The province was huge and would to-day include half of Delaware and Maryland, two-thirds of New Jersey and the sourthern half of eastern Pennsylvania including the city of Philadelphia. Edmund Plowden asserted a right to be an Irish peer by virtue of the charter but his claim to that dignity was unsuccessful. Probably because of his quarrelsome and combative nature, his colonizing venture ended in mutiny and failure.[15]

Shiplake remained in the possession of the Plowden family until 1689 when, twelve years after the death of her husband, Penelope Plowden and her son Francis sold it to Robert Jennings who had been a fellow of St. John's College, Oxford and headmaster of Reading Grammar School. The house was demolished in 1803.[16]

14. See the memorial tablet in Shiplake parish church.

15. See Carter and Lewis, in *Pennsylvania Mag. of History and Biography* lxxxiii (1959), 150–79. See also Bodl., Rawl. MS A 247 for a copy of the charter, Plowden's appointment as governor and earl palatine, and legal opinions in favour of his claim to be thereby a peer of Ireland.

16. Bodl., MSS ch. Oxon. c. 15, n. 2445 a-b, and ch. Oxon. c. 46, no. 4386; Climenson, *History of Shiplake*, 281–2. Penelope Plowden (whose husband, Edmund, died on 23 Nov. 1677) was the daughter and co-heiress of Sir Maurice Drummond, and the great-granddaughter of Sir John Perrot. Her son Francis entered the Society of Jesus in 1682; he was sometimes known as 'Fr. Perrot'.

XII

EPILOGUE

Plowden can be numbered among that group of learned and widely read lawyers, men such as William Lambard, Edward Coke and Francis Bacon, whose enduring work was the adaptation of medieval law and institutions to the needs of their day. Some invention and imagination is a necessary part of any process of adaptation, and imagination is to be found in the work of those men; not only did they enunciate rules that are to be found in the modern law, but they provided legal and historical theories to account for those rules. Though much of those theories is now discredited, their soundness was considered by earlier generations of lawyers to be as incontestable as the statements of law; it is only recently that a distinction has been drawn between the validity of the statements of law and the correctness of the historical foundations which were constructed to support those statements.

Among Plowden's contributions to the development of English law was his theory of how statutes should be interpreted. It has been said many times that the history of the judicial interpretation of statutes begins in the sixteenth century. Before that time the courts had tended to regard statutes as isolated rulings on specific topics which had been enacted to supplement the common law; but in the sixteenth century lawyers were coming increasingly to regard statutes as being of supreme legal authority. The religious and other great changes that took place under the Tudors were buttressed by acts of parliament, a process that did much to enhance the authority and prestige not only of parliament but of the legislation that parliament enacted. And as Tudor society grew more complex and its problems more sophisticated, the scope and importance of legislation increased. The increasing penetration of the lives of the people by statute-made law brought with it a corresponding need for a uniform system of judicial interpretation of statutes according to known principles or canons of construction. The compilers of the later Year Books and the reporters down to Coke were all noting the impact of the new legislation on the common law, and Coke himself saw the principal function of law reporting as the exposition of statutes enacted since the cessation of the Year Books.[1]

The lawyers were faced with the task of applying the provisions of the new legislation, couched in general terms, to the particular affairs of their clients, and to do that they needed the guidance of a judicially established body of rules of interpretation that would enable them to know how the judges would apply the enacted law to particular factual circumstances as they arose. The evidence of the law reports of the time, both printed and manuscript, makes it clear that the courts were increasingly concerned with the interpretation of legal instruments of all kinds, and by Plowden's time the process of interpretation was being systematized. Plowden was

1. 3 Co. Rep., p. xvi, (Preface).

well aware of the growing significance of statute law and of the need for unambiguous rules of interpretation, and it is not, perhaps, without significance that more than one-third of all the cases which appear in his printed reports are concerned with the interpretation and application of acts of parliament. Those cases form a valuable corpus of learning that did much to systematize a branch of the law that was then in its early stages of development.

In his report of the case of *Eyston* v. *Studd*,[2] Plowden included a long note of his own in which he expounded at considerable length the concept of what he called Equity as applied to statute law. His note began:

'From this judgment and the cause of it, the reader may observe that it is not the words of the law but the internal sense of it that makes the law, and our law (like all others) consists of two parts viz. of body and soul, the letter of the law is the body of the law, and the sense and reason of the law is the soul of the law, quia ratio legis est anima legis.'[3]

He went on to say that 'it often happens that when you know the letter, you know not the sense, for sometimes the sense is more confined and contracted than the letter, and sometimes it is more large and extensive. And Equity, which in Latin is called Equitas, enlarges or diminishes the letter according to its discretion.'

In his earlier report of the case of *Reniger* v. *Fossa*,[4] he devoted a good deal of space to the argument of Robert Brooke, then recorder of London and later chief justice of the Common Pleas. In the course of his argument Brooke had said that 'the ancient fathers of the law, considering the said statute [the Second Statute of Westminster of 1285], saw that if it should be taken according to the words, great inconvenience would follow from thence . . . and therefore they construed the said statute according to Equity and Reason, although the words did not allow of it, but seemed against it; so that in all statutes there are some private cases excepted out of the general provisions by Equity and reason, in avoidance of a greater mischief.'[5]

The core of the doctrine which Plowden enunciated consisted in the application to statutes of what he called Equity. That application of Equity could, according to the circumstances of the statute, result either in the extension or the contraction of the literal meaning of its terms. Plowden held that 'a man ought not to rest upon the letter only, nam qui haeret in litera haeret in cortice,[6] but he ought to rely upon the sense, which is temperated and guided by Equity, and therein he reaps the fruit of the law. . . . And in order to form a right judgment when the letter of a statute is restrained and when enlarged by Equity, it is a good way, when you peruse a statute, to suppose that the law-maker is present, and that

2. Plowd. 459, at pp. 465-7 (1574).
3. *cf. Partridge* v. *Strange* (1553), Plowd. 77, at p. 82, *per* Saunders, serj.
4. Plowd. 1, at pp. 12-13 (1550).
5. Plowd., at p. 13a; with this, compare St. Germain, *Doctor and Student* (1531), lib. 1, ch. 16.
6. *cf.* Co. Litt. 283b.

you have asked him the question you want to know touching the Equity, then you must give yourself such an answer as you imagine he would have done if he had been present.'[7] Here is the germ of the rule that a statute must be construed according to the intention of its makers. One obvious guide to the intentions of parliament was to be found in the preamble to a statute; preambles had become a notable feature of Tudor legislation and Dyer described them as 'a key to open the minds of the makers of the Act and the mischiefs they intended to redress.'[8] Plowden, however, placed no restrictions upon the means that might by employed to determine the intention of parliament and everything was grist to his mill, but he did not, it seems, realize the practical difficulties that would arise if the field of inquiry were not limited. It is not, perhaps, surprising that Plowden's attempt to build a coherent system of statutory interpretation based on Equity was not entirely successful, but it is indisputable that he made a considerable contribution to the development of the canons of construction. Although his conception was too broad for practical implementation, so that it came to be restricted to the investigation of the legislators' intention as found in the statute itself, his lasting influence was due to the care he took to demonstrate the means by which judges dealt with changing conditions.

Plowden's elaboration of a doctrine of interpretation of statutes, in which he insisted that it was the 'internal sense' of a statute that made the law, was only one aspect of a more general approach to the law, which was first to understand the reason of the law and then to enunciate clearly the relevant rule. As Coke said, 'Then are we said to know the law when we apprehend the reason of the law, that is, when we bring the reason of our law to our reason that we perfectly understand it as our own.'[9] That was what Plowden did in his *Reports,* and what he did in his *Treatise* on the succession where he 'searched the reasons and grounds of the law in the point'.[10]

Plowden's learning was not confined to the law, and it is clear that he was a widely read man. He was, for example, well versed in the philosophy of Aristotle and his knowledge of Aristotle's work is reflected in his argument on the natural law in the case of *Sharington* v. *Strotton*[11] and his note on the interpretation of statutes appended to his report of *Eyston* v. *Studd.*[12] The note which he added to his report of the *Case of Mines*[13] shows that he had some knowledge of metallurgy and was acquainted with the writings of Georgius Agricola. He had, too, a considerable knowledge of the history of England, as is evident from the many references to historical writers which he had made in his *Treatise* on the succession: in

7. *Eyston* v. *Studd* (1574), Plowd. 459, at p. 467 (Plowden's note).
8. See *Stowel* v. *Lord Zouch* (1569), Plowd. 353, at p. 369.
9. Co. Litt. 394b.
10. Br. Lib., Harl. MS 849, f. 1; see p. 91, *ante.*
11. Plowd. 298, at pp. 303–07.
12. Plowd. 459, at pp. 465–67. Plowden evidently read Aristotle in a Latin translation, as his quotations are in that language.
13. Plowd. 310; see p. 98, *ante.*

addition to the *History* of Polydore Vergil he cited many of the chronicles, especially those of Thomas of Walsingham, Matthew Paris, William of Newburgh, Roger of Hoveden, and the Chronicle of St. Albans, and he frequently set out long quotations from those authors. In the *Treatise* he also cited such diverse works as the *Metamorphoses* of Ovid, the Old and New Testaments, and the writings of St. Augustine and Henry VIII. As the Middle Temple had no library in Plowden's time, it seems that he possessed a fairly extensive library of his own.

Today the most striking feature of Plowden's career seems to be his almost complete immunity from harassment on account of his religion which he never troubled to hide. That was due to several factors. In the first place was his membership of one of the Inns of Court which were privileged professional bodies whose chapels were ecclesiastical peculiars largely exempt from episcopal control. The closely knit corporate character of life in the Inns, whose members were concerned to maintain their substantial privileges and ancient customs, engendered a tolerance that allowed an unusual degree of freedom to those members who were out of sympathy with the Elizabethan religious settlement. Even the privy council was baffled in its attempts to enforce conformity in the Inns of Court.[14] Second, there was his own professional ability and standing, and the professional services of such men as Plowden were too valuable for the government to allow itself to be deprived of them. And third, there was his reputation not only for learning and ability as an advocate but for independence of mind and uprightness of conduct. Those who sought Plowden's advice looked to his legal abilities, not to his religion, and his clients included men of every kind of religious attitude, from papist to puritan. The earl of Northampton referred to that aspect of Plowden's career when, in the next century, he justified his choice of a convicted recusant as his attorney. He said that 'my lord Burghley, Lord Treasurer, did retain Mr. Plowden as one of his counsel, though he and everyone knew him to be a papist; he retained him as a lawyer and not as a professor of any religion'.[15]

The great reputation for learning and integrity which Plowden had acquired during his lifetime was recorded after his death by the historian of queen Elizabeth I, William Camden, who, in the first edition of his *Annals* published in 1615, wrote:

'Plowdeni mors. In Anglia nemo e vivis excessit memoria dignior quam Edmundus Plowdenus, qui ut in Iuris Anglici scientia de qua scriptis bene meruit, facilis primus: ita vitae integritate inter homines suae professionis nulli secundus.'[16]

That eulogy was richly deserved. His great gifts and his conspicuous honesty would, no doubt, have taken him to the highest places in his profession and the state, had it not been for his adherence to the Catholic

14. Parmiter, *Elizabethan Popish Recusancy in the Inns of Court*, 49–50, 54.
15. Letter of William Wentworth to Sir William Wentworth, Feb. [1614], printed in Cooper, *Wentworth Papers, 1597–1628*, 61.
16. Camden, *Annales*, 365.

faith in which he had been brought up. That adherence was among his most notable characteristics and, although it severely restricted his professional advancement, it enabled him to bear his disappointments without bitterness. For Plowden the law was never a mere means to personal or professional aggrandizement as it was for some of his contemporaries; he was a true servant of the law who took pride in being 'an apprentice of the law,' and his gifts were devoted to moulding the law to be a better and more effective instrument to serve the interests of his fellow countrymen. It was, therefore, a fitting tribute that was paid to him by another great lawyer, Sir Edward Coke, who concluded the fourth part of his *Institutes* by recalling 'the aphorism of that great lawyer and sage of the law, Edmund Plowden, which we have often heard him say, "Blessed be the amending hand" '.[17]

In his own Inn his memory has remained green to this day. Plowden was buried, as he had wished, against the north wall of the Temple Church, alongside the body of his wife, where there was erected a fine altar tomb under a coffered arch. The tomb displays a figure of Plowden, vested in a long close-fitting gown, lying upon his back with his hands joined together upon his breast; it is an excellent example of the work of the studio of Gerard Johnson, the elder, in Southwark. In the eighteen-forties the benchers of the two Temple societies, after taking the best architectural and artistic advice of the day, undertook extensive restoration of the Church during which considerable damage was done to the monuments, some of which disappeared. Along with many other monuments, Plowden's tomb was removed from its original position and re-erected in the triforium of the church. In order to make the tomb fit into the cramped space available there, it was seriously mutilated; for instance, the shield and part of the cresting, which had formerly been above the coffered arch, were wantonly broken off and the shield was fixed to the base of the tomb so as to destroy an essential part of the design.[18] In the nineteen-thirties Mrs. Arundell Esdaile, who had been asked to report upon the monuments, recommended that the tomb be repaired and replaced in its original position.[19] Unfortunately, her advice was not fully accepted. The tomb was removed from the triforium but it was re-erected in an inconspicuous position between the 'Round' and the north aisle. Fortunately it was bricked up before the church was seriously damaged during an air raid on the night of 10–11 May 1941 and thus escaped further injury, but it still bears traces of the damage done to it earlier.

17. 4 Co. Inst. 366.
18. For a description of the tomb in its mutilated state, see Esdaile, *Temple Church Monuments,* 81–2, and see ch. 1 for a description of the damage done during the 19th cent. 'restoration'. There is a photograph of Plowden's tomb in its mutilated state, when it was in the triforium, in Mrs. Esdaile's book and in Worley, *Church of the Knights Templars,* 56. Richardson, *Monumental Effigies of the Temple Church* is stated to be an account of the restoration of 1842 but is concerned only with the effigies in the 'Round'; in the copy of this work in the Middle Temple Library there has been pasted in an engraving (published in 1794) of the tomb in its original setting.
19. Esdaile, *Temple Church Monuments.*

The hall of the Middle Temple, to the building and beautifying of which Plowden devoted so much time, is his greatest memorial in the Inn. His arms and an inscription are displayed in one of the windows at the western end,[20] and at the eastern end, just inside the screen, there now stands a bust of him. The bust, which is carved from Carrara marble, was given to the Inn in 1868 by one of its oldest members, Robert Ingram. It was executed by the sculptor, Morton Edwards, and was copied from a terra cotta bust of Plowden at Plowden Hall which is said to have been made during his lifetime. The bust was unveiled in the hall before dinner on Grand Night in Trinity Term, 10 June 1868, by Robert Phillimore, the judge of the Admiralty Court, in the absence through illness of the Treasurer, John Monk, Q.C. A large company of some 200 members of the Society was present, as well as some ladies who were accommodated in the Minstrels' Gallery and among whom were two descendants of the great lawyer. After a short speech by Sir Robert Phillimore the bust was unveiled and then, after grace had been said by the Master of the Temple, Canon Thomas Robinson, the company sat down to dinner.[21]

The hall was seriously damaged during the war when, on the night of 15 October 1940, a land-mine attached to a parachute struck the south side of No. 3 Elm Court; the resulting explosion was tremendous and blew a large hole in the east gable of the hall, shattered the screen and the Minstrels' Gallery, and did much other damage.[22] After the war the damage was carefully and lovingly repaired and few who see it to-day would realize that the hall had ever been injured. It was in the restored hall that a reading was given on the evening of 12 November 1952, in the presence of Queen Elizabeth the Queen Mother who, as Queen Elizabeth, had taken her place as a bencher of the Inn on 12 December 1944 and was later elected Treasurer. The reader was Richard O'Sullivan, Q.C., and his subject was 'Edmund Plowden, 1518-1585.'

20. See p. 120, *ante*.
21. See *The Standard,* 11 June 1868 (reprinted in *B.M.P.,* 33-5).
22. See Anon., *Middle Temple Ordeal,* 18-19, 53. Two incendiary bombs fell on the roof of the hall on the night of 14-15 March 1941, and on 25 March 1944, when 140 incendiary bombs fell in the Middle Temple, the hall was again hit but, although the lantern was burned out, the roof was saved. The hall suffered further damage on 24 July and 3 Dec. 1944.

BIBLIOGRAPHY

[This bibliography is no more than a list of those manuscripts and printed books cited in the foregoing pages.]

I. MANUSCRIPT SOURCES

Public Record Office
C. 3   Chancery Proceedings, Series II.
C. 66   Chancery, Patent Rolls.
C. 142   Chancery, Inquisitions post mortem, Series II.
E. 23   Exchequer, Treasury of Receipt, Royal Wills.
E. 179   Exchequer, King's Remembrancer, Subsidy Rolls.
E. 310   Exchequer, Augmentation Office, Particulars of Leases.
E. 368   Exchequer, Lord Treasurer's Remembrancer, Memoranda Rolls.
K.B. 9   King's Bench (Crown Side), Ancient Indictments.
K.B. 27   King's Bench (Crown Side), Coram Rege Rolls.
K.B. 29   King's Bench (Crown Side), Controlment Rolls.
Prob 11   Prerogative Court of Canterbury, Probate of Wills.
S.P. 12   State Papers Domestic, Elizabeth I.
S.P. 14   State Papers, Domestic, James I.
S.P. 15   State Papers, Domestic, Addenda, Edward VI to James I.
S.P. 70   State Papers, Foreign, General Series, Elizabeth I.
Sta. Cha. 5   Star Chamber Proceedings, Elizabeth I.
Ward 7   Court of Wards and Liveries, Inquisitions post mortem.

British Library (*British Museum*)
Additional MSS 11681, 16577, 26647, 35951, 36078, 36081.
Cotton MSS, Caligula B iv, B ix; Titus B vii; Vitellius C ix.
Harleian MSS 35, 249, 293, 421, 537, 555, 736, 849, 1226, 1689, 1877, 2060, 2071, 4274, 4627, 4666, 5805, 6235, 6256, 6707.
Hargrave MSS 4, 6, 9, 15, 27, 55, 89, 95, 132, 251, 290, 291, 351, 353, 373, 388, 389.
Lansdowne MSS 15, 109, 622, 1072, 1078, 1088.
Royal MS 7 C xvi.
Sloane MS 827.
Stowe MSS 354, 419.

Bodleian Library, Oxford
Ashmolean MSS 826, 829.
Bankes MS 8.
ch. Oxon., a. 11, no. 142b; c. 15, no. 3445; c. 46, no. 4386.
Don. C 43.
Douce MS 66
Rawlinson MSS A 124, A 247, B 7, C 85.
Tanner MSS 283, 304.

Cambridge University Library
  MSS Dd.iii.84, 85; Dd.ix., 14; Ff.v.4; Gg.iii.34; Ii. v, 3, 20.

Christ Church, Oxford (Archives of the Chapter)
  MS Estates 67.
  MS D.P. xi.a.1.
  MS 1.C.2 (Book of Evidences).

Exeter College, Oxford
  MS 128.

Harvard Law School, Cambridge, Mass., U.S.A.
  MS 2079.

Henry E. Huntington Library and Art Gallery, San Marino, Cal., U.S.A.
  MS E1 7921.

Inner Temple Library
  Petyt MSS 47, 538.

Lincoln's Inn Library
  Maynard MSS 29, 82.
  Miscellaneous MS 361.

Longleat House, Wiltshire
  MS 240.

Middle Temple Library
  Bench Minute Books, vols. A, D and K.
  Brerewood MS.

St. Mary's Seminary, Oscott
  Oscott MS 545.

Worcestershire Record Office, Worcester
  Beoley Parish Register, vol. 1 (1538–1652) [Microfilm 985 Beoley].

II. PRINTED SOURCES

A to Z of Elizabethan London, comp. Adrian Prockter and Robert Taylor, Lympne, 1979.
L. W. Abbott, *Law Reporting in England, 1485–1585,* London, 1973.
Georgius Agricola [Georg Bauer], *De Re Metallica*, Basel, 1556; English translation by H. C. and L. Hoover, London, 1912.
A. F. Allison and D. M. Rogers, *A Catalogue of Catholic Books in English printed abroad or secretly in England, 1558–1640*, Bognor Regis, 1956 [printed in *Biographical Studies,* iii, 119–832].

168   EDMUND PLOWDEN

John Corbett Anderson, *Shropshire: its Early History and Antiquities,* London, 1864.

Anon., *Allegations against the surmisid title of the Quine of Scotts and the fauorers of the same,* London, 1565.

Anon., *Middle Temple Ordeal. Being an Account of what World War II meant to the Inn,* with a foreward by the Hon. Mr. Justice Cassels; privately printed for the Middle Temple, 1948.

Godfrey Anstruther, *The Seminary Priests. A Dictionary of the Secular Clergy of England and Wales, 1558–1850,* 4 vols., Ware and Great Wakering, 1969–77.

Edward Arber, *A Transcript of the Registers of the Company of Stationers of London, 1554–1640,* 5 vols., London, 1875–94.

Articles agreed on by the Bishoppes, and other learned menne in Synode at London, in the yere of our Lorde Godde, MDLII for the avoiding of controversie in opinions, and the establishment of a godlie concord in certain matters of Religion, London, 1553 [The Forty-two Articles].

W. Atwood, *The Fundamental Constitution of the English Government, proving King William and Queen Mary our Lawful and Rightful King and Queen,* London, 1690.

Francis Bacon; see J. R. Spedding, R. L. Ellis and D. D. Heath.

W. P. Baildon; see John Hawarde.

J. H. Baker, 'The Status of Barristers' in *Law Quarterly Review,* lxxxv (1969), 334–338.

J. H. Baker, 'Counsellors and Barristers' in *Cambridge Law Journal,* xxvii (1969), 204–229.

J. H. Baker, *The Order of Serjeants at Law,* Selden Society, supp. ser., vol. 5, 1984.

H. B., *Plowdens Quaeries: Or, a Moot-Book of Choice Cases,* London, 1662.

E. A. B. Barnard, *The Sheldons: being some Account of the Sheldon Family of Worcestershire and Warwickshire,* Cambridge, 1936.

Mary Bateson, ed., *A Collection of Original Letters from the Bishops to the Privy Council, 1564,* Camden Society, new ser., vol. 53 (Miscellany IX), 1895.

J. H. Beale, *A Bibliography of Early English Law Books,* Cambridge, Mass., 1926 [supplement, by J. A. Anderdon, 1943].

C. A. Bernaud, ed., *Sixteenth Century Marriages (1538–1600),* London, 1911.

S. T. Bindoff, *Ket's Rebellion, 1549,* London, 1949 (Historical Association pamphlet, General Series No. 12; reprinted 1968).

J. B. Blakeway, *The Sheriffs of Shropshire,* Shrewsbury, 1831.

J. B. Blakeway, 'The Isle, anciently Up Rossall', in *Transactions of the Shropshire Archaeological and Natural History Society,* 2nd scr., ix (1897), 107–170.

J. B. Blakeway (edited by Mrs. Baldwyn Childe), 'Notes on Kinlet' in *Transactions of the Shropshire Archaeological and Natural History Society,* 3rd ser., viii (1908), 83–150.

D. S. Bland, 'Henry VIII's Royal Commission on the Inns of Court' in *Journal of the Society of Public Teachers of Law*, new ser., x (1969), 178–194.

C. W. Boase, *Register of the University of Oxford*, vol. 1, Oxford Historical Society, i, 1884 [further parts of the Register appear in vols. 10, 11, 12 & 14 of the publications of the Oxford Historical Society].

W. C. Bolland, *The Year Books*, Cambridge, 1921.

P. A. Boyan and G. R. Lamb, *Francis Tregian, Cornish Recusant*, London, 1955.

R. I. Bradley, 'Blacklo and the Counter Reformation' in C. H. Carter, ed., *From the Renaissance to the Counter Reformation*, New York, 1965; London, 1966.

Norman G. Brett-James, *The Growth of Stuart London*, London, 1935.

Brewer's Dictionary of Phrase and Fable, revised by Ivor H. Evans, London, 1974.

Henry Brinklow, *The Complaynt of Roderyck Mors, somtyme a gray fryre, unto the parliament howse of England his natural cuntry: For the redresse of certen wicked lawes, evel customs and cruel decreys*, London, c. 1542 (ed. J. M. Cooper, Early English Text Society, extra ser. xxii (1874); reprinted 1973).

Robert Brook, *La Graunde Abridgement, collect & escrie per Syr R. Brooke*, 2 parts, London, 1573.

Gilbert Burnet, *The History of the Reformation of the Church of England*, second edition, 2 vols., London, 1681.

John Richard Burton, *Some Collections towards the History of the Family of Walcot of Walcot, and afterwards of Bitterley Court, Shropshire*, privately printed, Shrewsbury, 1930.

Sister Callista, 'John Talbot, of Grafton Manor, and his son George, the ninth Earl of Shrewsbury', in *Worcestershire Recusant*, no. 8 (1966), 15–23.

William Camden, *Annales Rerum Anglicarum et Hibernicarum regnante Elizabetha*, London, 1615.

E. Cardwell, *Documentary Annals of the Reformed Church of England, 1546–1716*, 2 vols, London, 1839.

Charles H. Carter, ed., *From the Renaissance to the Counter Reformation: Essays in honour of Garrett Mattingly,* New York, 1965; London, 1966.

George Cavendish, *The Life and Death of Cardinal Wolsey*, edited by Richard S. Sylvester, Early English Text Society, no. 243, 1959.

Edward C. Carter, and Clifford Lewis, 'Sir Edmund Plowden and the New Albion Charter, 1632-1785', in *The Pennsylvania Magazine of History and Biography*, lxxxiii (1959), 150–179.

C. R. Cheney, *Handbook of Dates for Students of English History*, Royal Historical Society Guides and Handbooks, no. 4, London, 1945.

J. M. Cleary, 'Dr. Morys Clynnog's Invasion Projects of 1575-1576' in *Recusant History*, viii (1965-6), 300–322.

H. Clifford, *The Life of Jane Dormer, Duchess of Feria*, edited by J. Stevenson, London, 1887.

Emily J. Climenson, *The History of Shiplake, Oxon.*, London, 1894.

R. H. Clive, *Documents connected with the History of Ludlow and the Lords Marcher*, London, 1841.

Henry S. Cobb, ' "Books of Rates" and the London Customs, 1507–1558' in *The Guildhall Miscellany*, iv (1971), 1–13.

William Cobbett, *The Parliamentary History of England from the Norman Conquest in 1066 to the year 1803*, 36 vols., London, 1806–1820.

J. S. Cockburn, *A History of English Assizes, 1558–1714*, Cambridge, 1972.

Edward Coke, *Institutes of the Laws of England*, 4 parts, London, 1628–1644.

Gustave Constant, *The Reformation in England*, 2 vols.: vol. 1, *The English Schism: Henry VIII (1509–1547)*, translated by R. E. Scantlebury, London, 1934; vol. 2, *Introduction of the Reformation into England: Edward VI (1547–1553)*, translated by E. I. Watkin, London, 1942.

C. H. Cooper and T. Cooper, *Athenae Cantabrigienses*, 2 vols., Cambridge, 1858–1861.

J. Cooper, ed., *The Wentworth Papers, 1597–1628*, Camden Society, 4th ser., xii, 1973.

Julian Cornwall, *The Revolt of the Peasantry, 1549*, London, 1977.

D. H. S. Cranage, *An architectural account of the Churches of Shropshire*, 2 vols., Wellington, Salop, 1901–1912.

J. R. Dasent, ed., *Acts of the Privy Council of England*, 32 vols., London, 1890–1907.

Alan Davidson, 'The Recusancy of Ralph Sheldon' in *Worcestershire Recusant*, xii (1968), 1–7.

Alan Davidson, 'The second Mrs. Sheldon' in *Worcestershire Recusant*, xiv (1969), 15–21.

John Dee, *General and Rare Memorials pertayning to the Perfect Arte of Navigation*, London, 1577.

Thomas Dekker, *The Batchelars Banquet; or a Banquet for Batchelars*, London, 1603.

Simonds D'Ewes, *The Journals of all the Parliaments, During the Reign of Queen Elizabeth, both of the House of Lords and House of Commons*, London, 1682.

A. G. Dickens, *The English Reformation*, London, 1964 [the revised edition of 1967 (paper back) has been used].

F. C. Dietz, *English Government Finance, 1485–1558*, University of Illinois Studies in Social Sciences, ix (1920), no. 3.

Charles Dodd [pseudonym for Hugh Tootel], edited by M. A. Tierney, *The Church History of England from 1500 to the year 1688, chiefly with regard to Catholics*, 5 vols., London, 1839–1843.

R. Doleman [pseudonym], *A Conference about the next Succession to the Crowne of Ingland, divided into two parts*, [Antwerp], 1594.

M. B. Donald, *Elizabethan Copper. The History of the Company of Mines Royal, 1568–1605*, London, 1955.

M. B. Donald, *Elizabethan Monopolies. The History of the Company of Mineral and Battery Works, from 1565-1604*, London, 1961.

William Dugdale, *Origines Juridiciales, or Historical Memorials of the English Laws, Courts of Justice, forms of tryall, punishment in cases criminal, law writers, law books, grants and settlements of estates, degree of serjeant, innes of court and chancery. Also a chronology of the lord chancellors, . . .*, London, 1666.

T. F. Dukes, *Antiquities of Shropshire, from an old manuscript of Edward Lloyd, Esq., of Drenewydd; revised and enlarged from private and other manuscripts, with illustrations*, Shrewsbury, 1844.

Thomas Egerton; see Samuel E. Thorne.

Eilert Ekwall, *The Concise Oxford Dictionary of English Place-Names*, Oxford, 4th ed., 1960.

John Elder, *The copie of a letter sent into Scotlande, of the arrivall of Phillippe Prynce of Spaine*, London, 1555.

A. B. Emden, *A Biographical Register of the University of Oxford, A.D. 1501 to 1540*, Oxford, 1974.

Mrs. [Katherine] Arundell Esdaile, *Temple Church Monuments. Being a Report to the two Honourable Societies of the Temple*, London, 1933.

R. W. Eyton, *Antiquities of Shropshire*, 12 vols., London, 1834-60.

Mary E. Finch, *The Wealth of five Northamptonshire Families, 1540-1640*, Northamptonshire Record Society, xix, 1956.

W. Fleetwood, *Annalium tam Regum Edwardi quinti, Richardi tertij, & Henrici septimi, quam Henrici octaui, Titulorum Ordine Alphabetico multo iam melius, quam ante, Elenchus. Studio & Labore Guilhelmi Fleetwoodi quondam Recordatoris Londinensis*, London, 1579 [another edition, 1597].

R. J. Fletcher, ed., *The Pension Book of Gray's Inn (Records of the Honourable Society)*, 2 vols., London, 1901-1910.

B. C. Foley, 'Bl. John Payne, Seminary Priest and Martyr—1582' in *Essex Recusant*, ii (1960), 48-75.

Henry Foley, *Records of the English Province of the Society of Jesus*, 7 vols., London, 1877-1884.

H. E. Forrest, *Shrewsbury Burgess Roll*, Shrewsbury, 1924.

John Fortescue, *De Laudibus Legum Anglie*, translated by John Selden, London, 1616.

Edward Foss, *The Judges of England, with sketches of their Lives and Notices connected with the Courts at Westminster, 1066-1864*, 9 vols., London, 1848-1864.

Joseph Foster, *Alumni Oxonienses: The Members of the University of Oxford, 1500-1714: Their Parentage, Birthplace, and Year of Birth, with a Record of their Degrees*, 4 vols., Oxford, 1891-1892.

John Foxe, *Actes and Monuments of these latter and perillous dayes touching matters of the Church*, London, 1563 [the edition used is that edited by S. R. Cattley and George Townsend, *The Acts and Memorials of John Foxe*, 8 vols., London, 1837-1841.

Thomas Fuller, *The History of the Worthies of England, endeavoured by Thomas Fuller, D.D.*, London, 1662.

Thomas Wemyss Fulton, *The Sovereignty of the Sea. An Historical Account of the Claims of England to the Dominion of the British Seas, and of the Evolution of the Territorial Waters: with special reference to the Rights of Fishing and the Naval Salute*, Edinburgh, 1911.

James Gairdner, *The English Church in the Sixteenth Century, from the Accession of Henry VIII to the Death of Mary*, London, 1902.

Joseph Gillow, *A Literary and Biographical History, or Bibliographical Dictionary, of the English Catholics from the breach with Rome to the present time*, 5 vols., London, 1885-1903.

N. S. B. Gras, *The Early English Customs System*, Cambridge, Mass., Harvard Economic Studies, xviii, 1918.

George Grazebrook and John Paul Rylands, *The Visitation of Shropshire, taken in the year 1623, by Robert Tresswell, Somerset Herald, and Augustine Vincent, Rouge Croix Pursuivant of Arms*, Part II, Harleian Society, xxix, 1889.

M. S. Gretton, *The Burford Records. A Study in minor Town Government*, Oxford, 1920.

Daniel Gurney, 'Extracts from the Household and Privy Purse Accounts of the Lestranges of Hunstanton, from A.D. 1519 to A.D. 1578' in *Archaeologia*, xxv (1834), 411-569.

William Hakewill, *The Libertie of the Subject: against pretended power of Impositions. Maintained by an Argument in Parliament An°. 7°. Jacobi Regis*, London, 1641.

G. D. H. Hall, 'Impositions and the Courts, 1554-1606' in *Law Quarterly Review*, lxix (1953), 200-218.

G. D. H. Hall, 'Bate's Case and "Lane's" Reports: the Authenticity of a seventeenth-century legal tract' in *Bulletin of the John Rylands Library*, xxxv (1952-3), 405-427.

Hubert Hall, *A History of the Custom-revenue in England, from the earliest times to the year 1827*, 2 vols., London, 1885.

Adam Hamilton, ed., *The Chronicle of the English Augustinian Canonesses Regular of the Lateran, at St. Monica's in Louvain*, 2 vols., London, 1904-1906.

[George Harbin], *The Hereditary Right of the Crown of England Asserted; the History of the Succession since the Conquest clear'd; and the True English Constitution vindicated from the Misrepresentations of Dr. Higden's View and Defence. By a Gentleman*, London, 1713.

Francis Hargrave, *Collectanea Juridica. Consisting of Tracts relative to the Law and Constitution of England*, 2 vols., London, 1791-2.

P. R. Harris, 'William Fleetwood, Recorder of the City, and Catholicism in Elizabethan London', in *Recusant History*, vii (1963-4), 106-122.

Christopher Hatton, *A Treatise concerning Statutes, or Acts of Parliament: And the Exposition thereof*, London, 1677.

John Hawarde, *Les Reports del Cases in Camera Stellata, 1593-1609*, edited by W. P. Baildon, privately printed, 1894.

Samuel Haynes and William Murdin, *Collection of State Papers relating to Affairs in the Reign of Queen Elizabeth . . . left by William Cecil, Lord Burghley*, 2 vols., London: vol. 1 (ed. by Haynes), 1740; vol. 2 (ed. by Murdin), 1759.

Historical Manuscripts Commission
  10th Rep., App., Pt. IV: The Manuscripts of the Earl of Westmorland, Captain Stewart, Lord Stafford, Lord Muncaster, and others (C. 4576 of 1885; re-issued, 1906).
  Bath, vol. 4: Calendar of the Manuscripts of the Marquis of Bath preserved at Longleat, Wiltshire; vol. 4, Seymour papers, 1532–1689.
  Rutland, vol. 1: 12th Rep., App., Pt. IV. The Manuscripts of the Duke of Rutland preserved at Belvoir Castle; vol. 1, Letters and papers, 1888; re-issued, 1911.
  Various Coll., vol. 1: The Manuscripts of the Corporations of Berwick-on-Tweed, Burford, and Lostwithiel; the counties of Wilts and Worcester; the bishop of Chichester; the deans and chapters of Chichester, Canterbury and Salisbury (Cd. 784 of 1901).

W. Herbert, *Antiquities of the Inns of Court and Chancery; containing historical and descriptive sketches relative to their original foundation, customs, ceremonies, buildings, government, &c. &c., with a concise history of the English Law*, London, 1804.

Leo Hicks, ed., *Letters and Memorials of Father Robert Persons, S. J.*, Catholic Record Society, Record Series, xxxix, 1942.

Ronald Hilton, 'The Marriage of Queen Mary and Philip of Spain' in *Proceedings of the Hampshire Field Club and Archaeological Society*, xiv (1938), 46–62.

History of Parliament, *The House of Commons, 1509–1558*, vols 1 and 3 (ed. S. T. Bindoff), History of Parliament Trust, London, 1982.

Michael Hodgetts, 'Elizabethan Priest-Holes' in *Recusant History*, xi (1971–2), 279–298; xii (1973–4), 99–119, 171–197; xiii (1975–6), 18–55. 254–279; xiv (1977–8), 97–126.

L. Fabian Hirst, *The conquest of Plague. A Study of the Evolution of Epistemology*, Oxford, 1953.

W. S. Holdsworth, 'The Year Books' in *The Law Quarterly Review*, xxii (1906), 360–382.

W. S. Holdsworth, *A History of English Law*, 13 vols., London, 1922–1952 (7th revised edition of vol. 1, 1956).

Geoffrey Holt, *St. Omers and Bruges Colleges, 1593–1773. A Biographical Dictionary*, Catholic Record Society, Record Series, lxix, 1979.

William Hudson, *A Treatise on the Court of Star Chamber* [printed in Francis Hargrave, *Collectanea Juridica*, ii, 1–240].

Paul L. Hughes and James F. Larkin, ed., *Tudor Royal Proclamations*, 3 vols., New Haven, Yale University Press, 1964–1969 [vol. 1, 1485–1553; vol. 2, 1553–1587; vol. 3, 1588–1603].

Philip Hughes, *The Reformation in England*, 3 vols., London, 1950–1954.

J. Humphreys, *Elizabethan Sheldon Tapestries*, Oxford, 1929.

Joel Hurstfield, *The Queen's Wards: Wardship and Marriage under Elizabeth I,* London, 1958.

Joel Hurstfield, 'Corruption and Reform under Edward VI and Mary: the Example of Wardship', in *English Historical Review,* lxviii (1953), 22–36 [reprinted in J. Hurstfield, *Freedom, Corruption and Government in Elizabethan England,* London, 1973, ch. 6 (pp. 163–182)].

F. A. Inderwick, ed., *A Calendar of the Inner Temple Records,* 5 vols., London, 1896–1937.

Ben Jonson, *Ben Jonson his Case is alterd,* London, 1609 [another issue, *A pleasant comedy, called the Case is alterd,* London, 1609].

Journals of the House of Commons, 17 vols., London, 1803.

Journals of the House of Lords, 9 vols., London, 1846.

Ernst H. Kantorowicz, *The King's Two Bodies; A Study in Mediaeval Political Theology,* Princeton, 1958.

W. P. M. Kennedy, 'The Imperial Embassy of 1553-4 and Wyatt's Rebellion'', in *English Historical Review,* xxxviii (1923), 251–258.

T. F. Knox, ed., *The Letters and Memorials of William Cardinal Allen (1532-1594),* London, 1882.

William Lambard, *Eirenarcha: or the office of the Justices of peace,* London, 1581.

Stephen K. Land, *Kett's Rebellion: the Norfolk Rising of 1549,* Ipswich, 1977.

G. T. Lapsley, *The County Palatine of Durham. A Study in Constitutional History,* Cambridge, Mass., Harvard Historical Studies, no. 8, 1900.

Gerard Legh, *The Accidens of Armory,* London, 1562.

Mortimer Levine, 'The Last Will and Testament of Henry VIII: a reappraisal appraised'', in *The Historian,* xxvi (1964), 471–485.

Mortimer Levine, *The Early Elizabethan Succession Question, 1558-1568,* Stanford, California, 1966.

David Lloyd, *State Worthies: or, the Statesmen and Favourites of England from the Reformation to the Revolution. Their Prudence and Policies, Successes and Miscarriages, Advancements and Falls,* edited by Charles Whitworth, 2 vols., London, 1766.

D. M. Loades, *Popular Subversion and Government Security in England during the Reign of Mary I,* Cambridge Ph.D. thesis, 1961.

D. M. Loades, *Two Tudor Conspiracies,* Cambridge, 1965.

Thomas Lodge and Robert Greene, *A Looking Glasse for London and England,* London, 1594.

W. J. Loftie, *A History of London,* 2 vols., London, 1883–1884.

A. J. Loomie, *The Spanish Elizabethans: The English Exiles at the Court of Philip II,* London, 1963.

Daniel Lysons and Samuel Lysons, *Magna Britannia: being a concise topographical account of the several counties of Great Britain,* 6 vols., London, 1806–1822.

J. D. Mackie, *The Earlier Tudors, 1485-1558,* Oxford, 1952.

Roger B. Manning, *Religion and Society in Elizabethan Sussex. A Study of the Enforcement of the Religious Settlement, 1558-1603,* Leicester, 1969.

Charles Trice Martin, ed., *Middle Temple Records. Minutes of Parliament of the Middle Temple,* 4 vols., London, 1904-1905.

Robert Megarry, *Inns Ancient and Modern. A Topographical and Historical Introduction to the Inns of Court, Inns of Chancery, and Serjeants' Inns,* Selden Society, 1972 [Selden Society lecture for 1971, amplified].

T. Brendan Minney, 'The Sheldons of Beoley', in *Worcestershire Recusant,* v (1965), 1-17.

Stuart A. Moore, *A History of the Foreshore and the Law relating thereto. With a hitherto unpublished Treatise by Lord Hale. Lord Hale's 'De Jure Maris', and Hall's Essay on the Rights of the Crown in the seashore,* 3rd ed., London, 1888.

Madge Moran, 'The Mediaeval Parts of Plowden Hall', in *Transactions of the Shropshire Archaeological Society,* new ser., lix (1973-4), 264-271.

John Morris, *The Troubles of our Catholic Forefathers related by themselves,* first series, London, 1872.

J. E. Neale, *Queen Elizabeth I,* London, 1934 [edition of 1952].

J. E. Neale, *The Elizabethan House of Commons,* London, 1949.

J. E. Neale, *Elizabeth I and her Parliaments, 1559-1581,* London, 1953.

John Nichols, *The Progresses and Public Processions of Queen Elizabeth,* illustrated with historical notes, 4 vols., London, 1788-1821 [2nd ed., 3 vols., 1823].

J. G. Nichols, ed., *Literary Remains of King Edward the Sixth,* 2 vols., Roxburghe Club, 1857.

J. G. Nichols, ed., *The Chronicle of Queen Jane, and of two years of Queen Mary, and especially of the Rebellion of Sir Thomas Wyat. Written by a resident in the Tower of London,* Camden Society, vol. 48, 1850.

M. M. Nolan, 'William Bendlowes, Serjeant-at-Law, 1516-1584', in *Essex Recusant,* v (1963), 105-113.

Laura Lucie Norsworthy, 'The Plowden interest in Oxfordshire' in *Transactions of the Shropshire Archaeological Society,* new ser., lii (1947-8), 179-190.

Edward F. Oakeley, 'Some Notes on the History of the Oakeley Family', in *Transactions of the Shropshire Archaeological and Natural History Society,* 4th ser., vi (1916-7), 147-160.

Richard O'Sullivan, *Edmund Plowden, 1518-1585. Autumn Reading given in the presence of Her Majesty Queen Elizabeth the Queen Mother at the Middle Temple Hall on 12 November, 1952,* Middle Temple, privately printed, 1952.

H. Owen and J. B. Blakeway, *A History of Shrewsbury,* 2 vols., London, 1825.

Geoffrey de C. Parmiter, 'Edmund Plowden and the Woolsack: a query', in *Downside Review,* xc (1972), 251-259.

176 EDMUND PLOWDEN

Geoffrey de C. Parmiter, 'Bishop Bonner and the Oath', in *Recusant History,* xi (1971-2), 215-236.

Geoffrey de C. Parmiter, 'Plowden, Englefield and Sandford: I, 1558-1585', in *Recusant History,* xiii (1975-6), 159-177.

Geoffrey de C. Parmiter, 'Plowden, Englefield and Sandford: II, 1585-1609', in *Recusant History,* xiv, (1977-8), 9-25.

Geoffrey de C. Parmiter, *Elizabethan Popish Recusancy in the Inns of Court,* Bulletin of the Institute of Historical Research, Special Supplement no. 11, 1976.

Geoffrey de C. Parmiter, 'Edmund Plowden as advocate for Mary Queen of Scots: some remarks upon certain Elizabethan succession tracts', in *Innes Review,* xxx (1979), 35-53.

Geoffrey de C. Parmiter, 'The Judge's widow and the Papist', in *Kent Recusant History,* no. 3 (1980), 74-76.

Nikolaus Pevsner, *The Buildings of England: Shropshire,* London, 1958.

James E. Phillips, *Images of a Queen: Mary Stuart in Sixteenth Century Literature,* Cambridge, 1964.

B. M. P. [Barbara Mary Plowden], *Records of the Plowden Family,* Privately printed, 1887.

Edmund Plowden, *Les Commentaries, Ou Reports de Edmund Plowden vn Apprentice de le Common Ley, de diuers Cases esteants matters en Ley, & de les Arguments sur yceaux, en les temps des Raignes le Roy Ed. le size, le Roigne Mary, le Roy & Roigne Ph. & Mary, & le Roigne Elizabeth,* 2 parts, London: pt. 1, 1571; pt. 2, 1578 [English translation, 2 vols., London, 1816].

Francis Plowden, *Historical Letter from Francis Plowden, Esq., to Sir Richard Musgrave, Bart.,* London, 1805.

T. F. T. Plucknett, 'Ellesmere on Statutes', in *Law Quarterly Review,* lx (1944), 242-249.

A. F. Pollard, *England under Protector Somerset,* London, 1900.

A. F. Pollard, *Thomas Cranmer, 1489-1556,* London 1927.

A. F. Pollard, *The Evolution of Parliament,* London, 1920 [an amended edition was published in 1926].

J. H. Pollen, ed., *A Letter from Mary Queen of Scots to the Duke of Guise, 1562,* Scottish History Society, vol. 43, 1904.

F. M. Powicke and E. B. Fryde, ed., *Handbook of British Chronology,* London, 2nd ed., 1961 (Royal Historical Society Guides and Handbooks, no. 2).

Wilfred R. Prest, *The Inns of Court under Ellizabeth I and the Early Stuarts, 1590-1640,* London, 1972.

Arthur E. Preston, *The Church and Parish of St. Nicholas, Abingdon,* London, 1929 [Also published, under the same title and with the same pagination, by the Oxford Historical Society, original series no. 99, 1935].

John Proctor, *The Historie of Wyate's Rebellion, with the order and means of resisting the same.* London, 1554 [reprinted in A. F. Pollard, ed., *Tudor Tracts, 1532-1588,* London, 1903].

Alexander Pulling, *The Order of the Coif,* London, 1884.

Max Radin, 'Early Statutory interpretation in England', in *Illinois Law Review,* xxxviii (1943), 16–40.

Hastings Rashdall, *The Universities of Europe in the Middle Ages,* 2 vols. in 3, Oxford, 1895; new edition by F. M. Powicke and A. B. Emden, 3 vols., Oxford, 1936.

Conyers Read, *Mr. Secretary Cecil and Queen Elizabeth,* London, 1955.

Return of the Name of every Member of the Lower House of Parliament, 1213–1874, House of Commons Parliamentary Papers, 69, 69–I, 69–II, 69–III of 1878 (issued in two parts consisting of one vol. of text and one vol. of index). [Additions to the foregoing lists are in *Interim Report of the Committee on House of Commons Personnel and Politics, 1264–1832,* Cmd. 4130, 1932].

Edward Richardson, *The Monumental Effigies of the Temple Church, with an account of their restoration in the year 1842,* London, 1843.

Jasper Ridley, *Thomas Cranmer,* Oxford, 1962.

Hastings Robinson, *Original Letters relative to the English Reformation written during the reigns of King Henry VIII, King Edward VI, and Queen Mary: chiefly from the archives of Zurich,* 2 vols., Parker Society, vols. 52 & 53, 1846–1847.

H. E. G. Rope, 'Edmund Plowden', in *The Month,* new ser., xvi (1956), 100–109.

Elliot Rose, *Cases of Conscience. Alternatives open to Recusants and Puritans under Elizabeth I and James I,* Cambridge, 1976.

Frances Rose-Troup, *The Western Rebellion of 1549; an account of the insurrection in Devonshire and Cornwall against religious innovation in the reign of Edward VI,* London, 1913.

A. L. Rowse, *Tudor Cornwall. Portrait of a Society,* London, 1941.

F. W. Russell, *Kett's Rebellion in Norfolk,* London, 1859.

W. Harry Rylands, ed., *The Four Visitations of Berkshire made and taken by Thomas Benolte, Clarenceux, Anno 1532; by William Harvey, Clarenceux, Anno 1566; by Henry Chitting, Chester Herald, and John Philipott, Rouge Dragon, for William Camden, Clarenceux, Anno 1623; and by Elias Ashmole, Windsor Herald, for Sir Edward Bysshe, Clarenceux, Anno 1665–66,* vol. 1; Harleian Society, vol. 56, 1907.

Thomas Rymer, ed. (and R. Sanderson, vols. 16–20), *Foedera, conventiones, leterae, et cujuscunque generis acta publica inter reges Angliae et alios quovis imperatores, reges, pontifices, principes vel communitates ab . . . anno 1101, ad nostra usque tempora, habita aut tractata; ex autographis . . . fideliter exscripta,* 20 vols., London, 1704–35.

Christopher St. Germain, *Hereafter foloweth the fyrste Dyaloge in Englysshe bytwyxt a Doctoure of Dyuynyte and a Student in the Lawes of Englande: of the groundes of the sayd Lawes, and of conscyence, newly correctyd: and eft sones Enprynted: with newe addycyons,* London, 1531.

Select Essays in Anglo-American Legal History, by various authors, 3 vols., Boston, 1907–1909.

D. Shanahan, 'The White Family of Hutton', in *Essex Recusant*, vii (1965), 78–85, and viii (1966), 33–37.

A. Mary Sharp, *History of Ufton Court*, London, 1892.

A. W. B. Simpson, 'The Early Constitution of the Inns of Court', in *Cambridge Law Journal*, xxviii (1970), 241–286.

A. W. B. Simpson, 'The Source and Function of the later Year Books', in *Law Quarterly Review*, lxxxvii (1971), 94–118.

Richard Simpson, *Edmund Campion. A biography*, London, 1867.

C. A. J. Skeel, *The Council in the Marches of Wales*, London, 1904.

L. B. Smith, 'The last will and testament of Henry VIII: a question of perspective', in *Journal of British Studies*, ii (1962), 14–27.

L. B. Smith, *Henry VIII. The Mask of Royalty*, London, 1971.

Robert Somerville, 'The Duchy of Lancaster Council and the Court of Duchy Chamber', in *Transactions of the Royal Historical Society*, 4th ser., xxiii (1941), 159–177.

Robert Somerville, *History of the Duchy of Lancaster*, vol. 1 (1265–1603), London, 1953 [vol. 2 not published].

A. C. Southern, *Elizabethan Recusant Prose, 1559–1582. A historical and critical account of the books of the Catholic Refugees printed and published abroad and at secret presses in England together with an annotated bibliography of the same*, London, 1950.

J. Spedding, R. L. Ellis and D. D. Heath, *The Letters and the Life of Francis Bacon, including all his occasional works . . .*, 14 vols., London, 1861–1874.

Granville Squiers, *Secret Hiding-Places. The Origins, Histories and Descriptions of English Secret Hiding-Places used by Priests, Cavaliers, Jacobites & Smugglers*, London, 1934.

State Papers during the reign of Henry VIII, 11 vols., London, Record Commissioners, 1830–1852.

Statutes of the Realm, 11 vols., London, Record Commissioners, 1810–1825.

Leslie Stephen and Sidney Lee, ed., *Dictionary of National Biography*, 63 vols., London, 1885–1900; 1st supplement, 3 vols., 1901; reprinted, 22 vols., 1908–1909; Index and epitome, 1903.

Stevenson's Book of Proverbs, Maxims and Familiar Phrases, selected and arranged by Burton Stevenson, London, 1949.

Lawrence Stone, *The Crisis of the Aristocracy, 1558–1641*, Oxford, 1965.

Agnes Strickland, *Lives of the Queens of England*, 12 vols., London, 1840–1848; revised ed., 8 vols., 1851–1852.

John Strype, *Annals of the Reformation and the Establishment of Religion, and other various occurrences in the Church of England during Queen Elizabeth's happy reign*, 4 vols., Oxford, 1820–1840.

John Strype, *Ecclesiastical Memorials relating chiefly to Religion, and the Reformation of it, and the Emergencies of the Church of England, under King Henry VIII, King Edward VI and Queen Mary I*, 3 vols., Oxford, 1820–1840.

John Strype, *The Life of the Learned Sir Thomas Smith, Kt., Doctor of the Civil Law; Principal Secretary of State to King Edward VI, and Queen Elizabeth*, Oxford, 1820.

John Strype, *The Life and Acts of Matthew Parker, the First Archbishop of Canterbury in the reign of Queen Elizabeth*, 3 vols., Oxford, 1821.

John Strype, *The History of the Life and Acts of the most reverend Father in God, Edmund Grindal, the first bishop of London, and the second Archbishop of York and Canterbury successively in the reign of Queen Elizabeth*, Oxford, 1821.

H. A. C. Sturgess, ed., *Register of Admissions to the Honourable Society of the Middle Temple. From the Fifteenth Century to the year 1944*, 3 vols., London, 1949.

J. R. Tanner, *Tudor Constitutional Documents, A.D. 1484-1603, with an historical commentary*, Cambridge, 2nd ed., 1930; reprinted 1951.

Samuel E. Thorne, ed., *A Discourse upon the Exposicion & Understandinge of Statutes: with Sir Thomas Egerton's Additions*, San Marino, California, 1942.

William Tidd, *The New Practice of the Courts of King's Bench, Common Pleas and Exchequer of Pleas, in personal actions; and ejectment*, London, 1837.

R. Titler, 'Plowden and the Woolsack: a reply', in *Downside Review*, xcii (1974), 62-67.

W. R. Trimble, *The Catholic Laity in Elizabethan England, 1558-1603*, Cambridge, Mass., 1964.

W. H. Turner, ed., *Selections from the Records of the City of Oxford (1509-1583)*, Oxford, 1880.

John Venn and J. A. Venn, *Alumni Cantabrigienses. A Biographical List of all known Students, Graduates and Holders of Office at the University of Cambridge from the Earliest Times to 1900*, 4 vols., Cambridge, 1922-1927.

R. A. de Vertot, *Ambassades de messieurs de Noailles en Angleterre. Rédigées par feu M. l'Abbé de Vertot*, 5 vols., Leyden, 1763.

A. W. Ward, G. W. Prothero and S. Leathes, ed., *The Cambridge Modern History*, 13 vols., and Atlas, Cambridge, 1902-1912 [first edition].

K. R. Wark, *Elizabethan Recusancy in Cheshire*, Chetham Society, 3rd ser., vol. 19, 1971.

Edward Waterhous, *Fortescutus Illustratus, or a Commentary on that Nervous Treatise De Laudibus Legum Angliae Written by Sir John Fortescue Knight, first Lord Chief Justice, after Lord Chancellour to King Henry the Sixth*, London, 1663.

Martin Weinbaum, *British Borough Charters, 1307-1660*, Cambridge, 1943.

Maureen Weinstock, *More Dorset Studies*, Dorchester, [1960].

Henry W. Weyman, 'Some Shropshire Incidents in the Fifteenth Century', in *Transactions of the Shropshire Archaeological and Natural History Society*, 4th ser., vi (1916-7), 193-200.

Christopher Whitfield, 'The Kinship of Thomas Combe II, William Reynolds, and William Shakespeare', in *Notes and Queries,* ccvi (1961) [n.s., viii], 364–372.

Christopher Whitfield, 'Some of Shakespeare's Contemporaries at the Middle Temple', in *Notes and Queries,* ccxi (1966) [n.s., xiii], 122–125, 283–286, 363–369, 443–448.

William H. Wiatt, 'The lost history of Wyatt's rebellion', in *Renaissance News,* xv (1962), 128–133.

Penry Williams, *The Council in the Marches of Wales under Elizabeth I,* Cardiff, 1958.

J. Bruce Williamson, *The History of the Temple, London. From the Institution of the Order of the Knights of the Temple to the close of the Stuart Period,* London, 1924.

J. Bruce Williamson, *The Middle Temple Bench Book. Being a Register of Benchers of the Middle Temple. From the Earliest Records to the present time, with historical introduction,* London, 2nd edition, 1937.

Anthony Wood, *Athenae Oxonienses. An Exact History of all the writers and bishops who have had their education in the University of Oxford. To which are added the Fasti or Annals of the said University,* ed. Philip Bliss, 4 vols., London, 1813–1820.

A. Vere Woodman, 'The Buckinghamshire and Oxfordshire Rising of 1549', in *Oxoniensia,* xxii (1957), 78–84.

H. W. Woolrych, *The Life of Sir Edward Coke,* London, 1826.

H. W. Woolrych, *Lives of Eminent Serjeants-at-Law of the English Bar,* 2 vols., London, 1869.

George Worley, *The Church of the Knights Templars in London. A description of the fabric and its contents, with a short history of the Order,* London, 1907.

Thomas Wright, ed., *Queen Elizabeth and her Times, a series of original letters selected from the inedited private correspondence of the Lord Treasurer Burghley, the Earl of Leicester, the Secretaries Walsingham and Smith, Sir Christopher Hatton, and most of the distinguished persons of the period,* 2 vols., London, 1838.

More than one entry on a page is not noted in the Index. E.P. = Edmund
Plowden; M.T. = Middle Temple.